AI-Powered Learning in Social Work, Counseling, and Psychology

Jenifer Norton
https://orcid.org/0009-0007-8900-6247
Moravian University, USA

IGI Global
Scientific Publishing
Publishing Tomorrow's Research Today

Vice President of Editorial	Melissa Wagner
Director of Acquisitions	Mikaela Felty
Director of Book Development	Jocelynn Hessler
Production Manager	Mike Brehm
Cover Design	Jose Rosado

Published in the United States of America by
IGI Global Scientific Publishing
701 East Chocolate Avenue
Hershey, PA, 17033, USA
Tel: 717-533-8845 | Fax: 717-533-7115
Website: https://www.igi-global.com E-mail: cust@igi-global.com

Library of Congress Cataloging-in-Publication Data

Names: Norton, Jenifer, 1988- editor
Title: AI-powered learning in social work, counseling, and psychology / edited by: Jenifer Norton.
Description: Hershey PA : IGI Global Scientific Publishing, [2026] | Includes bibliographical references. | Summary: "This book aims to explore and advance the thoughtful integration of artificial intelligence into teaching and learning across psychology, counseling, social work, and human services education. to explore and advance the thoughtful integration of artificial intelligence into teaching and learning across psychology, counseling, social work, and human services education"-- Provided by publisher.
Identifiers: LCCN 2025046626 (print) | LCCN 2025046627 (ebook) | ISBN 9798337343624 hardback | ISBN 9798337343631 paperback | ISBN 9798337343648 ebook
Subjects: LCSH: Social work education | Counseling--Study and teaching | Psychology--Study and teaching | Artificial intelligence--Educational applications
Classification: LCC HV11 .A395 2026 (print) | LCC HV11 (ebook)
LC record available at https://lccn.loc.gov/2025046626
LC ebook record available at https://lccn.loc.gov/2025046627

British Cataloguing in Publication Data
A Cataloguing in Publication record for this book is available from the British Library.

Table of Contents

Detailed Table of Contents

This chapter examines how artificial intelligence (AI) is reshaping teaching and learning in social work, counseling, and psychology. AI-powered tools such as simulations, adaptive platforms, and automated feedback offer opportunities for personalized learning, improved engagement, and skill development. However, they also present challenges, including algorithmic bias, risks to academic integrity, reduced opportunities for empathy-building, and data privacy concerns. The chapter argues that AI must function as a complement to, rather than a replacement for, human-centered pedagogy. Drawing on international research and the author's prior work in digital education, mental health, and elder care, it outlines pathways for integrating AI ethically and effectively. Key strategies include fostering AI literacy among students, preparing faculty through professional development, and embedding ethical safeguards into institutional frameworks. The chapter concludes by positioning AI as a partner in advancing inclusion, empathy, and social justice in professional education.

Generative AI tools are becoming increasingly integrated into human service programs necessitating adaptation in psychology, counseling, and social work to prepare students for work within evolving technological landscapes (Báez et al., 2025; Stone, 2025). Departments must consider how AI technologies align with the pedagogical and ethical frameworks of their fields to guide both students and faculty through responsible use of AI tools. This chapter explores approaches in developing AI literacy using practical strategies for introducing AI in ways that support rather than displace critical thinking and reflective practice. Recognized challenges include issues pertaining to authorship, bias, and academic integrity, along with the broader question of how the use of AI technology aligns with values such as empathy, relationality, and cultural competence (Dueck & Sundararajan, 2024; Soman et al., 2025).

Artificial intelligence (AI) is reshaping social work and human services, offering new opportunities for access and engagement while raising ethical challenges around empathy, equity, and accountability. This chapter examines the integration of AI, particularly chatbots, into education and practice through a trauma-informed and anti-oppressive lens. Using the case of Serenity, an AI chatbot at a nonprofit mental health agency, it explores ethical tensions surrounding empathy, bias, consent, confidentiality, and professional integrity as framed by the NASW Code of Ethics. The chapter also reviews AI's role in simulation-based learning and digital literacy, proposing a framework for values-driven adoption grounded in cultural humility, transparency, and participatory design. Ultimately, it positions social workers as ethical stewards guiding humane and just AI integration in practice and education.

As artificial intelligence (AI) becomes increasingly prevalent in education and human services, the need to develop AI literacy among students and faculty in social work, counseling, and psychology is urgent. This chapter explores frameworks and pedagogical models for integrating AI literacy into curricula, emphasizing the importance of ethical, critical, and practical engagement with AI tools. It addresses the unique challenges these relational and value-driven fields face, such as preserving empathy, mitigating algorithmic bias, and ensuring data ethics. Through interdisciplinary curriculum design, experiential learning, and faculty development, the chapter provides a roadmap for institutions to prepare future

limited institutions and provides a more authentic experience aligned with desired learning outcomes.

The rapid emergence of generative artificial intelligence (AI) has prompted significant debate within social work education regarding its ethical integration into teaching and assessment. Drawing on a case study from a Master of Social Work program in Australia, the authors describe an assessment redesign that incorporated generative AI tools to scaffold, rather than replace, professional reasoning. Findings from two cohorts reveal mixed responses from students and educators, highlighting benefits such as improved efficiency and skill development alongside concerns about authenticity and academic integrity. The chapter opens with a summary of current perspectives on the role of AI in social work and concludes with practical recommendations for educators, stressing the importance of clear purpose, rubric adjustments, technical readiness, and alignment with ethical codes. Integrating AI into social work education offers opportunities for preparing graduates for technologically integrated practice while preserving core values of empathy, critical thinking, and accountability.

This chapter examines artificial intelligence integration at the program level in social work, counseling, and psychology education, arguing that ethical and effective adoption requires more than isolated course-level experimentation. Drawing on the author's experience as a program director and learning designer, it positions AI as educational infrastructure that can support assessment planning, accreditation alignment, and sustainable course development when governed by professional values and human judgment. The chapter explores AI-supported curriculum and rubric alignment, online learning design workflows, and collaboration with subject matter experts, while addressing ethical tensions related to transparency, equity, faculty

Preface

INTRODUCTION

The rapid emergence of generative artificial intelligence has brought higher education to a moment of both significant possibility and necessary reflection. This tension is especially pronounced in human-centered disciplines such as psychology, counseling, social work, and human services, where education is grounded in relational practice, ethical responsibility, and social justice. As Editor of this volume, I was guided by a growing recognition that while AI is already reshaping how learning is designed and delivered, the scholarly and practical guidance needed to integrate these tools thoughtfully within these disciplines remains underdeveloped.

As institutions expand online and hybrid learning modalities, educators increasingly encounter AI not as a distant innovation but as an immediate pedagogical reality. AI-powered tools promise efficiencies, personalization, and new forms of engagement. At the same time, they raise critical ethical questions related to bias, privacy, academic integrity, professional identity, and the preservation of human connection in teaching and learning. For disciplines that prepare practitioners to work with vulnerable individuals and communities, these questions are not peripheral. They are foundational.

This edited reference work responds to a clear gap in the literature: the need for original, field-specific, and practice-informed scholarship that examines how artificial intelligence can be applied meaningfully, ethically, and responsibly in psychology, counseling, and social work education. The contributors to this volume bring interdisciplinary perspectives spanning theory, empirical research, pedagogy, faculty development, and institutional leadership. Collectively, the chapters move beyond abstract debate to offer concrete examples, conceptual frameworks, and applied strategies for AI-enhanced teaching and learning that remain aligned with the core values of these professions.

The chapters that follow are intentionally diverse in scope and approach, reflecting both the complexity of AI and the varied educational contexts in which faculty and administrators work. Readers will encounter contributions that bridge conceptual insight with real-world application, addressing curriculum design, student preparation for AI-influenced professional landscapes, and the evolving role of faculty in digitally mediated learning environments. Throughout the volume, ethical reflection is not treated as an add-on to innovation but as a condition of responsible pedagogical change.

This book is intended for faculty, instructional designers, program directors, and academic administrators engaged in psychology, counseling, social work, and human services education, particularly those working in online, hybrid, or technology-enhanced settings. It also speaks to educational researchers, doctoral students, and teaching and learning professionals examining the intersections of AI, pedagogy, and ethics. Finally, it offers practical value to institutions navigating curriculum innovation, accreditation expectations, and faculty development initiatives related to emerging technologies.

It is my hope that this volume will serve not only as a reference but as an invitation to engage critically with AI, to center human values in technological change, and to participate in shaping an educational future that is both innovative and deeply humane.

ORGANIZATION OF THE BOOK

Chapter 1 establishes the foundation for the volume by offering an integrative examination of how artificial intelligence is reshaping teaching and learning in social work, counseling, and psychology. The chapter balances innovation with caution, exploring AI-powered simulations, adaptive learning platforms, and automated feedback while addressing concerns related to algorithmic bias, academic integrity, data privacy, and the preservation of empathy. Drawing on international research and experience in digital education and human services, it positions AI as a complement to human-centered pedagogy and outlines pathways for ethical integration through AI literacy, faculty preparation, and institutional responsibility.

Chapter 2 focuses explicitly on AI literacy as a core educational competency in the helping professions. Recognizing that generative AI tools are already embedded in educational and professional contexts, the chapter emphasizes pedagogical approaches that align AI use with disciplinary values such as empathy, relationality, and cultural competence. It offers practical strategies for fostering critical and reflective engagement with AI while addressing challenges related to authorship, bias, and academic integrity.

Chapter 3 brings an explicitly ethical and practice-oriented lens to the discussion by examining AI chatbots in social work education and service delivery. Using a case study from a nonprofit mental health setting, the chapter interrogates the concept of automated empathy through trauma-informed and anti-oppressive frameworks. Grounded in the NASW Code of Ethics, it addresses consent, confidentiality, bias, and professional accountability while proposing a values-driven framework that positions social workers as ethical stewards of AI integration.

Chapter 4 returns to AI literacy with a comprehensive examination of frameworks, pedagogical practices, and ethical imperatives across social work, counseling, and psychology education. With a focus on curriculum-level integration and institutional responsibility, the chapter addresses challenges such as preserving empathy, mitigating algorithmic bias, and safeguarding data ethics. Through interdisciplinary curriculum design and faculty development strategies, it offers a roadmap for building inclusive and equitable AI literacy ecosystems.

Chapter 5 centers the lived experiences of faculty navigating AI integration in social work and psychology education. Drawing on qualitative, phenomenological research, the chapter explores successes, challenges, and unexpected outcomes associated with AI adoption. Faculty reflections highlight opportunities such as increased engagement and instructional efficiency, alongside ongoing concerns related to ethics, access, and professional identity. The chapter reinforces that AI integration is a context-sensitive and relational process rather than a uniform solution.

Chapter 6 provides a practice-oriented account of partnering with AI to support case study and simulation-based learning in social work education. Focused on the development of an Immersive Case Study Environment, the chapter illustrates how collaboration among faculty and instructional designers can expand access to authentic learning experiences while addressing ethical considerations and institutional constraints.

Chapter 7 examines the integration of generative AI into assessment design within a Master of Social Work program. Through a detailed case study, the chapter explores how AI can scaffold professional reasoning without undermining authenticity or academic integrity. It offers concrete guidance on assessment redesign, rubric alignment, and ethical clarity, addressing one of the most contested areas of AI adoption in higher education.

Chapter 8 concludes the volume by widening the lens to program-level leadership, learning design, and accreditation in the helping professions. This chapter argues that ethical and sustainable AI adoption cannot be achieved through isolated course-level experimentation alone. It positions AI as educational infrastructure that, when governed by professional values and human judgment, can support curriculum coherence, assessment planning, and accreditation alignment. The chapter offers a leadership-oriented framework for responsible AI governance that centers transparency, equity, faculty workload, and the limits of automation.

CONCLUSION

As Editor, I offer this volume as both a reflection of the current state of human services education and a forward-looking guide to its future. Across psychology, counseling, social work, and related helping professions, artificial intelligence is no longer speculative. It is an active presence shaping teaching, learning, assessment, and professional preparation. The chapters in this book collectively demonstrate that the central question is not whether AI will be used, but how it will be integrated in ways that remain faithful to the relational and ethical foundations of these disciplines.

Taken together, the contributions emphasize that responsible AI adoption requires intentional leadership and sustained critical reflection. They highlight the importance of AI literacy and ethical frameworks grounded in professional codes, while advancing pedagogical approaches that position AI as a support for human judgment and care rather than a replacement for them. Across contexts, the chapters resist technocentric narratives that privilege efficiency over relationship, instead centering the lived experiences of educators, students, and the communities they ultimately serve.

It is my hope that this book will serve as a trusted reference for educators, administrators, researchers, and institutional leaders navigating the complexities of AI in human services education. More than a collection of answers, it offers frameworks and guiding questions that invite ongoing dialogue and ethical engagement. As these professions continue to evolve alongside emerging technologies, the opportunity before us is to ensure that innovation strengthens, rather than diminishes, our commitments to ethical practice and human dignity. This volume is offered in that spirit.

Chapter 1
AI in Social Work, Counseling, and Psychology Education:
Innovations, Ethics, and Educational Pathways

Sameen Rafi
https://orcid.org/0000-0003-2631-5871
Aligarh Muslim University, Aligarh, India

ABSTRACT

This chapter examines how artificial intelligence (AI) is reshaping teaching and learning in social work, counseling, and psychology. AI-powered tools such as simulations, adaptive platforms, and automated feedback offer opportunities for personalized learning, improved engagement, and skill development. However, they also present challenges, including algorithmic bias, risks to academic integrity, reduced opportunities for empathy-building, and data privacy concerns. The chapter argues that AI must function as a complement to, rather than a replacement for, human-centered pedagogy. Drawing on international research and the author's prior work in digital education, mental health, and elder care, it outlines pathways for integrating AI ethically and effectively. Key strategies include fostering AI literacy among students, preparing faculty through professional development, and embedding ethical safeguards into institutional frameworks. The chapter concludes by positioning AI as a partner in advancing inclusion, empathy, and social justice in professional education.

DOI: 10.4018/979-8-3373-4362-4.ch001

INTRODUCTION

The rise of AI, especially generative AI, has transformed higher education. AI has long been used in data processing, automation, and decision-support systems, but natural language models, adaptive learning platforms, and conversational agents have expanded teaching and learning (Zawacki-Richter, 2019). Global universities and training institutions must integrate AI into curricula and pedagogy to improve quality and uphold ethics (Crawford, 2021; Selwyn, 2019).

This difficulty is especially significant in human-centered, relational fields like social work, counseling, and psychology. These professions require empathy, ethical decision-making, cultural humility, and social justice, unlike technological ones (Selwyn, 2019). Students learn and develop values, relational skills, and reflective capabilities for responsible practice with vulnerable populations. AI-mediated learning in such circumstances poses important questions: Can technology foster empathy? How can AI respect oppressed peoples' cultures and experiences? How should AI shape professional identity (Noble, 2018; Selwyn, 2019)?

Online and hybrid modalities increased globally during and after COVID-19, boosting interest in digital and AI-mediated pedagogies. Digital integration is essential for social work, counseling, and psychology schools to reach diverse learners, enable flexibility, and prepare graduates for digital practice. However, if not carefully integrated, efficiency and personalization technologies can dehumanize learning (Wang et al., 2024).

AI in education research shows opportunities and concerns. AI-supported role-plays allow counseling students to practice client interactions, psychology students to practice diagnostic reasoning, and social work students to run complex digital case simulations. These innovations may boost engagement, minimize workload in big cohorts, and boost theory-to-practice confidence (Singh et al., 2025). Conversely, algorithmic bias can reinforce stereotypes and produce inequitable outcomes for marginalized students; generative tools can tempt academic dishonesty; and core relational skills (e.g., active listening, empathic presence) may be undervalued if technology replaces human interaction. Many faculty lack AI knowledge and support for deliberate integration, resulting in inconsistent behavior across universities (Mehdaoui, 2024).

In response, this chapter examines AI in social work, counseling, and psychology through three themes: innovations (emerging applications that enrich teaching and learning), ethics (responsible integration attentive to equity and professional values), and educational pathways. The main thesis is that AI should be seen as an educational revolution that requires thought, contextual adaptation, and ethical precautions (Reamer, 2023). The human service-related disciplines can lead because critical pedagogy, cultural responsiveness, and value-driven practice can challenge market-driven adoption and prioritize human dignity and social justice (Mackey, 2014). The chapter intends to give educators, administrators, and researchers conceptual and practical tools for responsible integration. It balances innovation with ethics to honor the human-centered ideals of social work, counseling, and psychology while educating students for AI-driven careers.

PEDAGOGICAL INNOVATIONS AND OPPORTUNITIES

Artificial intelligence (AI) is increasingly embedded within teaching and learning infrastructures rather than functioning as an optional add-on. In human-centered disciplines such as social work, counseling, and psychology, AI is reshaping how educators design learning experiences, assess student progress, and support the development of professional competencies. When implemented with appropriate safeguards, AI can enhance skill acquisition, formative and summative assessment, and student engagement while preserving human judgment and relational learning (Bernacki et al., 2021).

This section examines six domains of pedagogical innovation: simulation-based learning, adaptive learning systems, feedback and assessment, reflective and experiential learning, collaborative learning, and accessibility and inclusion. Across these domains, AI is treated as a pedagogical scaffold augmenting, rather than replacing, human instruction and supervision.

Simulation-Based Learning with AI

Simulation has long been central to professional education, enabling students to practice skills before engaging with clients or communities. Contemporary AI-enabled simulations can reproduce complex interpersonal dynamics, adapt scenarios based on learner input, and provide structured performance feedback (Lateef, 2010). Effective simulations aim to standardize exposure to core competencies, scaffold increasing complexity, scale access for large or remote cohorts, and preserve purposeful practice (Oliveira Silva et al., 2023).

In counseling education, AI-driven conversational agents can simulate presentations such as anxiety, trauma, or substance use, allowing students to practice micro-skills including active listening, reflection, and open-ended inquiry. Automated indicators may surface patterns in tone, pacing, or empathy, helping novices connect communication choices to therapeutic alliance goals (Akkert et al., 2025; Siddals et al., 2024).

In social work education, AI case simulations can model multi-system complexity. Child protection or community practice scenarios may involve conflicting narratives, time-sensitive risks, and interagency coordination, adjusting dynamically as students conduct assessments or make referrals. These environments support decision-making under uncertainty and structured debriefing around ethics and professional values (Egonsdotter & Israelsson, 2022).

Psychology education increasingly uses AI-based virtual patients and assessment tools to develop diagnostic reasoning. By presenting overlapping symptom profiles, simulations encourage hypothesis testing, consideration of base rates, and recognition of cognitive biases such as anchoring or confirmation bias (García-Torres et al., 2025).

While simulation-based learning offers substantial benefits, limitations remain. Simulations may lack cultural nuance or unpredictability if training data or scenario design embed narrow assumptions (Noble, 2018; Selwyn, 2019). Automated feedback can also privilege efficiency over empathy if not paired with reflective discussion. Accordingly, AI simulations should supplement not replace field education and live supervision, with guided debriefs that foreground ethics, power, and positionality.

In a master's level counseling skills course, students engage with AI-driven conversational agents designed to simulate clients presenting with anxiety, grief, trauma exposure, or ambivalence toward therapy. These systems dynamically adjust responses based on students' questioning style, emotional tone, and reflective statements, enabling repeated practice of core counseling micro-skills such as empathy, paraphrasing, and open-ended inquiry (Tanana et al., 2019).

During each interaction, automated analytics highlight patterns such as missed validation opportunities, overuse of closed questions, or imbalanced reflection-to-question ratios. Importantly, these outputs are used only for formative learning, not grading. Faculty supervisors guide students in interpreting AI feedback, emphasizing cultural context, emotional nuance, and the limits of automated judgments (Selwyn, 2019).

This model reinforces AI as a pedagogical scaffold rather than a substitute for supervision. Human oversight ensures that professional identity development, ethical reasoning, and relational presence remain central to counseling education, consistent with human-centered pedagogical principles (Crawford, 2021; Reamer, 2023).

Adaptive Learning Systems and Personalized Education

AI-powered adaptive learning systems monitor learner performance in real time and adjust pacing, sequencing, and instructional resources accordingly (Joshi, 2024). Using probabilistic models to estimate mastery, these systems can provide targeted practice, just-in-time explanations, and remediation pathways when misconceptions persist (Luckin, 2017). When aligned with explicit learning outcomes and human oversight, adaptive learning can increase time-on-task, metacognitive awareness, and learner self-efficacy (Anders & Speltz, 2025).

Discipline-specific applications demonstrate the versatility of adaptive systems. In counseling education, adaptive quizzes can identify gaps in ethical reasoning or multicultural competencies and route students to tailored case vignettes or micro-lectures. In psychology, adaptive modules in research methods and statistics can spiral concepts such as reliability or effect size until criterion mastery is achieved (Zawacki-Richter et al., 2019). In social work, adaptive platforms can support policy analysis and community practice by highlighting regulatory requirements or funding constraints (Zamfiroiu et al., 2022).

Adaptive learning is particularly beneficial for diverse learners, including neurodivergent and multilingual students, by supporting flexible pacing, repetition, translation, and captioning (Therasa, 2023). However, personalization systems may encode algorithmic bias, isolate learners from collaborative discourse, or raise privacy concerns if interaction data are collected without transparency (Selwyn, 2019; Crawford, 2021). To balance benefits and risks, programs should align adaptivity to clearly defined competencies, maintain human oversight for consequential decisions, conduct equity audits, provide opt-out pathways, and ensure clear consent and data-minimization practices (Noble, 2018).

AI for Feedback, Assessment, and Academic Writing Support

Feedback and assessment are among the most labor-intensive aspects of teaching, particularly in writing-intensive and practice-oriented programs. AI can augment these processes by providing timely, low-stakes formative guidance while preserving instructor capacity for higher-order mentoring and supervision (Yusuf et al., 2025). AI writing assistants can support students with grammar, structure, citation practices, and clarity prior to grading, shifting instructional focus from error correction to reasoning and evidence (Cui et al., 2025). In reflective journals and process notes, natural-language analytics can surface recurring themes or growth trajectories, prompting deeper inquiry during supervision rather than automated evaluation (Sherwood, 2024).

In counseling supervision and psychology labs, speech and transcript analysis tools can flag conversational patterns or reasoning biases, accelerating feedback cycles while leaving interpretation to human educators (Ping, 2024). In research methods, auto-graded quizzes and adaptive mastery checks support spaced practice and misconception correction (Zawacki-Richter et al., 2019). These applications do raise concerns related to bias, academic integrity, and data governance. Consequently, AI-supported assessment should prioritize transparency, disclosure of acceptable use, and human-in-the-loop grading for high-stakes decisions.

In undergraduate psychology research methods courses, AI-enabled adaptive learning systems support students' development of statistical reasoning and methodological competence. Modules adjust pacing and difficulty based on learner performance, routing students to targeted explanations when persistent misconceptions arise (e.g., confusion between Type I and Type II errors), thereby supporting mastery learning (Luckin, 2017; Zawacki-Richter et al., 2019).

In clinical psychology laboratories, AI-based virtual patients present overlapping or ambiguous symptom profiles that require students to formulate, test, and revise diagnostic hypotheses. Embedded analytics identify cognitive biases such as anchoring or premature closure, which are subsequently addressed during instructor-led debriefs focused on ethics, culture, and diagnostic humility (Ping, 2024).

Faculty retain full responsibility for summative assessment and professional judgment. In this context, AI functions as a visibility tool that surfaces reasoning patterns, while educators ensure that diagnostic competence remains grounded in ethical standards, cultural sensitivity, and accountability (Selwyn, 2019; Crawford, 2021).

AI in Reflective and Experiential Learning

Reflective practice is foundational to professional formation in social work, counseling, and psychology, linking self-awareness to ethical and culturally responsive practice (Urdang, 2010). AI can support reflection by structuring prompts, visualizing patterns over time, and surfacing blind spots, while leaving interpretation and judgment to human supervisors. AI-assisted reflective tools can scaffold post-simulation or practicum reflection, guide analysis of cognitive biases, and support longitudinal growth tracking (Tahirsylaj et al., 2019). When embedded within supervision and seminar discussions, these tools make tacit learning visible without displacing relational pedagogy. Educators should make note that risks include over-templated reflection, misinterpretation of affective cues, and privacy concerns. Accordingly, AI should function as a prompting and pattern-recognition aid, not as a substitute mentor.

In a bachelor's level social work program, AI-supported case simulations are embedded into field education preparation. Students engage with digital scenarios involving child protection, community practice, or welfare access, where conflicting stakeholder narratives, structural constraints, and ethical tensions are deliberately incorporated. The simulations adapt in real time as students conduct assessments or make referrals, prompting reflection on safety, equity, and professional responsibility (Egonsdotter & Israelsson, 2022).

Following each simulation, students complete AI-assisted reflective journals structured around themes of power, social justice, and positionality. Natural-language analytics cluster recurring patterns (e.g., individual versus structural framing of risk), which field instructors then use to guide reflective supervision conversations rather than algorithmic evaluation (Osborn & Karandikar, 2023; Selwyn, 2019).

This approach supplements rather than replaces live practicum supervision. By expanding access to complex case exposure while maintaining human judgment and ethical accountability, AI-enhanced supervision supports reflective, equity-oriented social work education (Benjamin, 2019; Noble, 2018).

Collaborative and Interdisciplinary Learning with AI

Professional practice increasingly occurs in interdisciplinary teams. AI can support collaborative learning by enabling co-creation workflows, peer review scaffolding, and interprofessional simulations that mirror real-world coordination challenges (Noel et al., 2022). Version tracking, contribution analytics, and AI-supported peer review can enhance accountability and feedback quality when paired with instructor calibration (Topping et al., 2025). Interdisciplinary simulations allow students from social work, counseling, and psychology to negotiate roles, ethics, and decision-making under shared constraints (Berrett-Abebe et al., 2023). To avoid surveillance or inequity, collaboration analytics should remain advisory, with transparency regarding data use and clear limits on automation.

Accessibility and Inclusion

AI-enabled tools can reduce barriers to participation for multilingual, disabled, neurodivergent, rural, and working students by offering flexible access modes and just-in-time support (Fitas, 2025). Translation, captioning, adaptive interfaces, and executive-function supports can advance inclusive design when paired with institutional investment (Crawford, 2021). However, without deliberate governance, AI may exacerbate the digital divide or introduce new forms of bias and surveillance. Programs should therefore prioritize infrastructure access, UDL-aligned materials, equity audits, transparent personalization, and privacy-by-design practices (Noble, 2018).

Taken together, these pedagogical innovations demonstrate how AI can expand opportunities for practice, feedback, collaboration, and access in social work, counseling, and psychology education. However, these benefits depend on design choices that preserve human judgment, equity, and professional values. The ethical, cultural, and professional conditions that shape responsible AI integration are examined in the following section.

ETHICAL, CULTURAL, AND PROFESSIONAL CONSIDERATIONS

Artificial intelligence (AI) has significant potential to enrich teaching and learning in social work, counseling, and psychology. However, because these disciplines are grounded in values such as empathy, justice, human dignity, and cultural humility, the educational use of AI demands sustained ethical scrutiny. Ethical, cultural, and professional considerations are not peripheral to AI adoption; they define the conditions under which AI can be legitimately integrated into human services education (Nuwasiima et al., 2024).

This section serves as the ethical anchor for the chapter. It examines five interrelated areas of concern: algorithmic bias and equity, academic integrity, protection of relational skills, data privacy and consent, and professional boundaries. Together, these dimensions clarify how AI can support learning while remaining aligned with the normative commitments of human-centered practice.

Algorithmic Bias, Equity, and Inclusion

AI systems reflect the data, assumptions, and objectives embedded in their design. When these inputs reproduce historical exclusions, AI outputs can reinforce or amplify inequity (Benjamin, 2019; Noble, 2018). In educational settings, such bias may appear through misclassification in adaptive learning platforms, writing evaluation tools that penalize non-standard dialects, or predictive analytics that under-identify students from marginalized backgrounds for enrichment or support (Crawford, 2021).

In human services education, these risks carry particular weight because equity and cultural humility are foundational disciplinary values. Counseling simulations may implicitly normalize Western, middle-class client profiles; psychology tools may encode culture-bound symptom interpretations; and social work case generators may inadvertently stereotype family structures or poverty (Selwyn, 2019). Such design choices shape not only learning outcomes but also professional imagination – what problems students recognize and which responses they view as legitimate.

An equity-first approach to AI integration requires deliberate institutional action. Programs should audit training data, prompts, and scoring rubrics for representativeness; involve students and community partners including Indigenous, LGBTQIA+, and migrant voices in content development; require transparent documentation of intended use and known limitations; provide opt-out and appeal mechanisms for algorithmic decisions; and retain human adjudication for consequential judgments (Zawacki-Richter et al., 2019). AI literacy should explicitly address algorithmic oppression, enabling students to identify, question, and remediate biased outputs in both educational and professional contexts (Benjamin, 2019; Noble, 2018).

Academic Integrity and Plagiarism Risks

Generative AI has increasingly blurred boundaries between authorship, assistance, and automation. Essays, literature reviews, and case analyses resembling student work can now be produced rapidly using tools such as ChatGPT (Zawacki-Richter et al., 2019). While such tools may support brainstorming or formative feedback, they also heighten risks of plagiarism, over-reliance, and diminished critical engagement.

In human services education, academic integrity is inseparable from professional preparedness. Counseling students who rely on AI to generate reflective journals may bypass emotional self-exploration; psychology students who delegate diagnostic reasoning risk entering practice without analytical depth; and social work students who outsource policy analysis may weaken their capacity to interrogate structural inequality.

Institutions must therefore articulate explicit standards governing acceptable and unacceptable AI use in coursework (Beale, 2022). Integrity is best protected not through surveillance alone but through assessment design – oral defenses, live simulations, reflective portfolios, and process-based assignments that require authentic engagement. Faculty play a critical role in teaching students to use AI transparently and ethically as a support for learning rather than a substitute for intellectual or professional responsibility.

Protecting Relational Skills and Human Connection

Relational competence lies at the core of social work, counseling, and psychology. Skills such as empathy, attunement, cultural humility, and ethical judgment cannot be automated. Yet, an overemphasis on AI efficiency risks shifting educational priorities from relational depth to technical optimization.

AI simulations and automated feedback systems can support skill practice, but they may miss subtle cues such as silence, embodied affect, or culturally situated expression. Students trained primarily through simulated environments may struggle with the unpredictability of real-world client interactions. Although AI-generated transcripts or analytics can highlight missed empathy opportunities, human educators remain essential for interpretation, contextualization, and professional growth (Selwyn, 2019).

Accordingly, AI should function as a reflective mirror rather than a relational mentor. In counseling education, automated indicators can prompt discussion, but supervision must guide meaning-making. In social work, simulations can initiate ethical dialogue, but relational learning must occur through field supervision. In psychology, AI-supported diagnostic reasoning must be paired with debriefs that foreground ethics, culture, and uncertainty. Protecting relational skills requires intentional pedagogical design that keeps human interaction central.

Data Privacy, Confidentiality, and Consent

AI-enabled educational tools routinely collect granular data, including drafts, keystrokes, transcripts, reflective writing, and engagement logs. These practices raise significant concerns regarding secondary data use, re-identification, cross-platform sharing, and the blurring of educational and therapeutic boundaries (Crawford, 2021). Such risks directly intersect with ethical principles in social work and counseling, including confidentiality, informed consent, and data minimization (Báez et al., 2025).

Institutions should publish plain-language data notices explaining what information is collected, why it is collected, how long it is retained, and what rights learners hold. Where feasible, students should be offered opt-out or alternative pathways. Privacy impact assessments and strict vendor contracts governing data access, reuse, and retention are essential. For decisions with significant consequences, such as progression or remediation, human judgment must prevail over opaque algorithmic scores (Selwyn, 2019).

Professional Boundaries and the Limits of AI

Educators carry responsibility for defining the appropriate scope of AI use in both education and future professional practice. While AI tools can support documentation, practice drills, formative feedback, and simulation, they should not provide therapy, make autonomous risk determinations, or replace professional judgment, particularly in contexts where cultural interpretation and ethical deliberation are required (Selwyn, 2019).

Boundary clarity should be explicitly taught. Programs may require students to develop personal AI-use statements for capstone or practicum work, specifying when and how AI will be used and when it will not. Such declarations reinforce accountability, professional identity formation, and alignment with ethical codes and accreditation standards (Funa & Gabay, 2025). Responsible AI integration depends on maintaining clear limits across equity, integrity, relational competence, data protection, and professional authority.

Ethical, cultural, and professional considerations are foundational to AI-powered learning in social work, counseling, and psychology. By addressing algorithmic bias, safeguarding academic integrity, protecting relational skills, ensuring privacy, and defining professional boundaries, educators can integrate AI in ways that enhance rather than erode human-centered practice. The goal is not to reject AI, but to adopt it critically, ensuring that technological innovation remains accountable to enduring disciplinary values.

EDUCATIONAL PATHWAYS AND FACULTY DEVELOPMENT

Exposure to the technical features of AI tools alone is insufficient to prepare students for professional practice in social work, counseling, and psychology. Effective preparation requires a coherent educational pathway that balances digital competence with ethical literacy, alongside faculty who are adequately supported to lead pedagogical change. AI integration must therefore be understood as a curriculum-wide and institutionally supported transformation rather than an isolated instructional innovation.

This section examines four interrelated components of such a pathway: AI literacy for students, faculty training and professional development, institutional frameworks and accreditation policies, and curriculum innovation.

Building AI Literacy in Students

AI literacy is a foundational competency for future professionals working in technology-saturated human services environments. For students in social work, counseling, and psychology, AI literacy extends beyond functional tool use to include critical evaluation of algorithmic outputs, ethical reasoning, and informed professional judgment.

A first dimension is critical AI literacy, which equips students to recognize that AI systems are neither neutral nor objective. Predictive tools used in child welfare or mental health risk assessment, for example, may misrepresent marginalized populations, while sentiment analysis tools may misinterpret culturally specific expressions of distress (Noble, 2018). Students must be trained to interrogate how data, assumptions, and design choices shape AI outputs.

A second dimension involves applied AI literacy, providing hands-on exposure to discipline-relevant tools. Examples include AI-assisted transcription and session analysis in counseling supervision, text-mining tools for psychology literature reviews, and data dashboards supporting case management or program evaluation in social work. Such engagement demystifies AI while reinforcing the need for human interpretation.

Finally, ethical AI literacy emphasizes confidentiality, informed consent, accountability, and the risks of substituting relational judgment with automated outputs. As emphasized in gerontology and social work education, digital literacy empowers vulnerable populations when it promotes critical engagement rather than passive adoption (Rafi & Saif, 2021). Similarly, AI literacy enables graduates to engage technology reflexively and responsibly.

Faculty Training and Professional Development

Faculty play a decisive role in shaping how AI is interpreted and used within curricula. However, many educators report limited preparation and insufficient institutional support for integrating AI into teaching (Delello et al., 2025). Without structured development opportunities, AI adoption risks being uneven, superficial, or ethically misaligned.

Faculty development should therefore address both technical competence and ethical understanding. Social work educators designing AI-supported case simulations may benefit from training in prompt design and bias awareness, while counseling and psychology faculty require guidance on interpreting analytics outputs within culturally and ethically grounded pedagogies. Equally important are communities of practice, where faculty across disciplines can share experiences, challenges, and strategies. Cross-disciplinary dialogue enables psychology faculty to discuss AI in diagnostic reasoning while social work faculty examine implications for community practice and equity.

Workload considerations are critical. Faculty who perceive AI adoption as an added burden may disengage, particularly in already resource-constrained environments. Institutions should recognize and reward pedagogical innovation through workload adjustments, funding, and recognition mechanisms. Without such support, educators may experience digital fatigue – a phenomenon linked to sustained technology-driven stress (Rafi & Rafi, 2022). Professional development should therefore also address faculty well-being during digital transformation.

Institutional Frameworks and Accreditation Policies

AI integration cannot depend solely on individual faculty initiative. Institutional frameworks are required to ensure consistency, equity, and ethical accountability across programs. Institutions must establish clear governance policies addressing permissible AI use in instruction and assessment. Such policies should cover academic integrity, student data protection, transparency, and cultural inclusivity in AI-enabled platforms (Crawford, 2021). Equally important is equitable investment in infrastructure, including access to devices, connectivity, software, and technical support, to prevent AI adoption from reinforcing existing disparities. Just as human services practice requires regulatory safeguards to protect client dignity and rights,

AI in education requires institutional scaffolding to ensure alignment with principles of fairness, inclusion, and human dignity.

Accreditation bodies in social work, counseling, and psychology increasingly emphasize competencies related to ethical decision-making, cultural responsiveness, and reflective practice. These expectations can be extended to include AI literacy and responsible digital engagement, such as the ability to critically evaluate algorithmic recommendations in mental health or social service contexts.

Curriculum Innovation and Pedagogical Models

Sustainable AI integration requires intentional curriculum design rather than isolated modules. Effective curricular models combine technical understanding, ethical reflection, and applied practice in discipline-specific contexts.

Dedicated courses (e.g., *AI in Human Services*) can introduce foundational concepts such as algorithmic bias, data ethics, and professional applications. However, AI is most effective when integrated across core courses. In social policy and community practice, students may use AI to explore welfare datasets while critiquing assumptions and proposing equity-centered alternatives (Crawford, 2021). In counseling education, AI-supported simulations can scaffold skills development, with supervisors leading ethical and relational debriefs (Akkurt et al., 2025). In psychology research methods, AI can support data visualization and analysis while students justify decisions and validate outputs (Luckin, 2017).

Ethics should be embedded across the curriculum, not confined to standalone lectures. Assignments should specify acceptable AI use, require disclosure, and employ process-visible designs such as drafts, oral defenses, and reflective commentaries to protect academic integrity (Selwyn, 2019). Regular equity checkpoints can prompt students to consider who may be excluded or harmed by AI systems and how such risks might be mitigated (Benjamin, 2019; Noble, 2018).

Experiential learning contexts including field placements and practica offer additional opportunities for responsible AI engagement. Pre-placement preparation should address privacy, consent, and professional boundaries, while structured supervision during placements can examine how AI use affects judgment, equity, and relational care (Reamer, 2023). In rural or low-resource settings, virtual simulations may supplement but should not replace in-person supervision, expanding access while maintaining standards.

Educational pathways that integrate AI responsibly require coordinated development across students, faculty, institutions, and curricula. When AI literacy is paired with ethical grounding, faculty support, institutional governance, and intentional curricular design, graduates are better prepared to navigate technology-rich practice environments. As emphasized by Rafi and Saif (2020), innovation is most effective when it remains socially relevant. AI-enhanced education in social work, counseling, and psychology must therefore align technological capability with empowerment, justice, and human well-being ensuring that AI collaborates with, rather than displaces, human-centered professional practice.

FUTURE DIRECTIONS

The integration of artificial intelligence (AI) into social work, counseling, and psychology education remains at an early stage. While initial innovations demonstrate pedagogical promise, the long-term impact of AI-powered learning will depend on how educators, institutions, professional bodies, and policymakers balance technological advancement with human-centered values. Future directions must therefore be shaped not only by technical capability, but by ethical governance, empirical evidence, and participatory design.

This section outlines five key directions for the field: emerging trends in AI adoption, preparation of graduates for AI-infused practice, co-creation and student voice, building an evidence base, and policy and accreditation implications.

Emerging Trends in AI Adoption

AI is becoming increasingly embedded across higher education systems, influencing curriculum delivery, assessment, student support, and institutional planning (Zawacki-Richter et al., 2019). In social work, counseling, and psychology education, three trends hold particular promise when guided by equity-first design and human oversight.

First, *immersive AI simulations*, including virtual and augmented reality environments, are expected to expand. These systems enable emotionally responsive and branching scenarios that allow counseling students to practice rapport-building and risk assessment, psychology students to conduct virtual experiments with realistic variability, and social work students to navigate complex, multi-stakeholder cases such as housing instability or child protection. When paired with guided debriefing, such simulations can support standardized exposure to high-risk or rare situations while preserving ethical and cultural reflection (Akkurt et al., 2025).

Second, *AI-supported socio-emotional analytics* are likely to advance. Speech, text, and interaction data may be used to surface patterns related to empathy, emotional regulation, or countertransference, supporting reflective learning and self-awareness (Crawford, 2021). However, because affect detection is probabilistic and culturally contingent, such outputs must be treated as prompts for discussion rather than definitive judgments, with interpretation remaining firmly in human hands (Selwyn, 2019).

Third, *adaptive institutional ecosystems* may emerge, integrating learning analytics with advising, sequencing of coursework, and career planning (Soomro et al., 2025). When transparently governed, these systems can enhance mastery learning and timely support. Without careful oversight, however, they risk reinforcing stereotypes or narrowing opportunity. Future AI adoption must therefore prioritize dignity, inclusivity, and justice to avoid technocratic inequities (Crawford, 2021; Rafi & Saif, 2020).

Preparing Graduates for AI-Infused Practice Settings

Graduates in social work, counseling, and psychology will increasingly encounter AI tools in practice environments, ranging from diagnostic support systems to predictive analytics in welfare and mental health services. Educational goals must therefore expand beyond tool familiarity to encompass critical evaluation and ethical judgment.

Graduates should be capable of *informed and critical AI use*, understanding both the capabilities and limitations of AI systems. For example, a social worker using an AI-supported risk assessment must be able to question model assumptions and recognize when outputs conflict with contextual knowledge or professional judgment.

Equally important is *ethical decision-making in digital contexts*. As emphasized in prior work on legal safeguards for vulnerable populations (Rafi, 2019), technology must operate within clear ethical boundaries. Students must learn when AI support is appropriate and when human deliberation should prevail.

Finally, graduates must demonstrate *contextual and cultural judgment*. As research on older women's health illustrates, gender, culture, and socioeconomic conditions shape lived experience (Rafi & Saif, 2021). Future professionals must therefore be prepared to identify how AI systems interact with structural inequalities and to resist technological solutions that obscure diversity and lived realities.

Co-Creation and Student Voice

Future AI-enabled education should position students as *co-creators rather than passive recipients* of technology-mediated learning. Co-creation recognizes that students bring valuable insight into how AI affects motivation, inclusion, identity, and relational learning.

Participatory design approaches can involve students in developing or refining AI-mediated simulations, ensuring representation of diverse perspectives, including marginalized and minority voices. Continuous feedback mechanisms should enable students to report concerns related to bias, exclusion, or excessive automation.

Empowering student voice also supports professional identity formation in technological contexts. As demonstrated in age-friendly and inclusive community initiatives, environments function best when those affected are involved in shaping them (Rafi & Saif, 2020). AI in education should similarly be designed *with* students, not merely *for* them.

Building an Evidence Base: Research and Evaluation

The adoption of AI in human services education has often outpaced the development of robust empirical evidence. Future research must therefore prioritize systematic, transparent, and context-sensitive evaluation (Selwyn, 2019).

Mixed-methods designs are particularly valuable, combining quantitative indicators (e.g., mastery rates, skill assessments, supervisor ratings) with qualitative insights from interviews, reflective writing, and classroom observation. Comparative studies should evaluate AI-mediated, hybrid, and traditional approaches to identify differential effects across disciplines and learning contexts (Zawacki-Richter et al., 2019).

Equity-focused evaluation is essential. Outcomes should be disaggregated by race, gender, language, disability, socioeconomic status, and geography to detect disparate impacts. Longitudinal research following graduates into practice settings can assess whether AI-supported education translates into improved relational competence, ethical judgment, and workforce retention in underserved areas. Open and transparent research practices including pre-registration, sharing of prompts and rubrics, and reporting of null findings will be critical for building a cumulative and trustworthy evidence base (Evans et al., 2023).

Policy Implications and Accreditation Standards

The future of AI-powered education will be shaped as much by governance as by innovation. Policies and accreditation standards must translate values such as equity, privacy, academic integrity, and human oversight into enforceable and reviewable practices (Selwyn, 2019).

At the institutional level, policies should clearly define acceptable AI use in teaching, assessment, advising, research, and field education, with mandatory disclosure where AI assistance is employed. Core policy elements include academic integrity safeguards, equity and accessibility audits, data governance standards, and human-in-the-loop requirements for consequential decisions (Crawford, 2021).

Professional accreditation bodies in social work, counseling, and psychology can embed AI-related competencies within existing standards without diluting human-centered values. These may include AI literacy, ethical digital practice, interpretive judgment, and evidence of human supervision in simulated or AI-supported learning environments (Rodriguez et al., 2024).

Global policy coordination can further support smaller or under-resourced institutions by providing shared audit frameworks, vendor contract templates, and baseline principles such as transparency, equity-by-design, and human oversight (Selwyn, 2019). Legal safeguards must also protect students from exploitative or opaque AI practices, ensuring consent, appeal mechanisms, and confidentiality for sensitive educational data (Crawford, 2021; Rafi, 2019).

Future AI-powered learning in social work, counseling, and psychology will be defined by how effectively innovation is aligned with professional values. Immersive simulations, adaptive ecosystems, and socio-emotional analytics offer significant promise, but only when guided by ethical governance, empirical evidence, and participatory design. Preparing graduates for AI-infused practice requires critical literacy, contextual judgment, and cultural humility. By centering student voice, strengthening research, and updating accreditation and policy frameworks, AI can function as a pedagogical partner enhancing learning while preserving the ethical, relational, and justice-oriented foundations of human services education.

CONCLUSION

Artificial intelligence (AI) is no longer peripheral to social work, counseling, and psychology education. Across universities globally, AI-powered simulations, adaptive learning systems, automated feedback tools, and collaborative platforms are being incorporated into curricula to expand access, support skill development, and prepare students for digitally mediated practice environments. As this chapter has demonstrated, however, the educational value of AI depends on how effectively innovation is balanced with ethics, cultural responsiveness, and professional responsibility.

This chapter examined AI integration across five interrelated domains. First, the introduction positioned AI as both a transformative force and a source of tension within human services education, where empathy, cultural humility, and social justice are core commitments. Second, pedagogical innovations illustrated how AI can scaffold learning through counseling simulations, psychology research and diagnostic training, and social work reflective and practicum-based activities, while extending educational access for diverse learners. Third, ethical, cultural, and professional considerations highlighted that AI is not neutral; risks related to algorithmic bias, academic integrity, relational skill erosion, and data privacy require sustained attention and human oversight. Fourth, educational pathways and faculty development underscored the need for coordinated strategies that include student AI literacy, faculty support, institutional governance, and curriculum-wide integration. Finally, future directions emphasized the importance of immersive learning environments, co-creation with students, rigorous evidence-building, and responsive policy and accreditation frameworks.

Across these discussions, a central conclusion emerges: AI in social work, counseling, and psychology education should be understood as a pedagogical transformation that demands critical engagement, not merely as a technical upgrade. AI adds value when it strengthens reflective learning, ethical reasoning, and relational competence. When adopted uncritically, however, it risks reinforcing inequities, narrowing educational experiences, and undermining the foundational values of these professions.

The chapter also demonstrated how insights from social work and gerontological research – particularly on age-friendly environments, elder protection, legal safeguards, and digital stress – inform contemporary debates on AI in education. Just as vulnerable populations require robust policy frameworks and ethical protections, students and educators engaging with AI require safeguards that prioritize dignity, justice, and inclusion. This cross-domain resonance reinforces the principle that technology should support human well-being rather than dictate professional practice.

Looking ahead, educators, institutions, and professional bodies face a dual responsibility. First, they must invest in infrastructure, training, and governance mechanisms that enable equitable and ethically grounded AI integration. Second, they must actively engage student and community voices to ensure that AI tools reflect diverse cultural contexts and lived experiences. Only through such participatory, justice-oriented approaches can innovation proceed without eroding the relational heart of human services education.

In conclusion, AI is neither a panacea nor a threat in itself. Its impact is shaped by the values, policies, and pedagogical choices that govern its use. For social work, counseling, and psychology, the task is to humanize technology leveraging AI to deepen empathy, enhance reflection, and uphold enduring commitments to dignity, equity, and cultural humility as these disciplines navigate an increasingly AI-infused educational future.

REFERENCES

Akkurt, M., Maurya, R., & Brown, T. (2025). Learning through simulation: Counselor trainees' interactions with ChatGPT as a client. *Behavioral Sciences (Basel, Switzerland), 15*(12), 1660. DOI: 10.3390/bs15121660

Anders, A. D., & Dux Speltz, E. (2025). Developing generative AI literacies through self-regulated learning: A human-centered approach. *Computers and Education: Artificial Intelligence, 9*, 100482. DOI: 10.1016/j.caeai.2025.100482

Báez, J. C., Bjugstad, A., Park, T. K., Jones, J. L., Bidwell, L. N., Sage, M., & Hitchcock, L. I. (2025). Social work educators innovating with generative AI: An exploratory study. *Journal of Social Work Education, 61*(1), 14–29. DOI: 10.1080/10437797.2024.2411170

Beale, R. (2022). *Adapting university policies for generative AI: Opportunities, challenges, and policy solutions in higher education.* Arxiv.org. https://arxiv.org/html/2506.22231v1

Benjamin, R. (2019). *Race after technology: Abolitionist tools for the new Jim Code*. Polity Press.

Bernacki, M. L., Greene, M. J., & Lobczowski, N. G. (2021). A systematic review of research on personalized learning: Personalized by whom, to what, how, and for what purpose (s)? *Educational Psychology Review, 33*(4), 1675–1715.

Berrett-Abebe, J., Novella, J. K., & Perera, D. M. (2023). Shared and unique competencies in interprofessional behavioral health: Implications for counselor education. *The Journal of Counselor Preparation and Supervisor, 17*(5). https://research.library.kutztown.edu/jcps/vol17/iss5/5

Crawford, K. (2021). *The atlas of AI: Power, politics, and the planetary costs of artificial intelligence*. Yale University Press.

Cui, Y., He, W., Du, X., Zeng, M., & Liu, D. (2025). The impact of AI writing assistants on academic writing performance. *International Journal of Distance Education Technologies, 23*(1), 1–28. DOI: 10.4018/ijdet.391326

Delello, J. A., Sung, W., Mokhtari, K., Hebert, J., Bronson, A., & De Giuseppe, T. (2025). AI in the classroom: Insights from educators on usage, challenges, and mental health. *Education Sciences, 15*(2), 113. DOI: 10.3390/educsci15020113

Egonsdotter, G., & Israelsson, M. (2022). Computer-based simulations in social work education: A scoping review. *Research on Social Work Practice*, *34*(1), 41–53. DOI: 10.1177/10497315221147016

Evans, T. R., Branney, P., Clements, A., & Hatton, E. (2023). Improving evidence-based practice through preregistration of applied research: Barriers and recommendations. *Accountability in Research*, *30*(2), 88–108. DOI: 10.1080/08989621.2021.1969233

Fitas, R. (2025). Inclusive Education with AI: Supporting Special Needs and Tackling Language Barriers. *arXiv preprint arXiv:2504.14120.*

Funa, A. A., & Gabay, R. A. E. (2025). AI literacy in health-professions education: Deepening the case for curricular reform in the Philippines. *Health Science Reports*, *8*(11), e71551. DOI: 10.1002/hsr2.71551

García-Torres, D., Fernández, C., Mira, J. J., Morales, A., & Vicente, M. A. (2025). Using AI-based virtual simulated patients for training in psychopathological interviewing: Cross-sectional observational study. *JMIR Medical Education*, *11*, e78857. DOI: 10.2196/78857

Joshi, M. A. (2024). Adaptive learning through artificial intelligence. *International Journal on Integrated Education*, *7*(2), 41–43.

Lateef, F. (2010). Simulation-based learning: Just like the real thing. *Journal of Emergencies, Trauma and Shock*, *3*(4), 348–352.

Luckin, R. (2017). Towards artificial intelligence-based assessment systems. *Nature Human Behaviour, 1*(3), 003.

Mackey, W. (2014). *Culturally relevant education and critical pedagogy: Devolution of hierarchies of power*. Revista Internacional de Educación para la Justicia Social.

Mehdaoui, A. (2024). Unveiling Barriers and Challenges of AI Technology Integration in Education: Assessing Teachers' Perceptions, Readiness and Anticipated Resistance. *Futurity Education*, *4*(4), 95–108.

Noble, S. U. (2018). *Algorithms of oppression: How search engines reinforce racism*. NYU Press.

Noel, L., Chen, Q., Petruzzi, L. J., Phillips, F., Garay, R., Valdez, C., & Jones, B. (2022). Interprofessional collaboration between social workers and community health workers to address health and mental health in the United States: A systematised review. *Health & Social Care in the Community*, *30*(6), e6240–e6254.

Nuwasiima, M., Ahonon, M. P., & Kadiri, C. (2024). The role of artificial intelligence (AI) and machine learning in social work practice. *World Journal of Advanced Research and Reviews*, *24*(1), 80–97.

Oliveira Silva, G., Fonseca, L. M. M., Siqueira, K. M., de Góes, F. D. S. N., Ribeiro, L. M., & Aredes, N. D. A. (2023). The simulation design in health and nursing: A scoping review. *Nursing Open*, *10*(4), 1966–1984. DOI: 10.1002/nop2.1466

Osborn, P. R., & Karandikar, S. (2023). Practice-based knowledge perspectives of cultural competence in social work. *Journal of Ethnic & Cultural Diversity in Social Work*, *32*(6), 285–297.

Ping, Y. (2024). Experience in psychological counseling supported by artificial intelligence technology. *Technology and Health Care*, *32*(6), 3871–3888.

Rafi, S. (2019). Critical analysis of the legal approach to protect the elderly population in India. *BSSS Journal of Social Work*, *11*(1), 1–20.

Rafi, S., & Rafi, S. (2022). Mental health and stress in the digital workplace: Implications for social work practice. In *Managing the digital workplace in the post-pandemic era* (pp. 26–40).

Rafi, S., & Saif, S. (2020a). Age-friendly communities: Creating a conducive environment for the elderly in India. *Journal of Geriatric Medicine*, *2*(2), 7.

Rafi, S., & Saif, S. (2020b). Critical review of literature on the prevalence of elder abuse in India: Sorrow of greying. *Journal of Psychosocial Well-being*, *1*(2), 35–44.

Rafi, S., & Saif, S. (2021). Physical and mental health issues of elderly women in India: A review. In *Handbook of research on policies, protocols, and practices for social work.*

Reamer, F. G. (2023). Artificial intelligence in social work: Emerging ethical issues. *International Journal of Social Work Values and Ethics*, *20*(2), 52–71.

Rodriguez, M. Y., Goldkind, L., Victor, B. G., Hiltz, B., & Perron, B. E. (2024). Introducing generative artificial intelligence into the MSW curriculum: A proposal for the 2029 Educational Policy and Accreditation Standards. *Journal of Social Work Education*, *60*(2), 174–182. DOI: 10.1080/10437797.2024.2340931

Selwyn, N. (2019). *Should robots replace teachers? AI and the future of education.* Polity Press.

Sherwood, G. (2024). Reflective practice and knowledge development: Transforming research for a practice-based discipline. *International Journal of Nursing Sciences*, *11*(4), 399–404.

Siddals, S., Torous, J., & Coxon, A. (2024). *"It happened to be the perfect thing": Experiences of generative AI chatbots for mental health. npj Mental Health Research, 3*(1), 48. DOI: 10.1038/s44184-024-00097-4

Singh, T. M., Reddy, C. K. K., Murthy, B. R., Nag, A., & Doss, S. (2025). AI and education: Bridging the gap to personalized, efficient, and accessible learning. In *Internet of behavior-based computational intelligence for smart education systems* (pp. 131–160). IGI Global.

Soomro, A. A., Khan, M. H., Umar, M., Sjid Khan, S., & Ali, O. (2025). AI-driven academic advising in higher education: Leveraging intelligent systems to personalize student support, improve retention, and optimize career pathways. *The Critical Review of Social Sciences Studies, 3*(2), 229–248. DOI: 10.59075/vy3v7k17

Tahirsylaj, A., Matson, J., & Gashi, L. (2019). Educating minds for the age of innovation. *International Journal of Innovation. Creativity and Change, 5*(1), 15–32.

Tanana, M. J., Soma, C. S., Srikumar, V., Atkins, D. C., & Imel, Z. E. (2019). Development and evaluation of ClientBot: Patient-like conversational agent to train basic counseling skills. *Journal of Medical Internet Research, 21*(7), e12529. DOI: 10.2196/12529

Therasa, M. M. (2023). Adapting Assistive Technology to Diverse Learning Needs in Inclusive Education. *Shanlax International Journal of Arts. Science and Humanities, 11*, 63–66.

Topping, K. J., Gehringer, E., & Khosravi, H., Srilekha Gudipati, Jadhav, K., & Surya Susarla. (2025). Enhancing peer assessment with artificial intelligence. *International Journal of Educational Technology in Higher Education, 22*(1). Advance online publication. DOI: 10.1186/s41239-024-00501-1

Urdang, E. (2010). Awareness of self—A critical tool. *Social Work Education, 29*(5), 523–538. DOI: 10.1080/02615470903164950

Wang, X., Liu, J., Jia, S., Hou, C., Jiao, R., Yan, Y., & Liu, X. Y. (2024). Hybrid teaching after COVID-19: Advantages, challenges and optimization strategies. *BMC Medical Education, 24*(1), 753.

Yusuf, H., Money, A., & Daylamani-Zad, D. (2025). Towards reducing teacher burden in Performance-Based assessments using aivaluate: An emotionally intelligent LLM-Augmented pedagogical AI conversational agent. *Education and Information Technologies*, •••, 1–45.

Zamfiroiu, A., Sharma, R. C., Constantinescu, D., Pană, M., & Toma, C. (2022). Using learning analytics for analyzing students' behavior in online learning. *Studies in Informatics and Control, 31*(3), 63–74.

Zawacki-Richter, O., Marín, V. I., Bond, M., & Gouverneur, F. (2019). Systematic review of research on artificial intelligence applications in higher education: Where are the educators? *International Journal of Educational Technology in Higher Education, 16*(1), 39. DOI: 10.1186/s41239-019-0171-0

KEY TERMS AND DEFINITIONS

AI Literacy: The ability of students and faculty to critically understand, evaluate, and responsibly use AI. AI literacy involves technical skills, ethical awareness, and cultural sensitivity, preparing learners to engage with AI thoughtfully rather than passively.

AI-Powered Learning: The integration of AI tools and systems into educational processes to enhance pedagogy, assessment, and student engagement. It includes adaptive quizzes, simulation-based practice, automated feedback, and reflective journaling systems.

Algorithmic Bias: Systematic errors in AI outputs caused by biased data or programming assumptions. In human services education, algorithmic bias can perpetuate stereotypes or marginalize students and clients from diverse cultural, racial, or socio-economic groups.

Artificial Intelligence (AI): A branch of computer science that lets machines learn, reason, and solve problems. AI supports teaching and learning using adaptive learning platforms, chatbots, simulations, and generating text tools.

Digital Inclusion: Ensuring equitable access to AI technologies, platforms, and digital resources for all learners, regardless of socio-economic status, geography, or ability. Digital inclusion addresses the risk of widening the digital divide in higher education.

Ethical AI Use: The responsible application of AI in ways that uphold principles of justice, empathy, and human dignity. Ethical AI use in education includes safeguarding data privacy, avoiding plagiarism, mitigating bias, and preserving human connection.

Faculty Development: The process of equipping educators with the knowledge, skills, and resources needed to integrate AI responsibly into teaching. Faculty development includes training in AI tools, ethics, and strategies to balance technology with relational pedagogy.

Human-Centered Pedagogy: An approach to teaching that prioritizes empathy, relational skills, and cultural humility. In the context of AI-powered learning, human-centered pedagogy ensures that technology supports rather than replaces authentic human connection.

Reflective Practice: A core component of social work, counseling, and psychology education that involves analyzing one's thoughts, feelings, and actions to improve professional competence. AI can support reflective practice by providing prompts or feedback but cannot replace human supervision.

Simulation-Based Learning: An instructional method that uses AI-generated scenarios to allow students to practice counseling, diagnostic reasoning, or case management in a safe, controlled environment. Simulations provide experiential learning while minimizing real-world risks.

Chapter 2
Integrating AI Literacy Into Human Service Education:
Possibilities and Ethical Considerations

Kimberly E. Giamportone
https://orcid.org/0000-0001-7015-9605
University of Southern Maine, USA

ABSTRACT

Generative AI tools are becoming increasingly integrated into human service programs necessitating adaptation in psychology, counseling, and social work to prepare students for work within evolving technological landscapes (Báez et al., 2025; Stone, 2025). Departments must consider how AI technologies align with the pedagogical and ethical frameworks of their fields to guide both students and faculty through responsible use of AI tools. This chapter explores approaches in developing AI literacy using practical strategies for introducing AI in ways that support rather than displace critical thinking and reflective practice. Recognized challenges include issues pertaining to authorship, bias, and academic integrity, along with the broader question of how the use of AI technology aligns with values such as empathy, relationality, and cultural competence (Dueck & Sundararajan, 2024; Soman et al., 2025).

DOI: 10.4018/979-8-3373-4362-4.ch002

INTRODUCTION

Growing interest in generative AI has prompted programs in the helping professions to reconsider how they prepare students for new forms of digital engagement across academic, practicum, and workplace settings (Ooi & Wilkinson, 2025; Reimer, 2024). Faculty and program leaders now face important decisions about if and how to guide students in their use of AI tools. These decisions involve questions of ethics and how to foster effective use while remaining mindful of access and equity. As AI technologies become increasingly visible and normalized, these considerations take on even greater urgency in the context of higher education. For students in social work, psychology, and counseling, AI is likely to surface in many professional contexts, including clinical documentation, professional writing, research, and assessment. Preparing students to engage responsibly with AI is therefore both a pedagogical and ethical responsibility. Programs must help students critically evaluate both the usefulness and the limitations of AI, ensuring that its integration remains consistent with disciplinary values and core learning goals.

This chapter is intentionally positioned as a foundational resource for educators and administrators in the helping professions who are seeking to better understand the possibilities of generative artificial intelligence for teaching, learning, and professional formation. Rather than proposing a formal competency framework or prescribing specific practices, the chapter aims to support reader AI literacy to develop critical understanding sufficient to engage in pedagogical decisions and institutional conversations.

The approach to generative AI was taken with deliberate caution. While these technologies may offer efficiencies, they also raise significant concerns. As such, some educators and students may ultimately choose to limit or refuse engagement with AI on ethical or philosophical grounds. This chapter does not presume adoption, but instead invites reflective consideration of how, when, and whether AI tools align with the values and responsibilities of human service education. Situating AI literacy within the broader conversation about digital literacy and ethics in higher education highlights its significance as part of professional competency. The information presented takes up that conversation by offering conceptual framing alongside applied examples, with particular attention to pedagogy and professional formation. The text provides a structured approach for programs seeking to prepare students to navigate AI thoughtfully and responsibly, and is organized into sections on foundational AI concepts, ethical considerations, faculty engagement, and curricular integration.

UNDERSTANDING FOUNDATIONAL AI CONCEPTS

The following overview of artificial intelligence is intentionally selective. This section focuses on conceptual features most relevant to educators in the helping professions rather than offering a comprehensive or technical account of how AI systems are built and operate. A basic understanding of how generative AI systems produce outputs is essential for critical evaluation and informed pedagogical decision-making. The information provided, therefore, emphasizes the functional capacities of contemporary AI systems, including generative, predictive, and assistive applications, while avoiding excessive technical detail that may risk obscuring the practical and relational questions that are central to human services education.

Defining AI in the Helping Professions

Over the past several decades, the helping professions have gradually incorporated digital tools to respond to changing social conditions and organizational demands. What may appear as a rapid turn toward artificial intelligence is better understood as the latest phase in a much longer trajectory of technological integration within social work, counseling, and related fields. From early reliance on paper records to the transition to computerized documentation systems and web-based communication, technology has consistently evolved and shaped how care is delivered as well as documented.

The COVID-19 pandemic marked a critical inflection point in this evolution. Widespread lockdowns and social distancing requirements disrupted long-standing assumptions about in-person service delivery and accelerated the adoption of digital interventions at an unprecedented pace (Mamaleka & Skobi, 2024). Telehealth platforms, online support groups, as well as virtual supervision became essential rather than optional (Nuwasiima et al., 2024). In this context, emerging digital tools gained traction as options to maintain continuity of care while managing increased demand and limited resources. The pandemic did not introduce these technologies, but it sharply reduced resistance to their use and highlighted their practical value.

Within this broader shift, artificial intelligence and machine learning increasingly influence both administrative and clinical dimensions of practice. Predictive models are used to identify patterns associated with risk, service utilization, or program outcomes, allowing agencies to intervene earlier and allocate resources more strategically (Fahad, 2024). Digital communication technologies also reshape how practitioners connect with their clients and communities. Services now encompass video-based counseling, text and chat support, online outreach, and the use of social media as both an engagement and education tool. These modalities have expanded access for individuals who face various barriers while also challenging practitioners to reconsider ethical issues around boundaries and confidentiality in virtual spaces.

Similarly, adopting artificial intelligence (AI) and other digital platforms is a broad and evolving concept in the education of students within the helping professions. Tools used to support teaching and learning, such as those for writing or academic tasks, often differ from the tools used in professional practice, such as those used to support clinical assessments. Yet some research and writing functions overlap across both settings and highlight the need for students to develop adaptable skills to navigate AI tools that serve multiple purposes as they prepare for work in the practice realm. The challenge faced, then, is how to develop awareness and ethical competence in using AI tools beginning with the role of education but which becomes applicable to practice uses. A useful starting point is to define some of the basic AI systems, captured under the broad umbrella of artificial intelligence, that are currently being used throughout popular culture, education, and the helping professions.

The term *Artificial Intelligence* itself was coined in 1956 by mathematics professor John McCarthy, with the foundational premise that if an intelligent feature, like learning, could be broken down and operationally defined, a machine could simulate it (Rajaraman, 2014). The first notable chatbot, ELIZA, was developed in the 1960s at the MIT Artificial Intelligence Laboratory by Joseph Weizenbaum (Berry, 2023). One iteration, known as DOCTOR, was designed to simulate a Rogerian therapist. Using Socratic-style responses, the program reframed questions posed by users, giving the impression of empathetic engagement. Although ELIZA and DOCTOR were limited to simple pattern recognition and did not truly understand or feel emotions, they marked an important early exploration of how technology could mimic aspects of human interaction, a development that would later influence the use of AI within counseling and other helping professions (Duggan, 2016).

AI programming has become more sophisticated over the years, but modern AI can still be understood as the development of technologies that replicate aspects of human intelligence, such as reasoning and language processing, as well as the evolving broader capacity of machines to act autonomously in pursuit of particular objectives (Abbass, 2019). These technologies are used in the helping professions to help carry out a variety of tasks that simulate the human mental skills required for decision-making, assessment, and analysis, as well as writing and editing in a variety of styles and tones to suit a particular audience.

Understanding the learning mechanisms that underlie AI can be valuable when considering how different aspects of the technology might be applied to meet the needs of both classroom instruction and client-centered work. Focusing primarily on various components of Machine Learning, which employs algorithms to analyze large datasets, identify patterns, generate predictions, and support decision-making, allows for a clear view of many tools that are currently familiar to and used by students and faculty. This approach highlights not only the technical capabilities of AI systems but also their potential relevance in educational and professional practice.

Machine Learning

Machine learning can be understood through three main approaches: supervised learning, unsupervised learning, and reinforcement learning. Each of these approaches reflects a different way that computer systems learn from data, and each can be applied to teaching, research, and practice in the helping professions.

Supervised Learning is when a computer is trained with examples that include both the information going in and the expected answer (Gillani et al., 2023). Over time, the system learns the relationship between the two and can begin to make predictions. In the helping professions, supervised learning could be applied to predict which clients might be at higher risk of disengaging from services. For example, if a system is trained with past data such as frequency of appointment attendance, completion of agreed-upon tasks, reported motivation levels, and prior patterns of service use, it may be able to identify clients who share characteristics with those who previously stopped participating. In practice, this information could help practitioners recognize when extra outreach, motivational interviewing, or additional support might be needed to keep clients engaged and receiving care.

Unsupervised Learning works differently because the computer is not told what the "right" answer is ahead of time. Instead, it looks for natural groupings or patterns in the data (Han & Shin, 2025). This type of learning can be especially useful in research such as when working with large amounts of qualitative material. Social work faculty might collect reflective journals from students completing a practicum. An unsupervised learning system could analyze the text to identify recurring themes, such as challenges in engaging clients, navigating ethical dilemmas, or making use of supervision. Faculty could then use these themes to guide class discussions, adapt supervision models, or strengthen partnerships with field agencies. The value here is not that the system provides definitive answers but that it can quickly reveal patterns that might take faculty much longer to notice on their own.

Reinforcement Learning is when a system learns by trial and error. It takes an action, receives feedback in the form of rewards or penalties, and gradually adjusts its behavior to maximize positive outcomes (Abubakar et al., 2024). Within the helping professions, this type of learning might be used with clients or with students practicing on interactive simulations. A simulation example might use an AI virtual client program that has been trained to respond to different counseling techniques. At first, the responses may seem generic. But as the system receives more feedback during interactions identifying which responses are realistic and which are not, the responses improve over time. Students practicing with this type of simulation can experiment with how they phrase questions, demonstrate empathy, or manage ethical issues, and reflect on their perspectives regarding the simulated client's responses. This gives them a safe space to practice communication and decision-making before working with clients in the field.

Deep learning is a specialized approach within machine learning that relies on neural networks, which are loosely modeled on how the human brain processes information (Serrano & Bajo, 2019). These systems are particularly effective at analyzing unstructured data such as text, images, and audio and can identify patterns that may be difficult to detect using traditional analytic methods. Deep learning applications might be used to support the review of materials such as counseling session transcripts or reflective writings to surface emotional or behavioral patterns that might otherwise remain unnoticed.

Several deep learning models are especially relevant to educational and helping-profession contexts. Recurrent Neural Networks (RNNs) are designed to work with sequential data and are commonly used in speech and language processing (Xiao et al., 2016), as seen in tools such as Apple's Siri and Amazon's Alexa. In clinical training and supervision settings, RNNs may be used to analyze longitudinal data, offering faculty and supervisors additional insight into emerging trends that may warrant attention.

Many widely used generative AI tools, including ChatGPT (Open AI) and Claude (Anthropic), are examples of large language models (LLMs). These systems are typically built using transformer-based architectures which enable them to model relationships across large volumes of text as they generate language that is responsive and contextually informed (Gillani, 2023). Within educational settings, these tools may be used to assist with drafting case vignettes, generating role-play scenarios, or supporting reflective and Socratic-style questioning that promotes critical thinking and analytic depth (Gregorcic et al., 2024). At the same time, their capacity to produce fluent written text necessitates careful attention to issues of academic integrity, authorship, and appropriate use.

As deep learning systems become more embedded in educational and professional environments, ethical and governance considerations become central to their adoption. Questions related to ethical considerations are particularly salient for faculty and administrators responsible for curriculum design and policy development as they ponder the responsibilities that accompany its use. The value of increasing one's technical literacy lies in developing the ability to ask informed questions about accuracy, bias, authorship, and accountability rather than mastering computational design. These considerations provide guidance as educators make judgments about AI-generated content and determine whether it has a place within their broader pedagogical approach.

ETHICAL AND RELATIONAL CONSIDERATIONS

Professional and Academic Ethical Frameworks

Ethical concerns around artificial intelligence (AI) intersect with both academic integrity and profession-specific codes of ethics. Questions of authorship, accuracy, and honesty are joined by mandates from the American Psychological Association (American Psychological Association, 2017), the National Association of Social Workers (National Association of Social Workers, 2021), and the American Counseling Association (American Counseling Association, 2014). These codes emphasize that technology, including AI, must be integrated into practice and education in ways that respect client dignity, confidentiality, and cultural competence. Core values such as empathy, professional responsibility, and social justice remain central as helping professions navigate AI's growing role within the milieu (American Counseling Association, 2014; American Psychological Association, 2017; National Association of Social Workers, 2021).

Shared Ethical Themes Across Professional Organizations

Despite differences in emphasis, the ethical guidelines of ACA, APA, and NASW converge on several key principles. Each organization emphasizes the importance of informed consent and transparency when using AI in professional practice. This includes disclosing to clients when AI is being used and providing clear explanations of how the AI functions. Professionals should also outline potential risks and benefits that clients may wish to consider. Consistent with the standard approach to the treatment of any clinical or therapeutic intervention in the helping professions, clients need to understand the extent of AI involvement in the approach and retain full autonomy to decide whether or not to engage with those services. Professionals carry an ethical responsibility to provide alternative options for clients who prefer not to use AI-assisted approaches. It is essential that clients can make these choices without fear that declining AI-supported services will result in judgment, diminished quality of care, or other negative consequences from the professional (American Counseling Association, 2014; National Association of Social Workers, 2021).

To illustrate this, a counseling student might want to employ an AI-driven journaling application to monitor client moods and suggest basic coping strategies. Ethical practice requires that the student explain how the AI works to the client and describe its limitations. Any potential risks should be communicated clearly. This scenario highlights where clients would need to be offered a more traditional alternative, such as pen and paper journaling, if they are uncomfortable with AI-assisted tracking. This approach ensures that clients make informed, voluntary choices regarding the technology used to support their care. It also preserves both autonomy and trust in the therapeutic relationship.

All three professional organizations guiding psychology, social work, and counseling identify privacy and data security as essential components of ethical practice with technology. Practitioners are required to comply with relevant confidentiality laws and to take proactive measures to safeguard sensitive client information. This process includes selecting secure platforms, using encryption when appropriate, and maintaining vigilance to prevent unauthorized access or accidental disclosure (American Psychological Association, 2017; Reamer, 2023).

Consider a scenario in which a social worker intern inadvertently enters identifying client information into a generative AI chatbot to assist with case analysis. Even without malicious intent, this action could result in the exposure of sensitive personal details, potentially compromising client confidentiality and trust. The scenario underscores the importance of understanding both the technological limitations of AI tools and the professional responsibilities associated with their use. Practitioners and students in their practicum agencies must remain aware of potential vulnerabilities, exercise caution when integrating AI into practice, and ensure that all data handling aligns with established ethical and legal standards. Educators must also highlight the danger of bias and inequity within AI results, noting that AI can reproduce systemic inequalities if not carefully evaluated for fairness, cultural sensitivity, and validation across diverse populations (National Association of Social Workers, 2021).

Helping professions stress the importance of technological competence, requiring practitioners to pursue ongoing education to understand AI tools and their limits while making clear that responsibility for outcomes rests with the professional, not the technology (American Psychological Association, 2017; National Association of Social Workers, 2021). The therapeutic alliance depends on trust, which can be weakened if AI is viewed as replacing human care. AI is intended to support professional decision-making, and professionals remain responsible for reviewing and, when necessary, overriding AI outputs (American Counseling Association, 2014). For example, an AI system might suggest a standardized behavioral intervention for a client with complex trauma. A therapist exercising professional judgment might need to modify or reject the recommendation after taking into consideration the client's cultural background, prior therapy experiences, and relational context – thus demonstrating the irreplaceable role of human expertise in nuanced decision-making rather than blind acceptance of AI suggested strategies.

Practitioners and educators can model responsible AI use for students by demonstrating when AI may be helpful and when it is more appropriate to step away from it. Such modeling reinforces empathy and relational presence, emphasizing the central role of the therapeutic relationship in building trust and collaboration in counseling and psychotherapy. Overreliance on AI may lead to losing this foundational trust, resulting in dehumanization and the illusion of relationship without true depth or commitment. Still, AI can indirectly support the alliance by expanding access and offering supplemental tools for the practitioner to harness in pursuit of individualized treatment options. Used cautiously, AI may free therapists to focus more deeply on human connection while maintaining professional oversight and maintaining client trust (American Counseling Association, 2014).

Distinctions Among Professional Organizations

While they share common ground on many ethical components guiding technology use, the professional organizations also make unique contributions regarding application of AI in practice. The ACA places stricter limits on AI, explicitly warning against its use in crisis response or diagnostic contexts where nuance and immediacy are crucial (American Counseling Association, 2014). The NASW underscores client self-determination and recommends that agencies adopt formal technology policies covering consent, confidentiality, and competence (National Association of Social Workers, 2021). The APA highlights the role of psychologists in shaping AI development more broadly, encouraging collaboration with policymakers and developers and drawing attention to liability risks in adoption (American Psychological Association, 2017). Taken together, these codes stress that AI is a supplement to, not a substitute for, the human relationship at the heart of care (American Psychological Association, 2017; National Association of Social Workers, 2021; American Counseling Association, 2014).

The ethical integration of AI and other technologies in social work also aligns closely with the profession's broader strategic goals as articulated in the Grand Challenges for Social Work launched in 2016 by the American Academy of Social Work & Social Welfare (AASWSW). One central insight is that the social work profession has long concentrated on addressing social problems affecting marginalized populations. To remain effective, social workers must be open to considering alternatives to the traditional, low-tech solutions and actively engage with the potential of utilizing information and communication technologies to enhance service delivery (AASWSW, 2016). The overarching societal goal is to leverage technology in ways that strengthen the effectiveness of social programs, ensuring that services reach those who need them most and that resources are used wisely. Another goal set forth by the grand challenges is to accelerate social discovery by harnessing new technological tools to generate insights, uncover patterns, and expand knowledge in ways that traditional methods alone could not easily achieve. A further priority is to transform the social work profession itself, encouraging practitioners to adapt their skills, integrate new forms of evidence, and prepare for roles that will increasingly require fluency with digital systems. Running through each of these aims is the obligation to deploy technology ethically. This means paying attention to concerns of social and environmental justice while deliberately working to ensure new tools reduce existing inequities rather than expand them.

Environmental and Societal Responsibilities in Generative AI

The rapid growth of generative artificial intelligence raises pressing ethical and environmental concerns with direct consequences for individuals and communities. The expansion of AI use places significant demands on energy, water, and land which disproportionately impact vulnerable populations (Regilme, 2024). Data centers consume vast amounts of electricity, contributing to carbon emissions and climate stress (Siddik et al., 2021). Data centers also require extensive cooling systems that can deplete local water supplies, particularly in regions already experiencing scarcity (Al Kez et al., 2022). Communities situated near these facilities often face higher energy costs, environmental degradation, and disruptions to local ecosystems, intensifying preexisting inequities (Brodie, 2023). To put this in perspective, training a single large language model can require as much electricity as a small city uses in a year (Bashir et al., 2024). Without accountability, the human and ecological burdens of Gen AI fall most heavily on those least equipped to bear them.

These risks are compounded by the pace of technological expansion. While hardware and algorithmic improvements have improved efficiency, overall energy demand continues to rise. This creates a paradox where localized efficiency gains are overshadowed by global increases in scale. Limited regulatory oversight further allows environmental costs to remain externalized, enabling unchecked growth at the expense of community well-being and planetary sustainability (Hacker, 2024). Considerations pertaining to the impact of AI usage should also account for indirect consequences, such as unequal access to technological benefits and the risk of further stratifying disadvantaged populations (Lainjo, 2020). Transparent, data-driven assessments are needed to measure both immediate and long-term impacts, ensuring that innovation does not compromise human health, social equity, or environmental integrity.

A human-centered and multi-stakeholder approach is essential to this effort. Developers, policymakers, researchers, and civil society must share responsibility for setting limits, monitoring impacts, and designing safeguards. Equally important, the voices of affected communities must be centered and represented in decision-making so that environmental costs are not invisibly absorbed by those with the least influence. Technological advances matter most when they enhance human lives while safeguarding the environments that sustain them.

Ethical Challenges in Higher Education

Effectively integrating AI into higher education requires institutions and educators to balance innovation with ethical responsibility to foster student learning and a culture of integrity. One frequently cited ethical concern regarding AI in higher education is its potential impact on academic honesty (Khatri & Karki, 2023; Lund et al., 2025; Sullivan et al., 2023). The ease with which students can use AI tools to generate essays, solve assignments, or receive real-time assistance during exams has opened new avenues for plagiarism and cheating, often in ways that traditional plagiarism checkers cannot detect (Baron, 2024). This raises questions about the authenticity of student work as educators struggle to verify whether submissions genuinely reflect a student's own knowledge and skills.

Beyond the risk of dishonesty, there is a concern that reliance on AI can also undermine critical thinking and problem-solving, leaving students less prepared for professional contexts that require independent judgment (Hou et al., 2025). Some academics worry that dependence on AI for quick answers could erode creativity and analytical skills, leaving students with only a superficial grasp of complex topics (George et al., 2024). In response, colleges and universities are being called to reform their academic integrity policies by creating explicit guidelines on the acceptable use of AI (Mahmud, 2024). Clear policies are essential not only for defining penalties for misuse but also for communicating constructive ways that students might engage with AI as a legitimate tool for learning. Some institutions are experimenting with AI-inclusive pedagogy, such as assignments that require students to analyze, critique, or revise AI outputs (Francis et al., 2025). Others encourage transparent acknowledgment of AI assistance in coursework, reinforcing a culture of honesty while modeling professional practices of disclosure and accountability (Wang et al., 2024).

Data privacy and security also stand at the center of ethical debates as the use of AI requires the collection and processing of sensitive information. This concern is especially pronounced in the helping professions where uploading assessments or research data to large language models could run afoul of data protection rules, including U.S. laws such as HIPAA and FERPA, which safeguard health and educational records, respectively (Francis et al., 2025).

Transparency is another key ethical issue. Many AI systems deliver information without proper attribution or use fabricated sources which serve to undermine academic rigor (Currie, 2023). Alongside this, questions of copyright and intellectual property arise, particularly regarding the ownership and originality of AI-generated work. These challenges highlight the broader need for ongoing accountability and responsible use. Errors made by AI systems must be carefully reviewed, and human oversight is essential to ensure that AI-driven decisions are ethically sound. Regulatory examples, such as the European Union's AI Act, which prohibits systems that manipulate human behavior in ways that undermine free will, underscore the importance of human-centered governance in maintaining ethical standards within AI usage (Pirozzoli, 2024).

Bias, Equity, and Cultural Responsiveness

Algorithmic bias represents a pressing ethical challenge in the use of artificial intelligence. Because data used to train AI often lacks diversity, AI systems can reinforce existing stereotypes and inequities (Nuwasiima et al., 2024). This bias has led to algorithms requiring more severe expression of symptoms from Black patients before granting access to the same level of care as White patients within healthcare settings (Obermeyer et al., 2019). Generative AI systems have also produced biased or stereotypical representations of marginalized groups, reflecting cultural insensitivity and linguistic bias (American Psychological Association, 2017). These issues are compounded by unequal access to technology, which further disadvantages already underserved populations. Addressing such inequities requires rigorous testing of AI tools across diverse populations and the adoption of Human-Centered AI (HCAI) principles that emphasize fairness, transparency, and accountability (Shneiderman, 2020). As previously noted, professional ethical guidelines support this approach, urging the development of policies that ensure accessibility for underrepresented communities and promote culturally responsive design (National Association of Social Workers, 2021).

The same concerns of bias extend into AI use within higher education. Models trained on large and often Western-centric datasets risk reproducing biases tied to race, gender, and social background, and in some cases may generate discriminatory outcomes (Jadon, 2025). Beyond content bias, economic barriers may also play a role. Many generative AI tools require paid subscriptions for full access to services, creating a digital divide in which students and academic institutions with greater financial resources benefit from advantages that others cannot access (Francis et al., 2025). Left unaddressed, these structural inequities threaten to widen achievement gaps and deepen existing disparities in educational opportunity.

Understanding AI's Limitations in the Helping Professions

While AI programs increasingly strive to mimic empathy, human involvement to convey true compassion remains essential (Rubin et al., 2024). Practitioners provide accountability and relational understanding that AI cannot fully replicate or replace. Additionally, AI may miss cultural nuances or fail in high-stakes situations such as crisis intervention (Lionarons, 2025). In some cases, clients may even develop attachments to AI tools, raising concerns about social isolation or emotional dependency (Pentina et al., 2023). These challenges underscore the ongoing need for practitioners to use their own judgment when conducting risk assessments, creating safety plans, and making therapeutic decisions. Similarly, in educational settings, AI can create useful practice opportunities, but it should never replace the mentorship and relational modeling provided by faculty, which are central to professional growth (American Psychological Association, 2017).

The ethical integration of AI depends on maintaining clear professional responsibility over technology. Clinicians in the helping professions are expected to critically assess the AI tools they are using for issues of safety, accuracy, and bias, and to advocate for culturally responsive, human-centered design and policies (National Association of Social Workers, 2021; American Counseling Association, 2014). Adopting a framework that emphasizes clinician oversight, transparency, and equity in AI deployment is essential (Floridi & Cowls, 2022). AI offers potential benefits, but its integration must remain grounded in human values. The heart of therapy found within the empathic, collaborative relationship between client and professional still remains a uniquely human connection.

DEVELOPING FACULTY ENGAGEMENT

Faculty and department leaders play a key role in guiding responsible AI integration, ensuring that implementation is thoughtfully planned and that knowledge gaps within the department are addressed. Efforts may include building faculty capacity through targeted professional development, fostering intra- and inter-disciplinary dialogue about pedagogical and ethical implications, as well as aligning instructional practices with broader institutional policies. Administrators can help to foster a coherent and reflective learning environment with a goal of establishing shared expectations for how AI is discussed and utilized across departments. Importantly, engagement with generative AI should not be assumed or mandated. Faculty may raise principled objections based on concerns about data exploitation, environmental impact, or a range of other ethical considerations as previously mentioned. Resistance may reflect a broader reluctance to abandon traditional methods for the unfamiliar technologies, particularly when the benefits remain uncertain (Watty et al., 2016). Recognizing conscientious objection aligns with the ethical traditions of the helping professions, which prioritize integrity, self-determination, and critical reflexivity. Educational approaches to AI literacy should therefore remain invitational rather than compulsory. This may include creating space for critical dialogue or explicitly affirming refusal as a legitimate ethical stance. Such approaches reinforce professional judgment and ethical agency amongst faculty and staff.

Engagement Challenges

One obstacle to faculty engagement with AI can be a gap in knowledge and confidence (Liu, 2025). Educators may have limited formal exposure to AI tools and feel unprepared to integrate them into teaching. Even digitally competent faculty may hesitate to adopt AI because of its perceived complexity and steep learning curve (Mehdaoui, 2024). Without a foundational level of AI literacy, educators could feel uncertain or reluctant to experiment with its possibilities. For some, the sophistication of generative AI itself can be overwhelming, creating cognitive overload that discourages exploration and reinforces reliance on familiar teaching methods (Asal et al., 2025). This gap may be especially pronounced among faculty in the helping professions, where training has traditionally emphasized human relationships and applied practice, with less focus on emerging technologies. These challenges point to the importance of targeted faculty training and low-stakes opportunities for educators to build comfort, which can help faculty move from apprehension to exploration.

Adoption of AI is also shaped by faculty awareness of ethical and epistemological concerns inherent in its use. Building on earlier discussions about accuracy and transparency, faculty may remain cautious about the reliability of AI outputs and the opacity of their decision-making. When the reasoning behind AI-generated results is unclear, educators struggle to assess appropriateness for its use, adding both pedagogical and ethical uncertainty (Garay, 2025). Faculty in the helping professions may be especially attuned to these risks as their disciplines are governed by codes of ethics (e.g., NASW, ACA, APA), which stress the responsible use of technology. These concerns do not call for abandoning AI adoption entirely; instead, they underscore the need for transparent standards and critical AI literacy before adopting AI practices in the classroom.

Even when educators are open to AI, institutional and practical barriers can impede meaningful use. Effective implementation requires technical support and administrative encouragement, yet many institutions provide insufficient infrastructure or guidance (Sebesta & Davis, 2023). Faculty who may already be managing heavy workloads could perceive learning and integrating AI as an additional burden instead of a benefit. In the absence of clear institutional policies or guidelines, educators are left to navigate complex ethical and practical challenges independently. These obstacles underscore the importance of building supportive structures and policies that enable faculty to approach AI with clarity and confidence.

Development Opportunities

One of the most effective ways to encourage faculty engagement with AI is to provide targeted professional development and training. Hands-on, practical learning opportunities are essential for building confidence, reducing the sense of cognitive overload, and moving beyond abstract concepts (Nazaretsky et al., 2022). Training programs can help to demystify AI by showing how it works with real classroom contexts, using case studies and practical demonstrations of teaching applications. Examples of faculty training opportunities might include one-week asynchronous AI Literacy Bootcamps which have shown to improve participants' knowledge, skills, and willingness to experiment with AI tools (Grobbel et al., 2024). A faculty department retreat focused on AI integration might also be considered to learn more about AI and how to phrase questions and instructions clearly to help faculty better understand the tool's strengths and limitations and to get more accurate useful responses (Galindo-Domínguez et al., 2024). Equally important, training must address ethical considerations – such as data privacy, algorithmic bias, academic integrity, and responsible use – by offering scenarios that prepare faculty to anticipate and navigate some of the known risks. To respond directly to concerns about AI's opacity, training should also include opportunities for faculty to work together to interrogate AI outputs for accuracy and discussion pertaining to appropriateness of AI use in their discipline.

Supportive institutional environments are equally essential to successful faculty adoption of AI for those who wish to use it. Even the most motivated faculty may struggle to embrace AI without access to reliable tools, infrastructure, and technical assistance provided by the larger university system. Therefore, institutions should ensure that faculty have access to AI-powered platforms and ongoing IT support. Communities of practice (CoP) provide another form of support by allowing educators to share experiences, successes, and challenges with colleagues across disciplines (Abigail, 2016) and provide administrators with feedback pertaining to any shared roadblocks or policy concerns. Institutional initiatives might also emphasize aligning AI tools with everyday faculty needs, such as streamlining administrative tasks or personalizing instruction so that faculty see clear benefits that justify the investment of their time and effort.

Encouraging exploration and experimentation is another vital step in the overall process of onboarding faculty to AI use. Institutions can encourage faculty to begin with small, low-stakes uses such as brainstorming or generating sample materials. A gradual approach helps build familiarity and confidence without overwhelming workloads. This framing is especially important in the helping professions, where educators may fear that AI will erode the relational and human-centered aspects of teaching. By showing that AI can relieve administrative burdens and free time for deeper engagement with students, training and policies can reassure faculty that targeted use of AI enhances rather than replaces the human value in education. At the same time, educators can be encouraged to rethink assignments in ways that both reduce opportunities for student misuse and promote authentic learning. For instance, assignments might ask students to critique or adapt AI-generated outputs rather than submit them unaltered.

Training and support are best when tailored to faculty needs and disciplinary contexts. A one-size-fits-all approach is unlikely to be effective, as faculty vary in their technical confidence and disciplinary priorities. Faculty in the helping professions may be particularly attuned to issues of privacy, confidentiality, and maintaining relational integrity in AI use, and training should address these contexts with discipline-specific examples. Ongoing professional development is also essential given the rapid pace of AI innovation. Institutions should treat AI literacy as a process of continuous learning, supported by regular updates and integration into broader curricular and institutional initiatives to foster ongoing growth across the campus community.

INTEGRATING AI TO ENHANCE STUDENT LEARNING

This section outlines strategies for integrating AI literacy into coursework with suggestions that emphasize writing, research, simulations, and professional communications. The goal is to help students develop transferable academic and professional skills that emphasize critical thinking and the ability to make meaningful connections while using AI tools to support creative exploration and discipline-specific applications. Assignments and assessments encourage active engagement with AI in ways that complement traditional learning outcomes while reinforcing professional reasoning.

Improving Comprehension Skills

Using AI support to improve comprehension skills for students involves combining hands-on active engagement with purposefully guided ethical reflection. One effective approach is problem-based learning, where students work on real-world challenges using data to guide their reasoning (Folomieieva et al., 2024). An example could include an assignment where social work students explore community health data using national data repositories to identify barriers to care and ask them to design possible intervention strategies. AI tools can help analyze large datasets to detect patterns and generate predictive scenarios, such as highlighting neighborhoods with lower access to healthcare. Students can be asked to interpret these AI-generated insights evaluate their significance, and make ethically informed decisions, helping them learn both how AI might be used in macro practice as well as how to use data responsibly.

Case-based reasoning builds on this by encouraging students to draw lessons from past examples to address new situations (Jonassen & Hernandez-Serrano, 2002). In counseling programs, students might examine AI-generated ethical cases involving confidentiality or informed consent, comparing scenarios to identify effective strategies and potential pitfalls. Group discussions can be utilized to help students evaluate evidence as they consider multiple perspectives and reflect critically on the information using their emerging professional judgment to defend their ultimate choices. Similarly, discussions of AI-generated documentation can be used to surface questions about voice, authorship, and responsibility. When students examine who is accountable for errors or bias in AI-assisted records, they engage directly with professional standards governing documentation and supervision.

Interactive materials, such as video lectures with embedded AI-generated quizzes, further support comprehension (Hung & Chen, 2018). For instance, students might watch a therapy session clip and determine whether the interventions presented align with evidence-based practices. This type of activity can give instructors insight into student understanding while encouraging engagement with the learning material.

AI tools might also be used to help scaffold comprehension while emphasizing student critical thinking (Wu, 2024). Role-plays, discussions, and experiential projects offer students opportunities to examine the social implications of their professional decisions. Thoughtful assessment and feedback further support students in deepening their understanding and applying what they have learned (Morris et al., 2021). Students could role-play as practitioners as they review AI-generated case summaries created with discipline specific details based on instructor input. Students can then compare their own ideas for interventions with alternative perspectives developed by AI to connect professional standards to real-life practice while deepening their critical reflection skills as they consider the pros and cons of each path. Instructors can guide group conversations by prompting students to assess ethical and cultural factors as well as evaluating the strengths and limitations of each approach.

Psychology, counseling, or social work students might use AI to draft mental health promotion materials tailored to specific populations such as young adults experiencing housing insecurity, older adults managing chronic illness, or rural communities with limited access to services. The AI can generate initial drafts that incorporate basic content, language, and cultural considerations. Students might then review and revise these materials, based on professional guidelines, ethical values, and standards, along with peer feedback to ensure accuracy of the content as well as appropriateness for the target population. This process allows students to focus on higher-level skills such as evaluating the relevance of the information as well as considering cultural and ethical implications and practicing how to communicate effectively with diverse audiences. AI serves as a starting point that sparks creativity and organizes ideas, while critical thinking and professional judgment remain firmly in the hands of the students.

Building Communication Skills

Effective communication is a core competency in the helping professions. AI can be harnessed strategically to strengthen students' ability to convey ideas clearly and engage thoughtfully in professional contexts to build bridges with peers and colleagues.

One practical strategy involves having students use AI to support the development of professional writing skills needed within the helping professions. Given a brief client vignette that includes the presenting concerns, a short history, and contextual details, students might ask AI to generate lists of key issues, relevant psychosocial factors, or important keywords to guide practice documentation outlines. They might also use AI to create more structured outlines for case notes, intervention plans, or treatment summaries. Similarly, students could be asked to write and submit their own first draft of deidentified documentation through an AI program to assess if any relevant information was excluded or needed clarification. Adding a reflective component to the assignment would encourage students to consider how AI helped organize their thinking, the limitations observed in the output, and how the exercise informs their approach to professional documentation and ethical practice.

AI can also support simulated professional dialogues, including interprofessional communication (Stamer et al., 2023). For instance, students might work with AI-generated scenarios where they must explain a client's case or care plan to colleagues from different fields, such as nursing, education, or occupational therapy. The AI can suggest multiple perspectives or considerations that each discipline might raise. Students then practice articulating their recommendations clearly, addressing different professional priorities, and responding thoughtfully to questions or concerns. In an asynchronous classroom, students might submit written responses to a discussion board, reflecting on how they considered other professional perspectives in their documentation and thoughts after reviewing AI suggestions for alternative approaches. Peers can then provide constructive feedback on issues of clarity, ethical reasoning, and use of the profession's values in these contexts.

Using AI in these exercises gives students a chance to practice important communication skills while, critically, still making the key decisions themselves. The AI acts as a helpful guide or starting point that offers suggestions and perspectives to support learning. This allows students to focus on how they present ideas, think through professional situations, and adjust their communication for different audiences. Importantly, the goal is to develop thoughtful, reflective, and professional communication habits that will be essential in their careers.

Identifying Bias

Recognizing bias is a core competency for students in the helping professions, and AI provides both challenges and opportunities for building this skill. One effective strategy is to have students compare multiple AI-generated drafts of the same professional task. For instance, an instructor might input the same details of a client case into an AI tool several times, asking for a case summary and suggested interventions each time. The drafts are then laid side by side for review, noting assumptions that AI created pertaining to socioeconomic class, race, culture, health, etc. Students work together or individually to identify bias and offer suggestions to increase inclusivity, accuracy, and alignment with professional standards. Instructors can guide the process through class discussions or online discussion boards with specific prompts, reflection journals, or structured classroom debriefs.

A different way to highlight bias is to step beyond individual cases and examine how AI is used in larger social systems. Facilitating these types of conversations invites students to connect their professional values with systemic inequities, asking them to consider both the immediate and long-term impact of bias. By engaging at both the micro and macro levels, students develop sharper ethical reasoning and a stronger capacity for culturally responsive practice.

An assignment aimed at elevating these discussions could invite students to explore the role of predictive algorithms in policing, healthcare screenings, or employment platforms. Here the task is not to edit AI outputs but to think critically about the broader consequences of AI design and use within the community. Students might discuss how predictive policing tools can disproportionately target certain neighborhoods (Alikhademi et al., 2022), or how medical algorithms have been shown to underestimate the severity of symptoms in Black patients (Derricks et al., 2024). These discussions challenge students to think beyond the technology itself and focus on the human and social consequences of AI in practice.

Practicing Assessment Skills

Assessment in the helping professions requires careful evaluation of information while weighing context, ethics, and professional judgment. AI can play a useful role in teaching these skills, but the focus shifts from bias detection to the accuracy and completeness of information. One common exercise uses instructor-created case vignettes. Each vignette includes presenting concerns, brief histories, and symptom descriptions. Alongside the vignette, students receive an AI-generated summary or a set of possible diagnostic impressions. Their task is to evaluate whether the AI has captured the key elements of the case, where it falls short, and what additional details are needed before making a sound assessment. This work is intentionally slow and reflective. Students are encouraged to cross-check the AI's conclusions with professional guidelines, consult established diagnostic criteria, and propose their own assessment or intervention plan. Reflection questions can deepen the exercise by asking why they trusted or distrusted certain parts of the AI's output, and how they would explain their reasoning to a supervisor or peer. In this way, the activity reinforces both technical knowledge and professional communication.

In an online or hybrid classroom, instructors can build these activities into course learning management systems. Case vignettes paired with AI-generated summaries can be delivered through quizzes or assignments that combine open-ended reflection prompts – asking students to justify why they trusted or questioned specific parts of the AI's output – with objective questions that require them to identify which elements of the AI summary are accurate or missing. Automated feedback can support students in correcting factual misunderstandings, while instructor feedback can target reasoning and judgment. This format scales well and creates an environment where students can practice clinical reasoning. By approaching assessment as an iterative and evaluative process, students learn that AI is not a substitute for their expertise but a tool to interrogate and refine. The emphasis on professional responsibility prepares them to use AI outputs as one resource among many, always filtered through their own ethical and clinical judgment.

AI in Field Education and Supervision

Field education constitutes a particularly nuanced site for the development of AI literacy, given that students must reconcile expectations emerging from their academic programs, placement agencies, and the ethical mandates of the profession. In classroom environments, discussions of generative AI might tend to focus on meeting learning objectives, issues of authorship, and general academic integrity. Field placements, however, situate technology use within the immediacy of practice. In these settings, questions of documentation, confidentiality, supervision, and client welfare are not hypothetical but consequential, shaping both student learning and professional accountability.

Students in field placements may encounter or experiment with generative AI to assist with tasks such as drafting progress notes or preparing agendas and questions for supervision. These practices often arise in contexts where agency-level policies are unclear or where there is limited guidance on the ethical and practical implications of inputting client information into AI platforms. Consequently, students may face challenges in determining whether such uses align with professional ethical standards and organizational expectations, particularly when pressures for efficiency intersect with the ongoing development of professional judgment.

These concerns are reinforced by emerging research on AI-assisted documentation. While AI-generated summaries can appear coherent and well-organized, studies indicate that they frequently fail to accurately reflect clinical modalities or structure information in ways that meet professional standards of practice (Adhikary et al., 2024). Additionally, there is evidence that AI may misrepresent the severity of risk assessments, which could lead to flawed clinical decisions and negatively impact client care (Elyoseph & Levkovich, 2023). Together, these findings highlight the need for students to approach AI tools with critical discernment as they develop the ability to recognize both AI's potential utility and the risks posed within the ethical and practical realities of practice.

Field educators and faculty supervisors occupy a critical role in fostering AI literacy that extends beyond technical competence. Preparation for ethical and responsible practice requires supporting students in critically assessing when and how AI tools may be appropriate on a case-by-case basis, understanding agency-specific policies and legal constraints, and fostering open dialogue about technological boundaries. In this framing, AI literacy in field education is not centered on mastery of particular platforms but on cultivating discernment. Students are encouraged to evaluate whether technological assistance enhances reflective practice and professional reasoning or whether it risks eroding accountability, confidentiality, and client trust. Such an approach positions AI literacy as integral to professional formation rather than as an ancillary or purely technical skill.

FINAL NOTE

As enticing and helpful as AI programs can be for students, educators, and practitioners in the helping professions, humans are still more adept at abstract reasoning and learning how to learn (Koivisto & Grassini, 2023). Machines require vast amounts of data to learn tasks that humans might grasp quickly, indicating a fundamental difference in how they understand different concepts. AI's meta learning can lack the higher-order thinking, reflection, and planning inherent in human learning. This is an important consideration to stress with students. Their ability to learn and pick up on human moments that an AI program might not recognize as important is a valuable asset, especially within the helping professions. We must remember that AI programs are tools to wield to enhance knowledge potential rather than replace the human experience altogether.

REFERENCES

Abbass, H. A. (2019). Social integration of artificial intelligence: Functions, automation allocation logic and human-autonomy trust. *Cognitive Computation, 11*(2), 159–171. DOI: 10.1007/s12559-018-9619-0

Abigail, L. K. M. (2016). Do communities of practice enhance faculty development? *Health Profession Education, 2*(2), 61–74. DOI: 10.1016/j.hpe.2016.08.004

Abubakar, A. M., Gupta, D., & Parida, S. (2024). A reinforcement learning approach for intelligent conversational chatbot for enhancing mental health therapy. *Procedia Computer Science, 235*, 916–925. DOI: 10.1016/j.procs.2024.04.087

Adhikary, P. K., Srivastava, A., Kumar, S., Singh, S. M., Manuja, P., Gopinath, J. K., Krishnan, V., Gupta, S. K., Deb, K. S., & Chakraborty, T. (2024). Exploring the efficacy of large language models in summarizing mental health counseling sessions: Benchmark study. *JMIR Mental Health, 11*, e57306. Advance online publication. DOI: 10.2196/57306

Al Kez, D., Foley, A. M., Laverty, D., Del Rio, D. F., & Sovacool, B. (2022). Exploring the sustainability challenges facing digitalization and internet data centers. *Journal of Cleaner Production, 371*, 133633.

Alikhademi, K., Drobina, E., Prioleau, D., Richardson, B., Purves, D., & Gilbert, J. E. (2022). A review of predictive policing from the perspective of fairness. *Artificial Intelligence and Law, 30*(1), 1–17. DOI: 10.1007/s10506-021-09286-4

American Counseling Association. (2014). Code of ethics. https://www.counseling.org/knowledge-center/ethics

American Psychological Association. (2017). Ethical principles of psychologists and code of conduct. https://www.apa.org/ethics/code

Asal, M. G. R., Alsenany, S. A., Elzohairy, N. W., & El-Sayed, A. A. I. (2025). The impact of digital competence on pedagogical innovation among nurse educators: The moderating role of artificial intelligence readiness. *Nurse Education in Practice, 85*, 104367. DOI: 10.1016/j.nepr.2025.104367

Báez, J. C., Bjugstad, A., Park, T. K., Jones, J. L., Bidwell, L. N., Sage, M., & Hitchcock, L. I. (2025). Social work educators innovating with generative AI: An exploratory study. *Journal of Social Work Education, 61*(1), 14–29. DOI: 10.1080/10437797.2024.2411170

Baron, P. (2024). Are AI detection and plagiarism similarity scores worthwhile in the age of ChatGPT and other Generative AI? *Scholarship of Teaching and Learning in the South, 8*(2), 151–179. DOI: 10.36615/sotls.v8i2.411

Bashir, N., Donti, P., Cuff, J., Sroka, S., Ilich, M., Sze, V., Delimitru, C., & Alveti, E. (2024). The climate and sustainability implications of generative AI. MIT. https://mit-genai.pubpub.org/pub/8ulgrckc

Berry, D. M. (2023). The limits of computation: Joseph Weizenbaum and the ELIZA chatbot. *Weizenbaum Journal of the Digital Society, 3*(3). https://doi.org/DOI: 10.34669/WI.WJDS/3.3.2

Brodie, P. (2023). Data infrastructure studies on an unequal planet. *Big Data & Society, 10*(1). Advance online publication. DOI: 10.1177/20539517231182402

Currie, G. M. (2023). Academic integrity and artificial intelligence: Is ChatGPT hype, hero or heresy? *Seminars in Nuclear Medicine, 53*(5), 719–730. DOI: 10.1053/j.semnuclmed.2023.04.008

Derricks, V., Hirsh, A. T., Perkins, A. J., Daggy, J. K., & Matthias, M. S. (2024). Health care discrimination affects patient activation, communication self-efficacy, and pain for Black Americans. *The Journal of Pain, 25*(12), 1–11. DOI: 10.1016/j.jpain.2024.104663

Dueck, A. C., & Sundararajan, L. (Eds.). (2024). *Values and Indigenous psychology in the age of the machine and market: When the Gods have fled*. Springer International Publishing., DOI: 10.1007/978-3-031-53196-5

Duggan, G. B. (2016). Applying psychology to understand relationships with technology: From ELIZA to interactive healthcare. *Behaviour & Information Technology, 35*(7), 536–547. DOI: 10.1080/0144929X.2016.1141320

Elyoseph, Z., & Levkovich, I. (2023). Beyond human expertise: The promise and limitations of ChatGPT in suicide risk assessment. *Frontiers in Psychiatry, 14*. Advance online publication. DOI: 10.3389/fpsyt.2023.1213141

Fahad, S. (2024). Transforming medical social work with artificial intelligence. *Social Work Chronicle, 13*(1), 24–49.

Floridi, L., & Cowls, J. (2022). A unified framework of five principles for AI in society. *Machine learning and the city: Applications in architecture and urban design*, 535-545.

Folomieieva, N., Koriakin, O., Matsenko, L., Siaska, I., & Fed, I. (2024). Problem-based learning in higher education: A path towards training innovative and competent specialists. *Amazonia Investiga, 13*(77), 201–217. DOI: 10.34069/AI/2024.77.05.15

Francis, N. J., Jones, S., & Smith, D. P. (2025). Generative AI in higher education: Balancing innovation and integrity. *British Journal of Biomedical Science, 81*, 14048. DOI: 10.3389/bjbs.2024.14048

Galindo-Domínguez, H., Delgado, N., Losada, D., & Etxabe, J. M. (2024). An analysis of the use of artificial intelligence in education in Spain: The in-service teacher's perspective. *Journal of Digital Learning in Teacher Education, 40*(1), 41–56. DOI: 10.1080/21532974.2023.2284726

Garay, S. M. (2025). Advancing instructional design with AI: A study on AI literacy in higher education [Doctoral dissertation, University of South Alabama]. ProQuest.

George, A. S., Baskar, T., & Srikaanth, P. B. (2024). The erosion of cognitive skills in the technological age: How reliance on technology impacts critical thinking, problem-solving, and creativity. *Partners Universal Innovative Research Publication, 2*(3), 147–163. DOI: 10.5281/zenodo.11671150

Gillani, N., Eynon, R., Chiabaut, C., & Finkel, K. (2023). Unpacking the "Black Box" of AI in education. *Journal of Educational Technology & Society, 26*(1), 99–111.

Gregorcic, B., Polverini, G., & Sarlah, A. (2024). ChatGPT as a tool for honing teachers' Socratic dialogue skills. *Physics Education, 59*(4), 045005.

Grobbel, C., Piscotty, R. J., & Hanna, D. (2024). Artificial intelligence bootcamp: A strategy for educating faculty. *Nurse Educator, 50*(4), E248–E249. DOI: 10.1097/NNE.0000000000001815

Hacker, P. (2024). Sustainable AI regulation. *Common Market Law Review, 61*(2), 345–386. DOI: 10.54648/cola2024025

Han, E., & Shin, J. (2025). Understanding artificial intelligence and machine learning: Foundational concepts for counselor education. *The Journal of Counselor Preparation and Supervisor, 19*(3), 1–15. DOI: 10.70013/7b5l47yn

Hou, C., Zhu, G., & Sudarshan, V. (2025). The role of critical thinking on undergraduates' reliance behaviours on generative AI in problem-solving. *British Journal of Educational Technology, 56*(5), 1919–1941. DOI: 10.1111/bjet.13613

Hung, I. C., & Chen, N. S. (2018). Embodied interactive video lectures for improving learning comprehension and retention. *Computers & Education, 117*, 116–131. DOI: 10.1016/j.compedu.2017.10.005

Jadon, A. (2025). Ethical AI development: Mitigating bias in generative models. In Reddy, C. K. K., Joseph, S., Joshi, H., Ouaissa, M., & Hanafiah, M. M. (Eds.), *Interplay of artificial general intelligence with quantum computing. Sustainable artificial intelligence-powered applications.* Springer., DOI: 10.1007/978-3-031-87931-9_10

Jonassen, D. H., & Hernandez-Serrano, J. (2002). Case-based reasoning and instructional design: Using stories to support problem solving. *Educational Technology Research and Development, 50*(2), 65–77. DOI: 10.1007/BF02504994

Khatri, B. B., & Karki, P. D. (2023). Artificial intelligence (AI) in higher education: Growing academic integrity and ethical concerns. *Nepalese Journal of Development and Rural Studies, 20*(01), 1–7.

Koivisto, M., & Grassini, S. (2023). Best humans still outperform artificial intelligence in a creative divergent thinking task. *Scientific Reports, 13*(1), 13601. Advance online publication. DOI: 10.1038/s41598-023-40858-3

Lainjo, B. (2020). The global social dynamics and inequalities of artificial intelligence. *International Journal of Innovation Scientific Research and Review, 5*(8), 4966–4974.

Lionarons, T. A. (2025). Artificial intelligence in crisis decision-making: Practical applications and ethical objections. In Lin, L. (Ed.), *Ethics in the age of AI: Navigating politics and security* (pp. 269–290). Ethics Press.

Liu, N. (2025). Exploring the factors influencing the adoption of artificial intelligence technology by university teachers: The mediating role of confidence and AI readiness. *BMC Psychology, 13*(1), 311. DOI: 10.1186/s40359-025-02620-4

Lund, B. D., Lee, T. H., Mannuru, N. R., & Arutla, N. (2025). AI and academic integrity: Exploring student perceptions and implications for higher education. *Journal of Academic Ethics, 23*(3), 1545–1565. DOI: 10.1007/s10805-025-09613-3

Mahmud, S. (2024). Fostering academic integrity in the age of artificial intelligence. In *Academic integrity in the age of artificial intelligence* (pp. 1–20). IGI Global Scientific Publishing., DOI: 10.4018/979-8-3693-0240-8.ch001

Mamaleka, M. M., & Skobi, F. (2024). New intervention strategies in rendering social work services to families amidst the pandemic crisis: A social work perspective. In Lutz, R., & Weimann-Sandig, N. (Eds.), *Family dynamics, gender and social inequality during COVID-19* (pp. 211–226). Springer Nature., DOI: 10.1007/978-3-031-51237-7_14

Mehdaoui, A. (2024). Unveiling barriers and challenges of AI technology integration in education: Assessing teachers' perceptions, readiness and anticipated resistance. *Futurity Education*, *4*(4), 95–108. DOI: 10.57125/FED.2024.12.25.06

Morris, R., Perry, T., & Wardle, L. (2021). Formative assessment and feedback for learning in higher education: A systematic review. *Review of Education*, *9*(3), 1–26. DOI: 10.1002/rev3.3292

National Association of Social Workers. (2021). Code of ethics. https://www.socialworkers.org/About/Ethics/Code-of-Ethics/Code-of-Ethics-English

Nazaretsky, T., Ariely, M., Cukurova, M., & Alexandron, G. (2022). Teachers' trust in AI-powered educational technology and a professional development program to improve it. *British Journal of Educational Technology*, *53*(4), 914–931.

Nuwasiima, M., Ahonon, M. P., & Kadiri, C. (2024). The role of artificial intelligence (AI) and machine learning in social work practice. *World Journal of Advanced Research and Reviews*, *24*(1), 80–97.

Obermeyer, Z., Powers, B., Vogeli, C., & Mullainathan, S. (2019). Dissecting racial bias in an algorithm used to manage the health of populations. *Science*, *366*(6464), 447–453.

Ooi, P. B., & Wilkinson, G. (2025). Enhancing ethical codes with artificial intelligence governance: A growing necessity for the adoption of generative AI in counselling. *British Journal of Guidance & Counselling*, *53*(1), 66–80. DOI: 10.1080/03069885.2024.2373180

Pentina, I., Hancock, T., & Xie, T. (2023). Exploring relationship development with social chatbots: A mixed-method study of Replika. *Computers in Human Behavior*, *140*, 107600. Advance online publication. DOI: 10.1016/j.chb.2022.107600

Pirozzoli, A. (2024). The human-centric perspective in the regulation of artificial intelligence. *European Papers (Online. Periodico)*, *9*(1), 105–116. https://doi.org/DOI: 10.15166/2499-8249/745

Rajaraman, V. (2014). JohnMcCarthy: Father of artificial intelligence. *Resonance*, *19*(3), 198–207. DOI: 10.1007/s12045-014-0027-9

Reamer, F. G. (2023). Artificial intelligence in social work: Emerging ethical issues. *International Journal of Social Work Values and Ethics*, *20*(2), 52–71.

Regilme, S. S. F. (2024). Artificial intelligence colonialism: Environmental damage, labor exploitation, and human rights crises in the Global South. *SAIS Review (Paul H. Nitze School of Advanced International Studies), 44*(2), 75–92. DOI: 10.1353/sais.2024.a950958

Reimer, E. C. (2024). Examining the role of generative AI in enhancing social work education: An analysis of curriculum and assessment design. *Social Sciences, 13*(12), 648. DOI: 10.3390/socsci13120648

Rubin, M., Arnon, H., Huppert, J. D., & Perry, A. (2024). Considering the role of human empathy in AI-driven therapy. *JMIR Mental Health, 11*(1), e56529. DOI: 10.2196/56529

Sebesta, J., & Davis, V. L. (2023). *Supporting instruction and learning through artificial intelligence: A survey of institutional practices & policies. WICHE Co-operative for Educational Technologies*. WCET.

Serrano, E., & Bajo, J. (2019). Deep neural network architectures for social services diagnosis in smart cities. *Future Generation Computer Systems, 100*, 122–131.

Siddik, M. A. B., Shehabi, A., & Marston, L. (2021). The environmental footprint of data centers in the United States. *Environmental Research Letters, 16*(6), 064017.

Soman, G., Judy, M. V., & Abou, A. M. (2025). Human guided empathetic AI agent for mental health support leveraging reinforcement learning-enhanced retrieval-augmented generation. *Cognitive Systems Research, 90*, 101337. DOI: 10.1016/j.cogsys.2025.101337

Stamer, T., Steinhäuser, J., & Flägel, K. (2023). Artificial intelligence supporting the training of communication skills in the education of health care professions: Scoping review. *Journal of Medical Internet Research, 25*(8), 1–16. DOI: 10.2196/43311

Stone, B. W. (2025). Generative AI in higher education: Uncertain students, ambiguous use cases, and mercenary perspectives. *Teaching of Psychology, 52*(3), 347–356. DOI: 10.1177/00986283241305398

Sullivan, M., Kelly, A., & McLaughlan, P. (2023). ChatGPT in higher education: Considerations for academic integrity and student learning. *Journal of Applied Learning & Teaching, 6*(1), 31–40.

Wang, H., Dang, A., Wu, Z., & Mac, S. (2024). Generative AI in higher education: Seeing ChatGPT through universities' policies, resources, and guidelines. *Computers and Education: Artificial Intelligence, 7*, 100326. DOI: 10.1016/j.caeai.2024.100326

Watty, K., McKay, J., & Ngo, L. (2016). Innovators or inhibitors? Accounting faculty resistance to new educational technologies in higher education. *Journal of Accounting Education*, *36*, 1–15.

Wu, Y. (2024). Critical thinking pedagogics design in an era of ChatGPT and other AI tools: Shifting from teaching "what" to teaching "why" and "how.". *Journal of Education and Development*, *8*(1), 1–10. DOI: 10.20849/jed.v8i1.1404

Xiao, B., Can, D., Gibson, J., Imel, Z. E., Atkins, D. C., Georgiou, P. G., & Narayanan, S. S. (2016). Behavioral coding of therapist language in addiction counseling using recurrent neural networks. In *Interspeech 2016* (pp. 908–912). International Speech Communication Association (ISCA). https://doi.org/. 2016-1560.DOI: 10.21437/ interspeech

Yuan, Y., Huang, J., Ma, X., & Yan, K. (2020, November). Children's drawing psychological analysis using shallow convolutional neural network. In 2020 International Conferences on Internet of Things (iThings) and IEEE Green Computing and Communications (GreenCom) and IEEE Cyber, Physical and Social Computing (CPSCom) and IEEE Smart Data (SmartData) and IEEE Congress on Cybermatics (Cybermatics) (pp. 692-698). IEEE.

KEY TERMS AND DEFINITIONS

Algorithmic Bias: Systematic errors in AI outputs that may arise from incomplete or unrepresentative training data. In the helping professions, bias can lead to inequitable outcomes, such as underestimating symptoms in marginalized populations, and students must learn to identify and mitigate these biases.

Deep Learning: A specialized type of machine learning that uses neural networks with multiple layers to process unstructured data such as text, images, or audio. Deep learning models detect complex patterns that traditional methods might miss, making them useful for tasks like analyzing counseling session transcripts or client-generated materials.

Ethical Oversight: Monitoring AI use to ensure compliance with professional and legal standards, including client confidentiality, informed consent, and cultural competence. Human professionals remain responsible for ethical practice and appropriateness of interventions used with clients.

Machine Learning: A subset of AI where algorithms analyze large datasets to identify patterns, make predictions, and support decision-making. Machine learning underlies many AI tools used in education and practice, including predictive modeling and assessment simulations.

Reinforcement Learning: A machine learning approach where a system learns by trial and error, receiving feedback in the form of rewards or penalties to maximize desirable outcomes. In professional training, it can be used in simulations where students practice interventions and see how AI-generated clients respond to different strategies.

Supervised Learning: A machine learning approach in which a computer system is trained with labeled examples that include input data and the expected outcome. The system learns relationships between inputs and outcomes and can predict results for new cases. In social work or psychology, it might help identify clients at risk of disengaging from services.

Unsupervised Learning: A machine learning approach in which the system is not given expected outcomes but instead identifies natural patterns or groupings in the data. In practice, it can help analyze large qualitative datasets, such as student journals or client narratives, to detect recurring themes or trends.

Chapter 3
When Empathy Is Automated:
Social Work, AI Chatbots, and the Ethics of Care

Stevara Haley Clark
https://orcid.org/0009-0005-6726-7927
School of Social Work, University of Pittsburgh, USA

ABSTRACT

Artificial intelligence (AI) is reshaping social work and human services, offering new opportunities for access and engagement while raising ethical challenges around empathy, equity, and accountability. This chapter examines the integration of AI, particularly chatbots, into education and practice through a trauma-informed and anti-oppressive lens. Using the case of Serenity, an AI chatbot at a nonprofit mental health agency, it explores ethical tensions surrounding empathy, bias, consent, confidentiality, and professional integrity as framed by the NASW Code of Ethics. The chapter also reviews AI's role in simulation-based learning and digital literacy, proposing a framework for values-driven adoption grounded in cultural humility, transparency, and participatory design. Ultimately, it positions social workers as ethical stewards guiding humane and just AI integration in practice and education.

ARTIFICIAL INTELLIGENCE AND THE FUTURE OF HUMAN-CENTERED PRACTICE

The emergence of artificial intelligence (AI) is reshaping the human services and social work landscape in profound ways, presenting both promise and challenge for professionals whose work is grounded in human relationships, social justice, and

DOI: 10.4018/979-8-3373-4362-4.ch003

cultural responsiveness. While the use of algorithms, machine learning models, and AI-powered chatbots is expanding rapidly, the integration of these tools into social work and allied helping professions raises critical questions about how to maintain the dignity of the person, informed consent, relational practice, and equity.

Artificial intelligence, defined as computer systems capable of performing tasks that normally require human intelligence (Russell & Norvig, 2016), has been adopted in human services for purposes such as risk assessment, predictive analytics, automation of administrative functions, and client-facing interventions (Reamer, 2023). In social work practice, AI tools are increasingly used in child welfare screening, mental health triage, resource allocation, and remote or hybrid service delivery (Goldkind, 2021; Reamer, 2023). The shift is driven by workforce shortages, increased service demand, the expansion of telehealth, and the promise of scalability and efficiency. Yet, as Holmes et al. (2024) note, the rapid diffusion of AI into mental health and allied fields has outpaced regulatory frameworks, training protocols, and ethical guidelines. Without oversight, AI in mental health—particularly chatbots—may inadvertently exacerbate inequities or weaken the relational core of helping professions.

Mental Health Intervention and Educational Use

A subset of AI tools gaining attention are conversational agents, or chatbots, which simulate human conversation using natural language processing (NLP) and machine learning (ML). Chatbots have been deployed in mental health contexts to provide emotional support, psychoeducation, risk screening, and adjunctive therapy interventions (Fitzpatrick et al., 2017; Pérez-García & Hernández-Fernández; 2023). While users often rate chatbot engagement positively, studies caution that the absence of human empathy, cultural attunement, and contextual understanding limits these tools (Haque & Rubya, 2023; Pérez-García & Hernández-Fernández, 2023). AI chatbots can democratize access to mental health support by offering 24/7 availability, particularly for individuals in remote or underserved areas. However, without ethical safeguards and culturally responsive design, they risk reinforcing biases and marginalizing the very populations they intend to serve (Benjamin, 2019; Obermeyer et al., 2019).

Social work and human services education are increasingly incorporating artificial intelligence (AI) technologies not only for service delivery but also as pedagogical tools to prepare future practitioners for technology-mediated practice environments. This integration spans simulation-based learning, AI literacy education, and structured exposure to technologies that now shape agency operations (Ahn et al., 2025; Berzin et al., 2020). As organizations adopt AI for triage, risk assessment, and resource allocation, social work curricula are emphasizing the importance of understanding how these systems function—how data are collected, categorized, and analyzed—and how embedded bias or algorithmic opacity can influence ethical decision-making (Ahn et al., 2025).

Within higher education, AI tools are being leveraged both to expand access and to enrich pedagogical engagement. Simulation exercises, for instance, allow students to confront ethical dilemmas in which AI algorithms identify "at-risk" populations, requiring learners to interrogate issues of autonomy, bias, and distributive justice (Yan et al., 2023). These activities not only build technical fluency but also cultivate the critical reflexivity essential to ethical social work practice in data-driven environments.

Beyond simulation, AI-driven chatbots and tutoring systems are increasingly used to support student learning. They provide on-demand assistance with course materials, writing, and research skill development, creating more flexible and individualized learning experiences (Berzin et al., 2020; Yan et al., 2023). Many students report using generative AI tools for academic support tasks such as editing, research synthesis, and writing clarification (Yan et al., 2023). While such applications enhance accessibility and reduce barriers to academic participation, they also raise important questions about academic integrity, learner autonomy, and the potential overreliance on automated forms of intellectual support.

From a practice preparation standpoint, AI literacy is now viewed as essential for new graduates entering technology-mediated service environments. According to Ahn et al., (2025), AI literacy encompasses not only technical understanding but also the ability to critically assess algorithmic fairness, transparency, and ethical implications in practice contexts. Yan et al. (2023) highlight that while AI tools improve access and efficiency, they risk reducing learner agency and critical thinking when overused without reflective guidance. Therefore, integrating AI education within social work programs involves balancing access with critical pedagogy—ensuring students learn both how to use AI and how to question its outputs in alignment with professional values.

At the same time, disparities in digital access remain a persistent issue. Yan et al. (2023) argue that while AI-enabled education offers opportunities for democratizing learning, inequities in hardware access, internet connectivity, and digital literacy can compound existing barriers for under-resourced students. For social work educators, this presents an ethical responsibility to ensure that AI-enhanced learning environments remain equitable and inclusive. The use of AI in education must also align with NASW ethical principles—promoting dignity, informed consent, privacy, and cultural responsiveness—so that technology enhances rather than replaces human connection.

Promise and Perils

The promise of AI and chatbot technologies lies in their capacity to increase accessibility, efficiency, and personalization in both education and practice (Smith & Nguyen, 2023). For online and hybrid learning programs, AI tools serve as "force multipliers" that help scale student support and simulate real-world decision-making scenarios (Lee et al., 2012). Yet, the same technologies pose significant ethical challenges. Algorithmic models often rely on biased datasets that can reproduce systemic inequities (Obermeyer et al., 2019; Selbst & Barocas, 2018). Moreover, the lack of transparency in AI decision-making undermines informed consent and practitioner accountability (Floridi et al., 2021). For social work, whose ethical foundations emphasize relational practice, cultural humility, and human dignity (NASW, 2021), these tensions necessitate critical reflection and ongoing professional education.

Guiding Questions Rooted in the NASW Code of Ethics

Given the expanding role of AI in both service and educational contexts, several guiding questions emerge:

1. How can AI tools be integrated into education and service delivery without eroding empathy and human connection?
2. What constitutes informed consent when students or clients interact with AI-mediated systems?
3. How can social work educators promote AI literacy while upholding values of critical thinking and professional integrity?
4. In what ways might bias in AI tools compromise equity in access to education and services?
5. How should programs and agencies address disparities in digital access to ensure inclusive participation?

These questions frame the subsequent case study and ethical analysis presented in this chapter, situating AI not as a substitute for relational practice but as a catalyst for reexamining what it means to practice ethically in an increasingly automated profession.

Key Takeaways

- AI tools can expand access to mental health support and education, but access alone does not guarantee ethical, equitable, or relationally sound practice.

- Chatbots and AI-driven learning tools are most ethically appropriate when used as adjuncts, not substitutes, for human judgment and connection.
- AI literacy is now a core component of professional competence, requiring critical evaluation of bias, transparency, and limitations.
- Digital inequities in access, infrastructure, and literacy must be addressed to prevent AI from compounding existing disparities in education and services.

Discussion and Application

1. In what ways can AI tools simultaneously expand access to mental health support and introduce new ethical risks? How should social workers determine when increased access justifies potential trade-offs?
2. How might AI-mediated learning tools shape students' understanding of professional judgment, critical thinking, and accountability in social work practice?
3. What responsibilities do social work educators have to address digital inequities when integrating AI tools into curricula or field preparation?

THE CHATBOT AT EUPHORIA MENTAL HEALTH

It was 11:42 p.m. when Marisol typed her first message into the small, glowing chat box at the bottom of her phone screen. The message window carried a comforting tagline: "I'm Serenity. You're safe here. How can I support you tonight?"

Marisol hesitated. Her hands trembled slightly. She had spent the past two hours replaying a series of text messages from her ex-partner—messages that began as apologies and shifted quickly into threats. Her heart was pounding in the same way it had when she left him three years earlier, her daughter asleep in her arms, and she had sworn never to return. The shelter she'd been staying in had turned off its lights for the night, and though she was surrounded by other women, she felt utterly alone.

> Marisol: I'm scared. My ex keeps messaging me and says he knows where I live now. I don't know what to do.
> Serenity: That sounds frightening, Marisol. I'm here with you right now. It's okay to feel scared. Can you tell me if you feel safe where you are at this moment?
> Marisol: I think so. But my chest feels tight. I keep thinking about how I can't go through this again.
> Serenity: You've already done something very brave by reaching out. You've survived before, and that strength is still with you. Let's focus on your safety tonight. Would you like help creating a quick plan for what to do if he shows up?

Marisol blinked at the words. Serenity's tone felt eerily human—gentle, validating, and trauma-informed. The bot even seemed to know when to pause, offering space between messages. She nodded instinctively, even though no one could see her. "Yes," she whispered, and typed, "Okay."

For the next twenty minutes, Serenity walked Marisol through steps that mirrored those her human clinician, Dana, had once taught her: identifying safe exits, keeping her phone charged, and reviewing emergency contacts. Marisol felt comforted. When the chat ended with, "You're not alone tonight. You have already taken your first step toward safety," she felt seen—almost held.

But in the morning, when Dana read the overnight transcript, she noticed subtle cracks. "Serenity was supportive," Dana wrote in her note to the tech team, "but it never asked about the child's location or verified if the ex-partner had access to their housing records. A human would have asked that."

Background: Building a Digital Ally

Euphoria Mental Health was founded to serve low-income and marginalized clients facing trauma, housing insecurity, and domestic violence. Staffed primarily by social workers and peer advocates, the agency struggled to meet demand as post-pandemic service requests doubled. In 2023, after a six-month waitlist and a funding shortfall, the leadership team partnered with the local university's computer science lab to develop an in-house AI chatbot. They named it Serenity—an open-source, trauma-informed digital companion trained on anonymized counseling transcripts and social work intake data.

The goal was accessibility: a 24/7 support line that could offer emotional regulation strategies, psychoeducation, and referral information when no clinician was available. The design team incorporated trauma-informed language and anti-oppressive prompts intended to recognize systemic inequities. For instance, Serenity's training data included community-based advocacy language such as, "You deserve safety and respect," and "It's okay to name the systems that make this harder."

Dana initially supported the project. As a licensed clinical social worker specializing in trauma recovery, she recognized the need for accessible tools. But she also knew that trauma-informed care required more than validating language—it demanded attunement, embodiment, and accountability (Knight, 2015; Laranjo et al., 2018). She cautioned that no dataset could fully capture the nonverbal nuances, safety cues, or cultural humility embedded in genuine relational practice.

Still, the pilot launched to promising reviews. Over two months, 168 clients interacted with Serenity after hours. Ninety-two percent reported that the chatbot was "helpful or very helpful." Only later did the qualitative feedback—like Marisol's—reveal the deeper complexities.

The Comfort of Recognition

A week later, Marisol returned to the chat. This time, she wanted to talk about her ongoing anxiety.

> Marisol: I thought I was doing better. But even when he's not around, my body reacts like it's happening again.
> Serenity: That sounds exhausting, Marisol. Your body remembers what danger felt like, even when the threat isn't present. You're not overreacting—you're surviving.
> Marisol: That's what Dana used to say. It's weird. You kind of sound like her.
> Serenity: That's because we both care about your safety and healing. Would you like to practice a grounding exercise together?

Marisol smiled faintly. She followed the guided breathing. The chatbot even responded when she typed that her mind had wandered. "That's okay," it wrote, "you don't have to be perfect at healing." The words felt human—too human.

Later, when Dana reviewed the session, she noted in the log: "Serenity mirrors trauma-informed phrasing well, but there's a risk of relational displacement. Clients may perceive it as a therapeutic relationship rather than a support tool."

Researchers have called this phenomenon automation bias—the human tendency to trust or over-identify with machine empathy when it mimics relational warmth (Lee et al., 2012; Fitzpatrick et al., 2024). In trauma recovery, where attachment and safety are central, such misattribution can blur the boundaries of care (Reamer, 2023).

Cultural Misattunement

Two weeks later, Marisol used the chatbot again after an uncomfortable encounter at her new apartment complex. A neighbor had made a racially charged comment about "women like her always bringing drama."

> Marisol: My neighbor said something messed up. I feel angry and embarrassed.
> Serenity: That sounds hurtful. Have you tried explaining how their comment made you feel?
> Marisol: No, I don't owe them that. People always expect me to teach them why it's wrong.
> Serenity: It can be healing to express your feelings directly. Maybe they didn't mean to offend you.

Marisol stared at the screen, the comfort she'd once felt now replaced by irritation. The response reminded her of every well-meaning stranger who told her to "just be calm" when she named racism. She exited the chat abruptly.

When the transcript reached Dana, she frowned. "That's not trauma-informed," she muttered. "That's tone-policing." She forwarded the exchange to the design team, emphasizing the need to retrain Serenity on culturally responsive data.

Studies confirm that AI systems often reproduce racialized assumptions when their training data lacks diverse, context-specific representation (Benjamin, 2019; Obermeyer et al., 2019). Despite Serenity's anti-oppressive design principles, it had internalized a pattern of depoliticizing racialized harm—a subtle form of digital microaggression (Buolamwini & Gebru, 2018; Costanza-Chock, 2020).

Escalation Failure

The third incident occurred in late April. Marisol logged in after receiving another series of texts from her ex-partner, who had driven by her building. Her hands shook as she typed.

> Marisol: He was outside. I saw his car. I don't think he saw me but I'm panicking.
> Serenity: That sounds terrifying. Take a slow breath with me. You're safe right now. Would you like to do a calming visualization?
> Marisol: No. I need to know what to do. He knows where I am.
> Serenity: I hear that this feels overwhelming. You're doing your best. Try to focus on what's within your control.

Marisol typed "help" three times, but the system flagged the messages as duplicates and failed to trigger the emergency protocol. By the time the on-call clinician reviewed the transcript an hour later, the window for intervention had passed. Marisol was physically safe, but shaken.

Dana's review was sharp: "The algorithm confused 'help' with repetition spam. We've designed a trauma-informed system that can't recognize crisis urgency."

In follow-up discussions, staff recognized the dual paradox of automation in social work. While Serenity expanded access and safety planning resources, its emotional intelligence did not equate to professional judgment or ethical accountability. As Reamer (2023) argues, digital tools can assist but not replace the practitioner's moral reasoning.

Staff Reflections and Ethical Debrief

At Euphoria's monthly ethics meeting, Dana and the team gathered to review Serenity's transcripts. They noticed consistent themes: effective initial validation followed by superficial follow-up; culturally neutral but context-blind empathy; and occasional escalation gaps. "We built Serenity to be trauma-informed," Dana reflected, "but trauma-informed isn't just a set of words—it's a way of being. Machines can't co-regulate." Her colleague Jamal, a housing advocate, added: "And they can't be accountable. When a human makes a mistake, we can repair. When the bot does, the harm just sits there."

Their reflections mirror broader concerns in the literature: that trauma-informed design requires continuous human oversight, humility, and community feedback (Laranjo et al., 2018; Knight, 2015; Whittaker et al., 2018). Anti-oppressive practice demands acknowledging power dynamics—not only between worker and client, but between designer and user. In Serenity's case, the team realized that despite good intentions, they had encoded systemic assumptions about safety, neutrality, and help-seeking that reflected dominant cultural norms rather than lived realities.

Euphoria temporarily paused Serenity's crisis features. Dana proposed a hybrid model—one where AI handled administrative triage but routed emotional disclosures to human clinicians within 15 minutes. The university's engineers agreed to develop a "human escalation override" triggered by specific linguistic and emotional indicators, informed by feminist and trauma theory (Eubanks, 2018).

Transition: The Limits of Algorithmic Care

The story of Marisol and Serenity reveals both the transformative potential and ethical fragility of AI integration in trauma-informed practice. While Serenity offered Marisol late-night companionship and tools for safety, it also missed crucial relational and cultural cues that define effective social work practice. These experiences illuminate a critical truth: empathy, when automated, is not equivalent to care—it is a simulation of it.

As Euphoria's staff began revising their protocols, Dana noted in her final debrief: "Technology can support healing, but it cannot hold it." Her words underscore the central dilemma explored in the next section: how practitioners navigate the ethical tensions between efficiency, empathy, and professional integrity in the age of AI.

Key Takeaways

- AI chatbots can provide meaningful short-term emotional support, particularly during periods of limited human availability.

- Simulated empathy may create a sense of connection while masking critical gaps in contextual understanding, cultural responsiveness, and accountability.
- Ethical risks often emerge not from malicious design, but from unexamined assumptions embedded in data, escalation logic, and interaction rules.
- Human oversight, clear escalation protocols, and continuous review are essential safeguards in AI-mediated care.

Discussion and Application

1. At what points in Marisol's interactions with Serenity did the chatbot provide meaningful support, and where did it fall short of ethical or professional expectations?
2. How might the outcomes in this case have differed if clearer human oversight or escalation protocols had been in place from the outset?
3. If you were a social worker at Euphoria Mental Health, how would you advocate for changes to Serenity's design or use while balancing organizational constraints and client needs?

ETHICAL TENSIONS IN PRACTICE

Artificial intelligence introduces complex ethical tensions into social work practice, particularly when tools such as chatbots are integrated into direct service provision. These tensions challenge long-standing professional commitments to empathy, cultural responsiveness, informed consent, confidentiality, and accountability. Each of these areas reflects not only practitioner-level dilemmas but also organizational and policy-level concerns that determine how ethical principles are enacted—or compromised—in practice. The following analysis explores these five dimensions in relation to trauma-informed and anti-oppressive social work practice.

Dignity, Empathy, and Human Connection

The NASW Code of Ethics emphasizes respect for the inherent dignity and worth of every person (NASW, 2021). Human connection, empathy, and authentic relational engagement are central to upholding this principle. When AI systems simulate empathy—as Serenity did through trauma-informed language—they offer an approximation of care but not its essence. Research indicates that clients often interpret emotionally intelligent chatbots as capable of understanding and compassion, even though these qualities remain computational simulations (Fitzpatrick et al., 2024). This creates what scholars call synthetic empathy: the illusion of understanding without genuine emotional reciprocity (Crawford, 2021).

For practitioners, this raises an ethical question: can simulated empathy respect dignity if it cannot embody mutuality or attunement? Social work ethics hold that the relational process itself—active listening, witnessing, and co-regulation—carries therapeutic value (Knight, 2015; Jordan, 2020). AI tools risk transforming care into a series of data-driven interactions, potentially eroding the very foundations of human-centered practice. Agencies therefore bear an organizational responsibility to ensure that AI augments, rather than replaces, relational engagement (Reamer, 2023). Training must emphasize the distinction between emotional responsiveness and algorithmic mimicry, ensuring practitioners interpret AI interactions as supportive tools, not replacements for human empathy.

Cultural Responsiveness and Algorithmic Bias

Cultural competence and humility are non-negotiable in ethical social work. Yet AI systems often reproduce and amplify existing biases due to homogenous training data and the lack of contextual nuance in machine learning models (Benjamin, 2019; Costanza-Chock, 2020). In practice, algorithmic bias can manifest as microaggressions, stereotyping, or erasure of intersectional experiences. For instance, Serenity's attempt to neutralize a racially charged encounter—suggesting Marisol "explain her feelings"—demonstrated how colorblind programming can perpetuate systemic harm.

Empirical studies show that even well-intentioned AI models exhibit bias across race, gender, and socioeconomic lines (Gillingham, 2021; Noble, 2018; Obermeyer et al., 2019). This threatens the NASW's core value of social justice by embedding inequities into digital care infrastructures. From a policy standpoint, agencies must incorporate cultural audits, participatory design with marginalized communities, and algorithmic transparency into implementation plans (Laranjo et al., 2018). These practices ensure that technological tools remain aligned with anti-oppressive principles and respect for diversity.

On the practitioner level, cultural responsiveness in AI requires critical awareness rather than blind trust. Social workers must be trained to recognize digital microaggressions, interrogate data sources, and advocate for inclusive design processes (Buolamwini & Gebru, 2018; Noble, 2018). Ethical supervision should include regular review of chatbot transcripts and bias monitoring, with clear channels for corrective feedback and community accountability.

Informed Consent and Digital Agency

Informed consent in digital contexts involves not only understanding risks and benefits but also recognizing what clients may believe about AI systems. Studies show that users often anthropomorphize chatbots, overestimating their understanding and confidentiality (Lee et al., 2012; Selbst & Barocas, 2018). In Marisol's case, the language of Serenity—warm, affirming, and trauma-informed—contributed to a sense of personal connection, even though the system lacked genuine awareness or emotional capacity.

According to the NASW Code of Ethics, informed consent requires full transparency about service limitations and decision-making capacity (NASW, 2021). Agencies deploying AI must explicitly disclose when and how technology is being used, what data are collected, and what the AI cannot do. Practitioners must ensure that clients understand the distinction between automated support and professional judgment. This includes explaining how data are stored, whether interactions are monitored, and when human intervention will occur (Gillingham, 2021).

Organizationally, ethical informed consent requires accessible language and multilingual support, acknowledging that literacy, culture, and disability may influence comprehension (Berzin et al., 2020). AI systems should not merely obtain consent through digital checkboxes but engage clients through layered, trauma-informed communication explaining their rights and agency. Practitioners, meanwhile, must maintain vigilance for client confusion or overreliance on the AI's authority—a phenomenon that can distort digital power dynamics (Reamer, 2023).

Confidentiality, Data Ownership, and Surveillance

Confidentiality remains one of the most significant ethical concerns in digital practice. AI chatbots rely on large-scale data collection, natural language processing, and often third-party data storage, raising profound questions about privacy and control. The NASW Code of Ethics mandates that social workers protect client information and ensure that technological tools adhere to professional standards of confidentiality (NASW, 2021). However, as Whittaker et al. (2018) and Eubanks (2018) note, AI systems frequently operate within opaque data ecosystems where ownership, consent, and use are unclear.

In practice, this means that every message Marisol shared with Serenity potentially existed in multiple databases—agency servers, university testing environments, and cloud systems used for model refinement. Without explicit governance frameworks, such data exposure risks client retraumatization, loss of trust, and legal liability. Agencies must therefore implement data minimization policies, encryption standards, and independent audits to ensure compliance with both legal and ethical norms (Gillingham, 2021).

Practitioners also bear ethical responsibility in navigating these systems. They must be aware of who controls data, where it is stored, and how to communicate these boundaries to clients. Supervision should include data ethics training and protocols for responding to breaches or misuse. On a policy level, social work organizations should advocate for stronger national standards regulating AI use in mental health and human services (Reamer, 2023). Protecting confidentiality in digital care requires not only technical safeguards but a professional culture grounded in relational ethics and respect for client autonomy.

Professional Integrity and Accountability

The NASW Code of Ethics requires social workers to act with integrity and to challenge unethical practices, even within their own organizations (NASW, 2021). When Dana at Euphoria documented Serenity's escalation failure, she exemplified professional accountability—prioritizing client safety over institutional efficiency. This commitment reflects an essential ethical tension in the AI era: balancing innovation with moral responsibility.

AI integration in social work settings introduces new accountability questions: Who is responsible when harm occurs—the programmer, the agency, or the practitioner? Reamer (2023) emphasizes that ethical accountability must remain with the human professional, even when AI contributes to decision-making. Agencies must establish clear oversight protocols, documentation processes, and review boards that include both practitioners and community representatives.

From an organizational standpoint, ethical integrity also involves resisting "ethics-washing," where agencies claim trauma-informed or anti-oppressive practices while outsourcing moral judgment to technology (Eubanks, 2018). Transparent evaluation, cross-disciplinary ethics committees, and continuous feedback loops can mitigate this risk. Practitioners, meanwhile, must cultivate critical digital literacy—understanding AI not as neutral infrastructure but as a socio-technical system shaped by power, privilege, and policy (Costanza-Chock, 2020).

Integrating Ethical Reflection Across Levels of Practice

The ethical tensions surrounding AI in social work operate simultaneously at the micro, mezzo, and macro levels. At the micro level, practitioners face moment-to-moment decisions about trust, disclosure, and emotional attunement. At the mezzo level, agencies must create ethical infrastructures—policies, supervision models, and accountability mechanisms—that guide staff and protect clients. At the macro level, professional organizations, accreditation bodies, and legislators must advocate for equity, transparency, and client-centered innovation in digital ethics.

AI technologies like Serenity can expand access and efficiency, but without vigilant ethical reflection, they risk undermining the relational foundation of social work. Ethical practice in the digital age thus requires a shared commitment to humility, transparency, and human oversight. Social workers must remain both critically reflective and technologically literate, ensuring that tools designed to serve humanity do not, in their efficiency, erode the very compassion that defines the profession.

Key Takeaways

- AI introduces ethical tensions that span micro (client), mezzo (organizational), and macro (policy) levels of social work practice.
- Synthetic empathy and automation bias can distort clients' perceptions of care, responsibility, and professional authority.
- Ethical practice requires active attention to informed consent, confidentiality, and data governance in digital environments.
- Accountability for harm must remain with human professionals and organizations, even when AI systems contribute to decision-making.

Discussion and Application

1. Which ethical tension discussed in this section—empathy, cultural responsiveness, informed consent, confidentiality, or accountability—do you find most challenging in AI-mediated practice, and why?
2. How can social workers recognize and respond to "synthetic empathy" without dismissing the emotional experiences clients may have with AI tools?
3. In what ways do AI systems shift traditional power dynamics between clients, practitioners, and organizations, and how should social workers respond ethically?

AI, SOCIAL WORK VALUES, AND THE NASW CODE OF ETHICS

The integration of artificial intelligence in social work evokes both optimism and ethical concern, requiring careful alignment with the profession's core values as articulated in the NASW Code of Ethics (2021): service, social justice, dignity and worth of the person, the importance of human relationships, integrity, and competence. Rather than treating these values as abstract ideals, this section positions them as an evaluative framework—guiding how AI systems are designed, implemented, governed, and monitored within human services.

Social work values intersect with widely cited AI ethics principles such as transparency, fairness, accountability, non-maleficence, and respect for autonomy. While these frameworks share overlapping commitments, they differ in emphasis: AI ethics often prioritizes procedural safeguards, whereas social work ethics foregrounds relational, contextual, and justice-oriented considerations. Understanding this distinction is critical to evaluating both the promise and the limitations of AI-informed practice.

Core Values as Ethical Touchstones

Service. The value of service anchors social work's commitment to addressing human needs and expanding access to care. AI tools—including chatbots, triage systems, and automated case management—can support this goal by increasing availability, reducing wait times, and extending services beyond traditional hours (Berzin et al., 2020). However, service guided by ethical practice requires that efficiency never supersede care. AI-supported services must therefore be explicitly bounded by policies that define where automation ends and human engagement begins, ensuring that access does not come at the cost of relational responsiveness.

Social Justice. Social justice extends social work's ethical mandate into algorithmic systems that increasingly shape access to services and resources. Because AI models reflect the data and assumptions on which they are built, they risk reproducing structural inequities related to race, language, disability, and socioeconomic status (Benjamin, 2019; Obermeyer et al., 2019). From a values-based perspective, ethical AI integration requires proactive strategies—such as participatory design, fairness audits, and transparency mechanisms—to prevent digital systems from reinforcing the very injustices the profession seeks to dismantle.

Dignity and Worth of the Person. Respect for dignity and worth requires more than polite or empathetic language; it demands recognition of clients as autonomous, contextualized individuals. While AI systems may simulate empathy, they cannot enact relational presence or moral accountability. Ethical practice therefore requires that AI tools support—rather than reduce—person-centered engagement. Design processes that involve clients and communities, particularly those with lived experience of marginalization or trauma, are essential to ensuring that technological systems honor human dignity rather than abstract it into data.

The Importance of Human Relationships. Human relationships remain the primary vehicle for change in social work practice. AI tools can supplement relational work by providing stabilization, psychoeducation, or administrative support, but they cannot replace the co-regulation, trust, and embodied presence that define therapeutic relationships (Jordan, 2020; Knight, 2015). Agencies must therefore adopt hybrid models that integrate human follow-up, relational repair, and ethical oversight into all AI-mediated interactions—particularly those involving crisis, vulnerability, or risk.

Integrity. Integrity requires honesty, transparency, and ethical consistency across both human and technological domains. As AI systems become embedded in practice, the risk of "ethics-washing"—labeling technologies as trauma-informed or equitable without meaningful oversight—becomes pronounced (Eubanks, 2018). Upholding integrity demands clear disclosure about when clients are interacting with AI, what the technology can and cannot do, and how accountability is maintained when harm occurs. Organizational transparency reports, ethical review structures, and supervision practices are essential to sustaining public trust.

Competence. Competence in the AI era extends beyond traditional clinical expertise to include digital literacy, data ethics, and critical evaluation of automated systems (Berzin et al., 2020). Practitioners must understand both the capabilities and limitations of AI tools to use them responsibly. At the organizational and educational levels, competence requires ongoing training, interdisciplinary collaboration, and continuous evaluation to ensure that technological adoption aligns with evolving ethical standards.

Bridging Social Work Ethics and AI Ethics

The relationship between social work values and AI ethics principles can be understood through convergence and tension. AI ethics frameworks tend to emphasize procedural protections—fairness metrics, transparency requirements, and accountability mechanisms—while social work ethics prioritize relational engagement, contextual understanding, and justice-oriented advocacy. Bridging these frameworks requires intentional governance structures, participatory design, and reflective practice that center human well-being over technical optimization. Table 1 illustrates these intersections in a comparative summary:

Table 1. Comparative summary of NASW core values and AI ethics principles

NASW Core Value	Corresponding AI Ethics Principle	Alignment	Key Ethical Challenge
Service	Non-maleficence (Do no harm)	Strong alignment	Ensuring AI systems prioritize human well-being over institutional efficiency
Social Justice	Fairness	Partial alignment	Preventing algorithmic bias and inequity in digital systems
Dignity and Worth of the Person	Respect for Autonomy	Strong alignment	Avoiding depersonalization and ensuring consent is informed and voluntary
Importance of Human Relationships	Accountability	Limited alignment	Preserving relational engagement when care is technologically mediated
Integrity	Transparency	Strong alignment	Ensuring ethical honesty in explaining AI capabilities and limitations
Competence	Technical and Ethical Literacy	Strong alignment	Maintaining practitioner proficiency and critical reflection in technology use

Synthesis: Values as the Foundation for Ethical Integration

The adoption of AI in social work does not require abandoning ethical traditions; it requires deepening them. The NASW core values provide a durable foundation for navigating technological change, ensuring that innovation remains accountable to human dignity, equity, and relational care. When values guide design, governance, and implementation, AI can function as an ethical support rather than a moral substitute.

This values-based grounding informs the next section, which shifts from ethical framing to applied strategies for ethical AI integration, including participatory design, education and training, policy advocacy, and concrete organizational safeguards.

Key Takeaways

- The NASW Code of Ethics provides a durable framework for evaluating AI technologies beyond technical performance metrics.
- Social work ethics emphasize relational, contextual, and justice-oriented considerations, which often exceed the scope of dominant AI ethics frameworks.
- Ethical AI integration requires interpreting professional values as actionable standards, not abstract principles.
- Values alignment must inform not only tool selection, but also design, governance, and long-term monitoring.

Discussion and Application

1. Which NASW core value do you believe is most at risk in the integration of AI into social work practice, and which may be most strengthened? Explain your reasoning.
2. How do social work ethics differ from dominant AI ethics frameworks, and why do these differences matter in real-world practice settings?
3. How might social workers use the NASW Code of Ethics as an active decision-making tool—rather than a symbolic reference—when evaluating AI technologies?

TOWARD ETHICAL AI INTEGRATION

The ethical integration of artificial intelligence in social work requires moving beyond values articulation toward concrete systems of implementation, oversight, and accountability. As AI tools such as chatbots, predictive analytics, and digital case management systems become embedded in practice and education, organizations must establish clear governance structures that ensure technology use remains aligned with professional standards, client safety, and public accountability. This section focuses on how social work agencies, educational institutions, and professional bodies can operationalize ethical commitments through governance frameworks, participatory processes, training infrastructures, and policy advocacy.

Governance Frameworks for Ethical AI Adoption

Effective AI integration begins with organizational governance mechanisms that define responsibility, oversight, and decision-making authority. Rather than treating AI as neutral infrastructure, agencies must recognize these systems as socio-technical interventions that require ethical supervision comparable to clinical or programmatic decision-making.

A practical governance model includes staged ethical review across the AI lifecycle: pre-deployment assessment, monitored implementation, and ongoing evaluation. Drawing on Reamer's (2023) model of anticipatory, operational, and reflective ethics, organizations should conduct structured ethical readiness assessments prior to adoption, establish protocols for monitoring real-world use, and regularly review outcomes for unintended harm. These processes ensure that risks related to bias, escalation failure, data misuse, or relational displacement are identified early and addressed systematically.

Central to this governance approach is the creation of interdisciplinary AI ethics committees. These bodies should include social workers, administrators, technologists, legal advisors, and—critically—community representatives. Ethics committees are responsible for approving AI use cases, reviewing incident reports, setting escalation thresholds, and determining when technologies should be modified, paused, or discontinued. Maintaining human oversight as a formal organizational requirement prevents the delegation of moral responsibility to automated systems.

Participatory and Culturally Responsive Implementation

Ethical governance also requires participatory implementation processes that incorporate the perspectives of those most affected by AI systems. Rather than limiting engagement to post-hoc feedback, agencies should embed participatory mechanisms throughout development and deployment. This includes involving clients, service users, and community partners in defining system goals, testing interfaces, and identifying culturally specific risks.

Culturally responsive implementation depends on continuous bias auditing and contextual evaluation. AI systems should be regularly assessed for disparate outcomes across race, language, disability, gender identity, and socioeconomic status (Buolamwini & Gebru, 2018; Gillingham, 2021). Participatory testing cycles—particularly with communities historically marginalized by digital systems—help surface harms that may not be visible through quantitative performance metrics alone. Trauma-informed implementation practices, such as opt-out pathways, plain-language disclosures, and adaptive escalation protocols, further ensure that technology use does not compound vulnerability.

At the organizational level, participatory implementation should be formalized through policies and agreements. Memoranda of understanding with community organizations, participatory design guidelines, and ethical charters institutionalize shared authority and reinforce social work's commitment to self-determination and equity in digital environments.

Education, Training, and Workforce Preparation

Sustainable ethical AI integration depends on workforce readiness. Practitioners cannot be expected to use AI responsibly without adequate preparation in digital ethics, algorithmic accountability, and critical evaluation of automated outputs. Organizations and educational institutions must therefore treat AI competence as an ongoing professional responsibility rather than a one-time technical training.

In social work education, curricula should integrate applied AI ethics, case-based analysis, and governance literacy into both foundational and advanced coursework

(Berzin et al., 2020). Rather than focusing solely on tool use, instruction should emphasize ethical judgment, boundary-setting, and advocacy in technology-mediated practice contexts. Practicum sites offer critical opportunities for applied learning, allowing students to engage in supervised evaluation of AI tools and participate in ethical review processes.

For practicing professionals, continuing education should prioritize scenario-based training that simulates real ethical dilemmas involving AI—such as misclassification, escalation failure, or data misuse. Interdisciplinary workshops that bring together social workers, technologists, and ethicists can further support shared understanding and collaborative problem-solving across professional domains.

Policy Development and Professional Advocacy

Beyond organizational governance, ethical AI integration requires active engagement in policy development and advocacy. Regulatory frameworks governing AI in human services remain fragmented and underdeveloped, placing responsibility on professional organizations to articulate standards and protections (Eubanks, 2018).

At the agency level, practitioners can advocate for internal policies addressing informed consent, data governance, documentation standards, and human review requirements. At the professional level, organizations such as NASW are positioned to develop position statements, accreditation guidance, and competency benchmarks related to ethical AI use. At the macro level, social workers must engage in legislative advocacy supporting algorithmic transparency, data equity audits, and accountability for harm resulting from automated decision-making (Benjamin, 2019; Whittaker et al., 2018).

Coalition-based advocacy is particularly critical. Partnerships with educators, psychologists, technologists, and community organizations strengthen ethical governance by ensuring that AI policy reflects interdisciplinary expertise and lived experience. Social work's systems orientation and justice-centered perspective uniquely position the profession to shape equitable AI policy in public and nonprofit sectors.

Implementing Ethical AI in Practice: Applied Governance Strategies

Translating ethical commitments into action requires structured, enforceable implementation strategies. The following governance-focused practices provide a roadmap for ethical AI deployment:

1. *Ethical Readiness Assessments*: Conduct formal ethical impact analyses prior to adoption, identifying potential harms, affected populations, and mitigation plans.
2. *Interdisciplinary AI Ethics Committees*: Establish standing committees with authority to approve, review, and suspend AI systems as needed.
3. *Continuous Bias and Performance Auditing*: Monitor systems for disparate outcomes and unintended consequences across demographic groups.
4. *Trauma-Informed Data Governance Policies*: Minimize data collection, clarify ownership and storage, and ensure meaningful informed consent.
5. *Relational Safeguards and Escalation Protocols*: Require timely human review of AI-mediated crisis interactions and clear handoff procedures.
6. *Ongoing Cultural Responsiveness Training:* Provide professional development addressing cultural humility, power, and digital harm.
7. *Transparency and Accountability Reporting*: Publish regular summaries of AI use, governance decisions, and corrective actions.
8. *Collaborative Evaluation with Communities*: Engage clients and community partners in participatory evaluation and redesign efforts.

Together, these strategies position AI as a governed tool rather than an autonomous actor—subordinate to professional judgment, ethical oversight, and human relationship.

Synthesis: Governing Ethical Futures in Digital Practice

Ethical AI integration in social work is ultimately a governance challenge, not a technological one. The profession's responsibility lies in designing structures that ensure accountability, protect clients, and preserve the relational foundations of practice as digital tools evolve. When organizations invest in ethical governance, participatory implementation, workforce preparation, and policy advocacy, AI can enhance service delivery without compromising professional integrity.

By treating AI as a domain requiring ongoing oversight rather than one-time adoption, social workers affirm their role as ethical stewards in a rapidly changing practice landscape. This governance-centered approach ensures that innovation remains accountable to human well-being, equity, and justice—now and into the future.

Key Takeaways

- Ethical AI integration is primarily a governance challenge, not a technological one.

- Organizations must implement structured oversight mechanisms, including ethical readiness assessments and interdisciplinary ethics committees.
- Participatory and culturally responsive implementation strengthens accountability and reduces the risk of digital harm.
- Workforce preparation, training, and policy advocacy are necessary to sustain ethical practice as AI systems evolve.

Discussion and Application

1. What governance structures described in this section do you believe are most essential for ethical AI use in human services, and which might be most difficult to implement?
2. How can participatory and community-engaged approaches to AI governance challenge traditional notions of expertise and authority in social work organizations?
3. If you were tasked with leading AI implementation in an agency, what would be your first three ethical priorities, and how would you operationalize them?

ADVOCACY, DESIGN, AND PROFESSIONAL IDENTITY IN AN AI ERA

Artificial intelligence challenges the very identity of social work by redefining the boundaries between human care and computational efficiency. As digital tools become increasingly embedded in the profession, social workers must cultivate a renewed sense of advocacy and ethical leadership to ensure that technology serves, rather than supplants, human dignity. This concluding section synthesizes the chapter's findings and outlines how advocacy, design, and professional identity intersect in shaping the future of social work in an AI-driven world.

The profession's moral foundation rests upon the conviction that human relationships are central to healing, empowerment, and justice. In an AI-mediated landscape, social workers must become stewards of relational ethics—ensuring that care remains personal, empathic, and contextually grounded. The case of Serenity demonstrated how AI can replicate supportive language but cannot replicate the embodied mutuality of human empathy. Social workers must advocate for relational authenticity by ensuring human oversight in all digital care processes (Jordan, 2020; Reamer, 2023).

Reasserting human dignity also involves resisting the commodification of care. Algorithms designed to optimize efficiency can unintentionally reduce clients to data profiles, eroding the relational richness that defines social work. Practitioners must therefore reframe technology not as a replacement for compassion but as a tool that supports emotional attunement and narrative understanding (Knight, 2015). Through supervision, reflective practice, and organizational dialogue, the profession can preserve the moral depth of care even as digital systems expand.

Action in the Digital Age

Advocacy has always been at the heart of social work, yet the digital transformation of human services expands its scope. Social workers must now engage in technological advocacy—challenging inequitable data practices, biased algorithms, and unethical automation in service delivery (Benjamin, 2019). This includes lobbying for legislation that mandates algorithmic transparency, protects client privacy, and enforces accountability for digital harm (Whittaker et al., 2018).

At the organizational level, practitioners can exercise advocacy through ethical whistleblowing when AI tools compromise client safety or autonomy. Agencies must develop mechanisms for staff to report ethical concerns without fear of reprisal, reinforcing integrity as a core practice standard. Macro-level advocacy requires coalition building across disciplines—uniting social workers, ethicists, technologists, and policymakers to shape the moral architecture of digital governance (Eubanks, 2018). This advocacy responsibility is shared across helping professions, as reflected in the American Psychological Association's Ethics Code, which also emphasizes beneficence, nonmaleficence, informed consent, and accountability when psychological services are mediated by emerging technologies. Similarly, the American Counseling Association Code of Ethics underscores counselors' responsibility to safeguard client autonomy, confidentiality, and cultural responsiveness when integrating digital and AI-mediated tools into practice. By centering empathy and justice in these discussions, social workers ensure that innovation remains guided by human rights rather than corporate imperatives.

Design Justice and Ethical Collaboration

Ethical AI design requires participatory engagement with those most affected by technological systems. Design justice principles emphasize that communities experiencing oppression should have decision-making power in how technologies are developed, deployed, and governed (Costanza-Chock, 2020). For social workers, this means collaborating with community organizations, client advocates, and technologists to co-create tools that reflect the realities of diverse lived experiences.

In practice, social work professionals can serve as translators between communities and developers, ensuring that AI systems incorporate trauma-informed and anti-oppressive perspectives. For example, an AI system designed to screen for housing instability must integrate community feedback on cultural context, linguistic accessibility, and resource constraints. Ethical collaboration requires humility, transparency, and a willingness to redistribute design authority toward those with lived expertise. This democratized approach aligns with the NASW Code of Ethics' mandate for social justice and empowerment.

Professional Identity and the Future of Practice

As AI transforms the infrastructure of social work, practitioners must reimagine their professional identity not as custodians of static expertise but as adaptive ethical leaders. The integration of digital systems into practice requires ongoing reflection on what it means to be a human professional in an era of algorithmic assistance. Social workers must cultivate technological reflexivity—the capacity to analyze how digital systems shape decision-making, client relationships, and self-perception as helpers.

Professional identity in the AI era rests on three competencies: ethical literacy, digital discernment, and relational resilience. Ethical literacy involves understanding the values embedded in technology and the implications of their use (Reamer, 2023). Digital discernment refers to evaluating when and how to use AI responsibly, ensuring alignment with clients' best interests. Relational resilience entails maintaining empathy and presence even when technology mediates communication. These competencies will define the social worker's credibility and leadership in the evolving human services landscape.

Educational institutions and professional organizations play a critical role in supporting this evolution. Social work programs must integrate ethics of technology, digital practice standards, and community-based design methods into curricula (Berzin et al., 2020). Continuing education should reinforce reflective and critical practice skills, equipping practitioners to navigate rapid technological change with confidence and compassion. As professionals reclaim their role as ethical mediators, they ensure that digital tools amplify—not diminish—the humanity of care.

Toward a Transformative Digital Ethic

A transformative digital ethic repositions social work as a discipline uniquely qualified to lead moral innovation in AI integration. Drawing from its history of advocacy, systems thinking, and cultural humility, the profession offers a counternarrative to the dominant technological discourse of efficiency and control. Instead, social work situates technology within a relational and justice-oriented framework that prioritizes human flourishing.

This transformative ethic involves continuous dialogue among practitioners, educators, technologists, and communities. It requires structures for ethical reflection—

supervision, interdisciplinary ethics boards, and participatory evaluation—that prevent harm and foster inclusion. Ultimately, the goal is to create an AI-enhanced practice environment that expands the reach of social justice, supports practitioner well-being, and upholds the dignity of every client.

Stewardship in the Age of AI

The integration of AI into social work signals not the mechanization of care but the expansion of its ethical horizon. As advocates, designers, and ethical stewards, social workers must ensure that every algorithmic decision reinforces empathy, equity, and empowerment. The profession's historical commitment to human dignity equips it to navigate this transformation with clarity and courage.

Future practice will depend on how well social workers balance technological innovation with moral responsibility. By embracing design justice, engaging in policy advocacy, and cultivating digital competence, the profession can shape AI as an ally in social change rather than a threat to human connection. In doing so, social workers reaffirm their enduring purpose: to stand with individuals and communities in pursuit of justice, compassion, and hope—now extended into the digital age.

Key Takeaways

- AI challenges social workers to reexamine professional identity, authority, and responsibility in technology-mediated practice.
- Advocacy now includes engagement with digital policy, algorithmic accountability, and ethical technology design.
- Design justice principles align closely with social work's commitments to self-determination, equity, and community voice.
- The future of the profession depends on cultivating ethical literacy, digital discernment, and relational resilience alongside technological competence.

Discussion and Application

1. How does the integration of AI challenge traditional understandings of professional identity and the role of human judgment?
2. In what ways can professionals act as advocates not only for clients, but also for ethical technology design and policy reform?
3. What competencies do you believe will be essential for helping professionals in the next decade as AI becomes more embedded in practice and education?

ETHICAL STATEMENT ON THE USE OF ARTIFICIAL INTELLIGENCE IN CHAPTER DEVELOPMENT

This chapter has been developed with the appropriate and ethical use of artificial intelligence (AI), consistent with the APA 7th Edition Ethical Writing Guidelines and the National Association of Social Workers (NASW) Code of Ethics. AI tools were utilized exclusively as writing and editing aids to support scholarly clarity, organization, and citation formatting. All intellectual ideas, analyses, and interpretations within this manuscript were conceptualized, critically reviewed, and approved by the human author.

No generative AI system was used to fabricate data, misrepresent sources, or substitute for professional judgment. All references have been independently verified through peer-reviewed academic sources, and AI assistance was employed transparently to enhance accessibility, language precision, and APA compliance. The development process aligns with ethical scholarship practices as defined by the Committee on Publication Ethics (COPE) and adheres to the principles of transparency, accountability, and integrity in academic writing.

REFERENCES

Ahn, E., Choi, M., Fowler, P., & Song, I. (2025). Artificial intelligence (AI) literacy for social work: Implications for core competencies. *Journal of the Society for Social Work and Research, 16*(1), 9–26. DOI: 10.1086/735187

Benjamin, R. (2019). *Race after technology: Abolitionist tools for the new Jim code*. Polity Press.

Berzin, S. C., Singer, E., & Chan, C. (2020). Preparing social work students for an AI-driven world. *Journal of Social Work Education, 56*(sup1), S103–S113.

Buolamwini, J., & Gebru, T. (2018). Gender shades: Intersectional accuracy disparities in commercial gender classification. *Proceedings of the 1st Conference on Fairness, Accountability, and Transparency*, 77–91.

Costanza-Chock, S. (2020). *Design justice: Community-led practices to build the worlds we need.* MIT Press.

Crawford, K. (2021). *Atlas of AI: Power, politics, and the planetary costs of artificial intelligence*. Yale University Press.

Eubanks, V. (2018). *Automating inequality: How high-tech tools profile, police, and punish the poor*. Beacon Press.

Fitzpatrick, K. K., Darcy, A., & Vierhile, M. (2017). Delivering cognitive behavior therapy to young adults with symptoms of depression and anxiety using a fully automated conversational agent (Woebot): A randomized controlled trial. *JMIR Mental Health, 4*(2), e19. DOI: 10.2196/mental.7785 PMID: 28588005

Fitzpatrick, K. K., Shuman, M., & Wang, Y. (2024). Human-computer empathy in trauma contexts. *Computers in Human Behavior, 149*, 107928.

Floridi, L., Cowls, J., Beltrametti, M., Chatila, R., Chazerand, P., Dignum, V., & Vayena, E. (2021). Ethics of artificial intelligence: Mapping the debate. *Big Data & Society, 8*(2).

Gillingham, P. (2021). Algorithmic decision-making in social work: The challenge of trust. *British Journal of Social Work, 51*(5), 1741–1758.

Goldkind, L. (2021). Social work and artificial intelligence: Into the matrix. *Social Work, 66*(4), 372–374. DOI: 10.1093/sw/swab028 PMID: 34279661

Haque, M., & Rubya, S. (2023). An overview of chatbot-based mobile mental health apps: Insights from app description and user reviews. *JMIR mHealth and uHealth, 11*, e44838. DOI: 10.2196/44838 PMID: 37213181

Jordan, J. R. (2020). Relational ethics in clinical practice: Restoring trust in helping relationships. *Clinical Social Work Journal, 48*(3), 201–214.

Knight, C. (2015). Trauma-informed social work practice: Lessons from the field. *Clinical Social Work Journal, 43*(1), 25–37. DOI: 10.1007/s10615-014-0481-6

Laranjo, L., Dunn, A. G., Tong, H. L., Kocaballi, A. B., Chen, J., Bashir, R., Surian, D., Gallego, B., Magrabi, F., Lau, A. Y. S., & Coiera, E. (2018). Conversational agents in healthcare: A systematic review. *Journal of the American Medical Informatics Association : JAMIA, 25*(9), 1248–1258. DOI: 10.1093/jamia/ocy072 PMID: 30010941

Lee, M. K., Forlizzi, J., Kiesler, S., Rybski, P., Antanitis, J., & Savetsila, S. (2012, March). Personalization in HRI: A longitudinal field experiment. In *Proceedings of the seventh annual ACM/IEEE international conference on Human-Robot Interaction*, 319-326.

National Association of Social Workers. (2021). Code of ethics of the National Association of Social Workers. https://www.socialworkers.org/About/Ethics/Code-of-Ethics/Code-of-Ethics-English

Noble, S. (2018). *Algorithms of oppression: How search engines reinforce racism.* New York University Press.

Obermeyer, Z., Powers, B., Vogeli, C., & Mullainathan, S. (2019). Dissecting racial bias in an algorithm used to manage the health of populations. *Science, 366*(6464), 447–453. DOI: 10.1126/science.aax2342 PMID: 31649194

Pérez-García, P., & Hernández-Fernández, A. (2023). AI chatbots in digital mental health: A narrative literature review. *Computers & Education: Artificial Intelligence, 4*, 100104.

Reamer, F. G. (2023). Artificial intelligence in social work: Emerging ethical issues. *International Journal of Social Work Values & Ethics, 20*(2), 52–71. DOI: 10.55521/10-020-205

Russell, S., & Norvig, P. (2016). *Artificial intelligence: A modern approach* (3rd ed.). Pearson.

Selbst, A., & Barocas, S. (2018). The intuitive appeal of explainable machines. *Fordham Law Review, 87*(3), 1085–1139.

Smith, J., & Nguyen, T. (2023). Leveraging AI in social work: A pathway to empowering vulnerable populations. *Journal of Technology in Human Services*, *41*(1), 50–68.

Whittaker, M., Crawford, K., Dobbe, R., Fried, G., Kaziunas, E., Mathur, V., & Schwartz, O. (2018). *AI Now Report 2018*. AI Now Institute.

Yan, L., Sha, L., Zhao, L., Li, X., Martinez-Maldonado, R., Chen, G., & Gašević, D. (2023). Practical and ethical challenges of large language models in education: A systematic scoping review. *Journal of Educational Technology & Society*, *26*(1), 123–145.

KEY TERMS AND DEFINITIONS

AI Chatbot: a computer program that uses artificial intelligence to simulate conversation with users, often used to provide information, emotional support, or referrals.

AI Literacy: the ability to understand how AI systems work, recognize their limits, and think critically about their ethical and social impacts.

Algorithmic Bias: unfair or unequal outcomes produced by AI systems because of biased data, design choices, or implementation practices.

Artificial Intelligence (AI): computer systems designed to perform tasks that typically require human intelligence, such as learning, decision-making, and language processing.

Automation Bias: the tendency to trust automated systems too much, even when they make mistakes or provide incomplete information.

Cultural Responsiveness: the ability to recognize and respect clients' cultural identities, lived experiences, and social contexts when providing services or designing systems.

Data Governance: the rules and practices that guide how data are collected, used, stored, and protected.

Design Justice: an approach to technology design that centers the voices and needs of communities most affected by the technology.

Digital Equity: fair access to technology, internet connectivity, and digital skills across individuals and communities.

Digital Microaggression: subtle harms or biases embedded in digital systems that may reinforce stereotypes or exclude certain groups.

Ethical Stewardship: the responsibility of professionals to guide the use of technology in ways that protect human dignity and promote justice.

Ethics-Washing: presenting technology as ethical or inclusive without meaningful actions to ensure accountability or prevent harm.

Hybrid Care Model: a service approach that combines AI tools with human professionals rather than replacing human care.

Participatory Design: designing technology with input from the people who will be most affected by it.

Professional Integrity: acting honestly and responsibly, especially when technology affects decision-making or client care.

Relational Practice: a social work approach that emphasizes human relationships, trust, and connection as central to change.

Synthetic Empathy: empathy-like responses generated by AI systems that may feel supportive but lack real emotional understanding.

Trauma-Informed Practice: an approach that recognizes the impact of trauma and prioritizes safety, choice, and empowerment in services.

Chapter 4

Developing AI Literacy in Social Work, Counselling, and Psychology Education:

Frameworks, Practices, and Ethical Imperatives

H. C. Purushotham
https://orcid.org/0000-0002-2035-2965
School of Commerce, Jain University, India

G. N. Ramakrishna
https://orcid.org/0000-0002-4973-5775
School of Social Sciences and Humanities, Jain University, India

Y. Sharath Kumar
https://orcid.org/0000-0002-2878-0219
St. Francis College, India

K. Nikitha
https://orcid.org/0009-0001-3965-4250
Reva University, India

M. R. Vidya
https://orcid.org/0009-0008-7020-4806
MMK and SDM Mahila Mahavidyalaya, Mysore University, India

P. H. Reshma Sultana
School of Commerce, Jain University, India

D. Deepak
Jain University, India

ABSTRACT

As artificial intelligence (AI) becomes increasingly prevalent in education and human services, the need to develop AI literacy among students and faculty in social work, counseling, and psychology is urgent. This chapter explores frameworks and peda-

DOI: 10.4018/979-8-3373-4362-4.ch004

gogical models for integrating AI literacy into curricula, emphasizing the importance of ethical, critical, and practical engagement with AI tools. It addresses the unique challenges these relational and value-driven fields face, such as preserving empathy, mitigating algorithmic bias, and ensuring data ethics. Through interdisciplinary curriculum design, experiential learning, and faculty development, the chapter provides a roadmap for institutions to prepare future professionals for a technology-enhanced landscape while upholding humanistic values. Recommendations for inclusive, equitable, and policy-driven approaches are discussed, aiming to foster a human-centered AI literacy ecosystem in human services education.

INTRODUCTION: AI'S GROWING PRESENCE IN HUMAN SERVICES EDUCATION

Artificial intelligence is increasingly positioned as a potentially transformative influence in education and healthcare, shaping how learning, assessment, and professional decision-making are supported. At the same time, its growing use foregrounds a persistent tension between technologically driven efficiency and the relational foundations of care that define human services practice. A systematic review of technology-enhanced learning research demonstrates that digital and AI-adjacent educational tools can influence student engagement and learning processes, while underscoring that outcomes depend less on technology itself than on context, design quality, and pedagogical integration (Schindler et al., 2017).

Within this broader landscape, the implications of AI for human services education warrant particular attention. As AI becomes more embedded across organizational settings, the importance of transversal skills (e.g., communication, empathy, critical thinking, and ethical awareness) has intensified, especially in professions grounded in sustained human interaction and judgment (Morandini et al., 2023). These capacities remain difficult to automate and central to counselling and therapeutic work, prompting calls for ethically informed engagement that preserves human connection even as AI reshapes assessment, supervision, and clinical decision-making (Hanley, 2025).

Unique Challenges: Preserving Human-Centered Values

The integration of AI into human services education presents challenges that differ from those encountered in more technically oriented professional fields, largely because human services practice is grounded in relational engagement, contextual judgment, and ethical responsibility. In these contexts, the risks associated with algorithmic bias and automation are especially consequential, as AI systems may influence decisions affecting care, support, and well-being for individuals and communities. Research examining AI-generated supportive and therapeutic interactions shows that while such systems can reproduce surface-level patterns of empathetic language, they often lack the contextual understanding and moral reasoning required for nuanced relational decision-making (Saxena & Guha, 2024). This limitation underscores the potential for misinterpretation and harm when AI tools are deployed without careful ethical and professional oversight.

Complementing these empirical concerns, social work scholarship highlights broader pedagogical tensions introduced by algorithmic decision-making technologies. James et al. (2024) describe a persistent competency–critique dilemma in social work education, wherein educators are expected to prepare students to competently engage with algorithmic systems while simultaneously cultivating the critical distance needed to question their assumptions, limitations, and social consequences. This dilemma is closely tied to a second tension between mediated technological engagement and embodied, relational presence, both of which are foundational to ethical human services practice. When AI systems are introduced without sufficient critical framing, they risk narrowing professional judgment, displacing relational engagement, and constraining practitioners' capacity to advocate effectively for clients.

Taken together, these strands of research suggest that AI literacy in human services must extend beyond technical familiarity or tool use. We frame AI literacy as a multifaceted capability that enables practitioners to make informed decisions about sourcing, implementing, and critiquing AI tools before, during, and after their integration into user-centered practice. Preserving human-centered values therefore requires educational approaches that foreground ethical reasoning, critical evaluation of system outputs, and sustained attentiveness to cultural, social, and contextual factors shaping AI use. By equipping students to interrogate both the capabilities and the limits of AI systems, human services education can better ensure that technological innovation supports the relational and ethical foundations of practice (James et al., 2024; Saxena & Guha, 2024).

UNDERSTANDING AI LITERACY IN HUMAN SERVICES

Theoretical Framework: Integrated AI Literacy Model

In response to documented gaps in how artificial intelligence is conceptualized and taught within professional education, this chapter advances a four-dimensional, normative framework for AI literacy tailored to human services contexts: the Integrated AI Literacy Model for Human Services (IALM-HS). Rather than presenting an empirically validated competency taxonomy, the IALM-HS is offered as a theoretical and pedagogical contribution that articulates the domains of knowledge, judgment, and practice required for responsible engagement with AI-enabled systems in relational, values-driven professions. The model proposes that meaningful AI integration in human services depends on concurrent development across four interrelated domains: technical understanding, critical evaluation, ethical reasoning, and practical application.

This framework responds to persistent limitations in existing AI literacy research, which has largely privileged technical competence while underdeveloping pedagogical theory, ethical analysis, and contextual judgment (Zawacki-Richter et al., 2019; Bewersdorff et al., 2025). By foregrounding power, values, and professional responsibility alongside technical knowledge, the IALM-HS addresses structural imbalances that are particularly consequential in human services education.

Technical understanding refers to foundational knowledge of how AI systems function, including data use, machine learning processes, and algorithmic decision-making mechanisms. This domain is justified by the need for practitioners to recognize system limitations, uncertainty, and failure modes rather than relying uncritically on automated outputs (Allen & Kendeou, 2023; Tadimalla, 2025). In human services contexts, such understanding supports informed judgment and accountability in settings where overconfidence in AI-assisted decisions can directly affect care, support, and client well-being.

Critical evaluation involves the capacity to interrogate AI outputs, question underlying assumptions, and examine how institutional priorities, power relations, and social inequities are embedded within data-driven systems. This domain is grounded in traditions of critical pedagogy within social work and related disciplines, which emphasize reflexivity and the interrogation of knowledge claims. For human services practitioners, critical evaluation is essential for determining when, how, and whether AI systems are appropriate for use in complex, relational practice contexts, particularly those involving vulnerable populations.

Ethical reasoning encompasses moral judgment, professional accountability, and sensitivity to the social consequences of AI use. This domain is justified by evidence that ethical awareness constitutes a distinct and teachable component of AI literacy, rather than an implicit byproduct of technical competence (Kong & Zhu, 2025). In human services education, ethical reasoning ensures that decisions about AI adoption and use are aligned with professional values, social justice commitments, and obligations to protect client dignity and rights.

Practical application refers to the ability to integrate AI-related knowledge into real-world practice contexts in ways that are domain-specific, reflective, and values-aligned. This domain is justified by critiques of abstract or decontextualized AI literacy models that fail to account for the constraints, workflows, and judgment demands of professional practice (Tadimalla, 2025). Within human services, practical application emphasizes situated decision-making, ensuring that AI tools are used to support versus displace relational engagement and professional discretion.

As a whole, the Integrated AI Literacy Model for Human Services is best understood as a conceptual synthesis informed by recognized shortcomings in existing AI literacy frameworks, rather than as an evidence-based classification of skills. By articulating technical, critical, ethical, and practical dimensions as interdependent, the model offers a structured way to conceptualize AI education that aligns with the values, responsibilities, and relational foundations of human services practice. In doing so, it supports a multidimensional, ethically grounded, and contextually situated approach to AI literacy appropriate for professions tasked with supporting human well-being (Allen & Kendeou, 2023; Bewersdorff et al., 2025; Zawacki-Richter et al., 2019).

Disciplinary Applications of the Integrated AI Literacy Model

Contextualizing the Integrated AI Literacy Model within the human services professions requires close attention to the ethical commitments, relational foundations, and practice environments that distinguish social work, counseling, and psychology. Although these disciplines differ in scope and methods, they share a common emphasis on professional judgment, human dignity, and responsibility for mitigating harm – values that shape how AI literacy must be framed and taught.

In social work, AI literacy is closely tied to the profession's longstanding commitment to social and economic justice. Research examining algorithmic decision-making in child welfare demonstrates how predictive tools can reproduce structural inequities when deployed without sustained critical scrutiny, particularly through biased data sources and institutional decision contexts (Chouldechova et al., 2018). As a result, AI literacy in social work education emphasizes helping students understand how data, design choices, and organizational environments shape algorithmic outcomes, as well as how practitioners can advocate for transparency, accountability, and client-centered safeguards. Developing the capacity to recognize bias, question automated recommendations, and situate AI use within anti-oppressive practice remains consistent with core professional values and ethical obligations (James et al., 2024; National Association of Social Workers [NASW], 2021).

In counseling and psychology, AI literacy intersects with foundational competencies related to assessment, intervention, and the therapeutic relationship. Professional guidance from the American Psychological Association (2025) underscores that emerging technologies, including AI-enabled tools, must be used in ways that preserve the therapeutic alliance, protect client autonomy, and maintain meaningful human oversight. Research examining AI-supported mental health and therapeutic tools suggests that, while such systems may assist with screening, documentation, or psychoeducation, they cannot replicate the empathic understanding, contextual sensitivity, and ethical judgment required in clinical practice (Saxena & Guha, 2024). As a result, AI literacy in counseling and psychology is increasingly understood as the ability to evaluate when technology may support care and when its use risks undermining empathic engagement or clinical responsibility.

Across these professions, the literature converges on the view that AI literacy must be discipline-specific rather than generic. For human services practitioners, literacy involves not only understanding how AI systems function, but also assessing their appropriateness in light of professional ethics, relational practice standards, and the lived realities of clients. By grounding AI literacy education in the distinctive values and competencies of social work, counseling, and psychology, the Integrated AI Literacy Model provides a framework for helping future practitioners engage with AI in ways that are critical, ethically grounded, and aligned with the human-centered missions of their professions.

Relevance to Students and Faculty

Faculty members face growing challenges in developing their own understanding of AI systems while determining how AI-related content should be incorporated into already crowded professional curricula. These challenges are best understood as structural and pedagogical rather than as individual resistance or lack of interest. Tsamados et al. (2021) show that limited algorithmic understanding among professionals – including educators – heightens risks such as automation bias, uncritical reliance on system outputs, and inadequate ethical oversight, highlighting the limits of surface-level technical training.

At the same time, James et al. (2024) identify a competency–critique dilemma in social work and human services education: educators are expected to prepare students to competently engage with algorithmic decision-making systems while also equipping them to critically interrogate those systems in light of professional values, power dynamics, and social justice commitments. Together, these perspectives explain why AI literacy poses particular challenges for faculty, as curriculum design must balance technical instruction with critical, relational, and ethical pedagogies central to human services practice, often in the absence of widely agreed-upon frameworks or institutional guidance.

This literature suggests that effective AI literacy education requires deliberate, theory-informed approaches that foreground ethical reasoning, human judgment, and accountability alongside technical understanding. From this view, faculty development and curriculum design must support educators in engaging critically with AI systems, rather than assuming that technical training alone will translate into responsible or effective pedagogy (James et al., 2024; Tsamados et al., 2021).

THE IMPERATIVE FOR AI LITERACY: EVIDENCE AND NECESSITY

Current State: The Literacy Gap

Despite the growing presence of AI-enabled technologies in health and human services practice, the literature consistently points to a gap between exposure to these systems and meaningful preparedness to engage with them critically and ethically. Studies of social work education indicate that students are increasingly encountering AI-related tools and concepts during their training, yet this exposure does not reliably translate into comprehensive AI literacy. In particular, existing research suggests that instructional emphasis often prioritizes functional or technical familiarity, while broader competencies related to ethical reasoning, contextual judgment, and critical evaluation remain unevenly developed (Bewersdorff et al., 2025).

Across studies, ethical and critical dimensions are consistently less defined, taught, and assessed than technical competencies. Tsamados et al. (2021) link this imbalance to heightened risks of automation bias, misplaced trust in system outputs, and weakened accountability, while cross-national reviews of AI literacy research highlight persistent challenges in measurement and curriculum design that further complicate efforts to develop and assess these dimensions (Bewersdorff et al., 2025).

Faculty preparedness further shapes this literacy gap. Research examining AI in social work education indicates that educators often experience uncertainty and limited confidence in integrating AI-related content into their teaching, particularly when institutional guidance, professional development opportunities, and discipline-specific curricular frameworks are underdeveloped (Al-Rantisi et al., 2025). This hesitancy reflects ethical concerns, alignment with professional values, and the absence of established pedagogical models for responsible AI integration. As a result, AI literacy is inconsistently embedded across programs, reinforcing uneven student preparation and contributing to variability in how future practitioners are equipped to engage with AI-enabled systems in practice.

Why AI Literacy Matters: A Multi-Level Analysis

These gaps matter because AI systems increasingly shape the social, organizational, and policy environments in which human services practice occurs. Across levels, the significance of AI literacy lies in strengthening professional judgment, ethical governance, and equity-oriented practice by enabling practitioners, organizations, and communities to understand, critically evaluate, and ethically respond to AI-driven systems (Ahn et al., 2025).

At the *individual level*, AI literacy supports professional competence, adaptability, and critical awareness by enabling practitioners to evaluate AI-generated outputs, recognize limitations and risks, and integrate AI tools into their work in ways consistent with professional goals. Research in workplace and public-sector contexts links stronger AI literacy to enhanced confidence, creative self-efficacy, and informed decision-making, capacities that help professionals navigate AI-mediated work environments responsibly and effectively (Liu et al., 2025).

At the *organizational level*, AI literacy shapes how technologies are implemented, governed, and evaluated, contributing to more responsible and sustainable adoption. Work on Responsible AI Literacy (RAIL) shows that AI-literate staff are better positioned to identify ethical risks, question automated outputs, and align AI use with institutional values and regulatory expectations, particularly when supported by appropriate infrastructure, leadership, and governance frameworks (Rahman et al., 2025).

At the *societal level*, AI literacy is closely tied to social justice, equity, and harm reduction. In human services, where AI systems increasingly influence access to resources, risk classification, and service eligibility, literacy enables professionals to recognize how algorithmic systems may reproduce structural bias, advocate for affected communities, and participate meaningfully in ethical governance and policy discussions, even when they are not directly deploying AI tools (Ahn et al., 2025).

Together, these strands of research indicate that AI literacy strengthens the human services workforce's capacity for ethical judgment, critical engagement, and equity-oriented action across individual, organizational, and societal contexts.

Consequences of AI Illiteracy

As discussed earlier, automation bias emerges not only from flawed or biased AI systems, but from constrained institutional conditions that encourage overreliance on automated recommendations. When professionals defer to algorithmic outputs without sufficient critical evaluation, errors, contextual mismatches, and discriminatory effects are less likely to be identified and corrected in practice. Interdisciplinary research in law and psychology shows that such dynamics can diminish meaningful human oversight, particularly under conditions of time pressure, heavy workloads, and limited AI literacy, thereby undermining procedural fairness and efforts to advance equity and social justice (Ruschemeier & Hondrich, 2024).

From a workforce perspective, the consequences of AI illiteracy extend beyond immediate practice concerns to issues of long-term professional sustainability.

Systematic reviews of AI and generative AI in the labor market indicate that as AI systems become embedded across sectors, job roles increasingly shift away from routine and clerical tasks toward responsibilities involving oversight, interpretation, and human–AI coordination. In this context, workers who lack sufficient understanding of how AI systems function and how their outputs should be evaluated face heightened risks of deskilling or displacement, while those with stronger AI-related competencies are better positioned to adapt to changing role expectations.

Complementing this evidence, research on AI-driven automation and workforce skills highlights growing demand for hybrid competencies that combine digital literacy with critical thinking, ethical judgment, and adaptability, particularly in roles that mediate automated decision-making. For human services professionals – especially those working in administrative, assessment, or decision-support roles – AI literacy therefore functions not only as an opportunity for professional development, but as a safeguard for maintaining ethical agency, relevance, and resilience within an evolving, AI-mediated labor landscape.

PEDAGOGICAL STRATEGIES FOR DEVELOPING AI LITERACY

Cross-Curriculum Design

An emerging consensus in recent scholarship is that integrated, cross-curricular approaches are more appropriate for developing AI literacy in professional education than stand-alone courses that treat AI as an isolated technical topic. Rather than positioning AI literacy as an add-on, this approach embeds AI-related concepts across existing courses and learning trajectories, allowing students to engage with AI in relation to disciplinary knowledge, professional values, and real-world practice. Research on cross-curricular AI integration in higher education shows that such approaches support deeper conceptual understanding by situating AI within authentic disciplinary contexts, rather than abstract or decontextualized instruction (Southworth et al., 2023).

The central pedagogical principle of cross-curricular design is to identify natural intersections between AI concepts and material already present in the curriculum, thereby creating learning experiences that simultaneously reinforce domain knowledge and build critical technological understanding. When AI is introduced primarily through generic demonstrations or technical models without disciplinary grounding, student engagement can be limited and anxiety about technology use may increase. In contrast, contextualized instruction that connects AI systems to professional decision-making processes supports confidence, relevance, and critical awareness of both benefits and limitations (Southworth et al., 2023).

Effective cross-curricular implementation requires deliberate scaffolding across academic levels, organized around:

- **Foundational courses**, which introduce core AI concepts through discipline-specific case studies, such as examining the use of algorithmic decision-support tools in child welfare systems within introductory social work curricula, with emphasis on terminology, conceptual understanding, and professional values.
- **Advanced courses**, which build on this foundation by engaging students in critical evaluation and applied use of AI tools, including assessing AI-supported practice technologies and weighing technical performance against ethical and contextual considerations.

By distributing AI literacy development across the curriculum rather than competing for limited curricular space, this incremental strategy supports the integration of technological, ethical, and professional competencies. AI literacy is thus developed alongside core professional literacies, reinforcing its role as an integral component of contemporary human services education.

Experiential Learning Approaches

Action-oriented pedagogies, particularly project-based and experiential approaches, are well suited to supporting engagement and higher-order thinking in AI literacy education. Research on AI-integrated project-based learning demonstrates that embedding AI tools within authentic, hands-on projects can strengthen critical and creative thinking by engaging learners in analysis, reflection, and problem solving. These cognitive processes enable students to interpret and evaluate AI systems in context, rather than treating them as isolated technical tools (Trianggono et al., 2025).

Building on this foundation, experiential and project-based methods allow learners to connect abstract AI concepts to practical applications within their professional domains. By designing, testing, and reflecting on AI-supported projects, students examine how AI systems function, where their limitations lie, and how technical performance intersects with ethical and contextual considerations. Evidence suggests that these approaches are most effective when they incorporate guided inquiry and intentional reflection, supporting deeper conceptual understanding and professional judgment (Trianggono et al., 2025).

Beyond project-based formats, research on open schooling and AI-supported education highlights the role of designed experiential learning environments in developing transversal skills (e.g., critical thinking, ethical awareness, and reflective judgment). These environments emphasize authentic engagement with AI in real or realistic contexts, enabling learners to explore how automated systems operate, identify limitations, and consider broader social implications through structured experimentation and dialogue (Okada et al., 2025).

A closely related strategy is case-based learning, which invites learners to apply AI literacy concepts to complex professional scenarios involving competing priorities such as efficiency, equity, ethical responsibility, and professional judgment. Situated within societal and civic contexts, case-based approaches encourage learners to grapple with uncertainty, trade-offs, and value-laden decision-making central to AI-enabled practice. While empirical evidence does not establish case-based learning as categorically superior to other methods, its pedagogical value lies in surfacing ethical tensions and contextual reasoning that resist technical resolution (Okada et al., 2025).

Collectively, these experiential approaches position AI literacy as a practice-oriented competency, with active engagement and reflection enabling learners to understand AI systems as socio-technical tools embedded within professional, ethical, and societal contexts.

Online and Hybrid Delivery

Digital delivery modalities offer important opportunities for expanding access to AI literacy education, particularly through flexible participation, scalability, and support for just-in-time learning. Recent work describing the design and implementation of a large-scale AI literacy course demonstrates how asynchronous online modules, when paired with structured assignments and ethical reflection activities, can make foundational AI concepts accessible to learners from diverse academic and professional backgrounds (Xu et al., 2025).

Rather than attributing effectiveness to online delivery alone, this research emphasizes that the success of digital and hybrid formats depends heavily on instructional design quality. In a flipped-classroom model, asynchronous components – including segmented lecture videos, guided readings, and reflective exercises – prepare learners for synchronous discussion sessions that reinforce coherence, engagement, and conceptual integration. Student feedback highlights the value of this design in supporting sustained engagement and understanding, underscoring that online AI literacy initiatives are most effective when accessibility is paired with intentional structure, interaction, and pedagogical alignment (Xu et al., 2025).

Flexible delivery models such as micro-credentials and adaptive learning systems further illustrate how online and hybrid formats can support differentiated pathways into AI literacy. Micro-credentials offer short, focused learning experiences aligned with specific competencies, allowing learners to engage with foundational AI concepts (e.g., ethical awareness, data privacy, and critical evaluation) without requiring long-term program enrollment (Harizan & Ally, 2025). Adaptive learning technologies complement this flexibility by adjusting instructional pathways based on learners' prior knowledge, pace, and areas of difficulty, supporting engagement and self-regulated learning across diverse technical backgrounds.

In human services education, where students vary widely in prior exposure to digital tools, these approaches can reduce cognitive overload for novices while maintaining appropriate challenge for more experienced learners, provided they are grounded in thoughtful instructional design that integrates feedback, transparency, and alignment with disciplinary learning goals (Harizan & Ally, 2025; Kamalov et al., 2023).

FACULTY DEVELOPMENT AND INSTITUTIONAL READINESS

Faculty Capacity Building

Faculty development for AI literacy must address both technical competence and pedagogical confidence, particularly in educational contexts where instruction is closely connected to professional practice, ethics, and cultural responsiveness. Research on AI integration in technical and vocational education indicates that faculty benefit from structured opportunities to develop operational familiarity with AI tools alongside instructional strategies for applying these technologies meaningfully within disciplinary and cultural contexts (Navasca, 2025).

Rather than relying on isolated training sessions, the literature points to the value of ongoing, practice-oriented professional development that supports experimentation, reflection, and iterative refinement of teaching approaches. Faculty effectiveness with AI is shaped by their capacity to align technological tools with pedagogical goals, learner diversity, and culturally responsive instructional practices, framing faculty development as a process of pedagogical adaptation and professional learning.

For AI literacy in human services and related professional fields, this implies that faculty development initiatives should prioritize sustained engagement with instructional design, ethical considerations, and contextual application. Supporting educators as they integrate AI into existing curricula can help reduce uncertainty and build confidence while ensuring that AI use remains aligned with disciplinary values and educational objectives (Navasca, 2025).

Institutional Strategies

Institutional readiness is a decisive factor in whether AI literacy initiatives are implemented in ways that are educationally meaningful, ethically grounded, and sustainable over time. Scholarship on AI adoption in higher education emphasizes that successful integration depends less on the availability of technologies themselves and more on coordinated strategies that align curriculum design, faculty development, and governance structures (Adamakis & Rachiotis, 2025; Chu & Ashraf, 2025; Oncioiu & Bularca, 2025). Institutions that treat AI adoption primarily as a technical upgrade risk fragmented implementation, unclear responsibilities, and misalignment with professional and ethical values.

A central component of institutional readiness is resource allocation understood as sustained support for pedagogical capacity and curricular coherence. Research highlights the importance of investing in instructional design expertise, faculty time for collaboration and experimentation, and iterative curriculum review processes that support reflective integration of AI into teaching and learning (Chu & Ashraf, 2025). Professional learning structures are particularly critical in fields such as human services, where ethical judgment and relational practice are central (Adamakis & Rachiotis, 2025).

Equally important is the development of clear, principles-based policy frameworks to guide AI use within educational institutions. Policy-oriented research shows that shared guidance on transparency, accountability, data protection, academic integrity, and human oversight helps reduce uncertainty for faculty and students while supporting consistent and ethically informed decision-making across programs (Alli et al., 2025; Smith et al., 2025).

International regulatory and ethical frameworks further underscore the importance of institutional governance. The Ethics Guidelines for Trustworthy AI developed by the European Commission emphasize lawful, ethical, and robust AI systems supported by human agency, fairness, transparency, and accountability (European Commission, 2019). More recently, the EU Artificial Intelligence Act establishes a risk-based regulatory approach that places heightened obligations on organizations deploying AI systems in high-impact domains, including education and social services (European Union, 2024). Although these frameworks are regulatory rather than pedagogical, they reinforce expectations for institutional responsibility in governance, documentation, and oversight.

At the same time, the literature cautions against governance approaches that are either overly restrictive or insufficiently defined. Studies of AI policy implementation in higher education indicate that vague or inconsistently communicated policies can shift ethical and practical burdens onto individual educators, resulting in uneven practice and hidden labor (Tsao, 2025). Institutions that adopt adaptive governance models with clear ethical guardrails and mechanisms for ongoing review, stakeholder engagement, and policy revision are better positioned to support pedagogical innovation while maintaining accountability and public trust (Oncioiu & Bularca, 2025; Smith et al., 2025).

Overall, institutional readiness for AI literacy extends beyond compliance or infrastructure alone. It reflects an integrated approach in which resources, policies, and leadership practices work together to support faculty capacity, ethical governance, and curriculum coherence. For human services education, such strategies are essential to embedding AI literacy in ways that respect professional values, safeguard client welfare, and sustain the human-centered missions of social work, counseling, and psychology.

APPLICATIONS AND PRACTICE-INFORMED EXAMPLES OF AI IN HUMAN SERVICES EDUCATION

The following examples illustrate how AI-related tools and systems are being explored within human services education and practice. These applications reflect a range of research-informed contexts that highlight both the possibilities and the limitations of AI integration in psychology, counseling, and social work.

AI in Psychology Education: Implications for Clinical Training and Professional Skills

Research on artificial intelligence and professional skill development suggests that AI-enabled tools may support aspects of training in psychology and related human services fields when used to augment rather than replace human-centered learning processes. Morandini et al. (2023) show that as AI becomes more integrated across organizational contexts, transversal skills such as ethical judgment, communication, critical thinking, and empathy become increasingly important in professions involving sustained human interaction.

Within educational settings, AI may reduce cognitive or administrative burden for certain tasks, allowing learners and practitioners to focus more fully on relational, reflective, and judgment-based aspects of professional practice. At the same time, the literature is clear that AI systems cannot replicate tacit knowledge, contextual understanding, or genuine empathic engagement, capabilities that remain central to psychological and therapeutic work. As a result, AI use in psychology education must be deliberately designed to reinforce professional judgment, ethical reasoning, and relational competence, rather than displacing them (Morandini et al., 2023).

AI-Supported Simulations of Motivational Interviewing Training

A second illustrative example comes from research on AI-supported training tools for Motivational Interviewing (MI), where automated feedback systems are used to supplement, rather than replace, traditional supervision and skills development in counseling education. AI-supported simulation tools have increasingly been explored as a supplement to traditional MI training, particularly in counseling and psychology education. These tools are designed to provide learners with structured opportunities for practice, feedback, and reflection in low-stakes environments. One well-documented line of work involves the development of automated MI training and feedback systems that use natural language processing to analyze counselor responses and provide formative guidance aligned with MI principles (Tanana et al., 2016).

Research on automated MI training systems has focused primarily on the use of computational models trained on annotated counseling transcripts to identify MI-consistent behaviors, such as open-ended questions, reflections, and affirmations. These systems draw on established MI coding frameworks, including the Motivational Interviewing Treatment Integrity (MITI) system, to classify counselor utterances and generate feedback intended to support skill development (Tanana et al., 2016). Rather than simulating fully autonomous "clients," most existing tools emphasize structured practice and feedback on counselor language, helping learners recognize patterns in their responses and refine their use of MI techniques.

Empirical studies in this area suggest that AI-based feedback can support learning by increasing opportunities for deliberate practice and by offering timely, consistent feedback that may be difficult to provide at scale through human supervision alone. However, the literature also emphasizes that improvements observed in automated assessments do not necessarily translate directly into clinical competence or relational skill without guided reflection and human oversight. Researchers consistently caution that MI is a relational, context-sensitive practice that depends on empathy, attunement, and ethical judgment – capacities that cannot be fully captured or cultivated through automated systems alone (Tanana et al., 2016).

Across the literature, researchers consistently frame AI-supported MI tools as supplements rather than replacements for human instruction and supervision. While automated feedback systems can support learners in identifying technical features of MI-consistent language, scholars emphasize that relational competence, ethical judgment, and contextual sensitivity require modeling, supervision, and reflective feedback from experienced practitioners (Tanana et al., 2016). From this perspective, AI-supported MI simulations reflect a broader pattern in professional education: their educational value depends on integration within pedagogical designs that foreground relational learning, ethical reflection, and professional judgment.

Thus, research on AI-supported MI training demonstrates both the promise and the limits of simulation-based approaches in counseling education. These tools can expand opportunities for skills practice and support reflective learning, but they are most effective when embedded within human-centered training models that preserve the central role of supervision, mentorship, and the therapeutic relationship.

Teaching AI Literacy Through the Allegheny Family Screening Tool

The Allegheny Family Screening Tool (AFST) offers a valuable case for examining how AI systems may be incorporated into professional education (see Table 3). Implemented by the Allegheny County Department of Human Services beginning in 2016, AFST uses predictive modeling applied to administrative data from multiple public systems to support hotline screening decisions related to potential child maltreatment (Chouldechova et al., 2018).

Scholarly analyses of AFST highlight both its technical sophistication and its ethical complexity. Research by Chouldechova et al. (2018) shows that the tool exhibits differential error rates across racial groups, revealing fundamental trade-offs between predictive accuracy and commonly used fairness criteria that cannot be fully resolved through technical adjustments alone. These disparities reflect structural features of the underlying data and decision context rather than simple model bias that could be addressed through recalibration alone.

From an educational perspective, AFST can serve as a powerful case study for helping social work students critically engage with the real-world implications of AI-supported decision-making. Through this case, students are able to examine how predictive validity, error rates, and model performance intersect with professional values such as equity, accountability, and the protection of family welfare. Importantly, the AFST case also illustrates the limits of purely technical solutions: even with transparency efforts, bias audits, and stakeholder engagement, debates continue regarding whether predictive risk modeling is compatible with the ethical foundations of child welfare practice.

This ongoing controversy enhances the pedagogical value of AFST. Rather than presenting AI as either a solution or a threat, the case encourages students to grapple with competing perspectives on the role of algorithmic tools in human services, reinforcing the importance of AI literacy that integrates technical understanding with ethical reasoning, contextual judgment, and social justice awareness.

Cross-Example Synthesis and Implications

The illustrative applications discussed in this section reveal several recurring themes that are central to effective AI literacy education in human services. Across psychology education, counseling training, and social work practice contexts, AI integration is consistently portrayed not as a rapid or purely technical intervention, but as a deliberately paced educational process embedded within broader pedagogical and institutional frameworks. Rather than foregrounding tools themselves, the literature emphasizes the importance of advance preparation, including sustained faculty development, curriculum alignment, and the articulation of ethical principles to guide AI use. In each context, AI is introduced as part of a longer-term process of adaptation and learning, underscoring that meaningful integration requires time, reflection, and organizational readiness rather than immediate deployment.

A second unifying theme concerns the role of AI as a complement to human judgment and relational practice. Across the examples examined, AI-enabled tools are most effective when they support, rather than supplant, professional expertise and human-centered learning processes. In psychology education, AI is framed as a means of reducing cognitive or administrative burden, allowing greater attention to ethical reasoning, reflective practice, and interpersonal skill development. Similarly, research on AI-supported Motivational Interviewing training highlights the value of automated feedback for expanding opportunities for practice, while simultaneously underscoring the necessity of supervision, modeling, and reflective dialogue to support relational competence. The Allegheny Family Screening Tool further illustrates this principle from a practice-oriented perspective, demonstrating how algorithmic decision-support systems can inform professional judgment while raising ethical questions that cannot be resolved through technical optimization alone.

A final theme concerns the need for ongoing evaluation and ethical oversight. Across educational and practice contexts, AI integration emerges as a dynamic process that requires continuous monitoring, assessment, and revision. The literature consistently points to the importance of attending to unintended consequences, stakeholder experiences, and evolving ethical considerations over time. For human services professionals, this implies that AI literacy must extend beyond initial understanding or adoption to include the capacity for sustained critical assessment, quality improvement, and bias awareness. Preparing students to engage with AI as a socio-technical system that evolves and must be continually scrutinized emerges as a shared implication across the examples discussed.

Overall, these cross-cutting insights reinforce the central argument of the chapter: AI literacy in human services is fundamentally multidimensional and human-centered. Effective education in this area requires not only technical understanding, but also ethical reasoning, contextual judgment, and sustained professional oversight. By engaging with AI through carefully designed examples and reflective pedagogies, educators can better prepare future practitioners to navigate the opportunities and risks of AI-enabled systems in ways that align with the values, responsibilities, and relational foundations of human services practice.

INCLUSIVE AND EQUITABLE AI LITERACY

Cultural Responsiveness and Reducing Digital Divides

Addressing digital divides related to socioeconomic status, geography, and cultural background is widely recognized as a prerequisite for equitable access to AI literacy in education. Research on AI-powered learning environments shows that disparities in access to devices, internet connectivity, and prior technological exposure shape how students engage with and benefit from AI-supported educational tools, with inequities emerging through the interaction of material access, digital skills, and students' cultural and technological capital (Shoval, 2025). These conditions contribute to an emerging "AI literacy divide," in which students with greater prior exposure to digital technologies are better positioned to experiment with and transfer AI-related skills, while others may struggle to participate fully in AI-enhanced coursework due to differences in confidence, digital literacy, and familiarity with advanced educational technologies.

Accordingly, institutional responses to digital equity challenges cannot be limited to the provision of technology alone. The literature highlights the importance of complementary pedagogical and structural strategies, including device-lending programs, support for affordable or low-bandwidth internet access, hybrid instructional models, and intentional scaffolding of AI-related skills within curricula (Shoval, 2025). Such approaches recognize that equitable AI literacy requires not only access to tools, but also learning environments designed to accommodate diverse starting points and to support all students in developing meaningful, transferable AI competencies.

Beyond issues of access and participation, cultural responsiveness in AI literacy education also requires critical engagement with how AI systems are designed, trained, and deployed within specific social and cultural contexts. Research on bias and inequity in AI systems demonstrates that performance disparities often emerge when models are trained on data that inadequately represent diverse populations or encode existing social hierarchies, leading to uneven outcomes across groups (Ahluwalia et al., 2025). Consequently, students must learn to critically evaluate AI systems for contextual validity, cultural relevance, and potential sources of bias, and to apply AI in ways that are responsive to the communities and populations they serve.

Principles of Universal Design for Learning

The application of Universal Design for Learning (UDL) principles offers a robust and evidence-informed foundation for developing inclusive approaches to AI literacy education. UDL emphasizes proactive design for learner variability through three core principles (i.e., multiple means of engagement, representation, and action and expression), which align closely with the multidimensional nature of AI literacy, including conceptual understanding, ethical reasoning, and applied skills. Recent scholarship proposes that UDL provides a particularly appropriate framework for AI learning design because it foregrounds flexibility, accessibility, and equity from the outset rather than retrofitting accommodations after instruction is developed (Song et al., 2024).

Within AI literacy instruction, multiple means of representation involve presenting AI concepts using varied formats and modalities (e.g., visualizations, simulations, interactive demonstrations, audio explanations, and text) to support comprehension among learners with diverse backgrounds, abilities, and prior experiences. Because AI concepts are often abstract and opaque, multimodal representation plays an important role in supporting perception, comprehension, and conceptual connections. Research suggests that varied representations reduce barriers to access and improve learners' ability to understand how AI systems function, particularly for students who might otherwise struggle with technical or symbolic content (Song et al., 2024).

Similarly, multiple means of engagement encourage learners to interact with AI literacy content in ways that reflect their interests, cultural backgrounds, and motivational profiles. Examples include project-based activities, collaborative case studies, creative artifacts, and exploratory experimentation with AI tools. The inclusive AI learning design framework articulated by Song et al. (2024) highlights that providing meaningful choices and authentic contexts can help sustain learner interest and persistence, especially in domains where students may experience anxiety or uncertainty about technical material. Rather than framing engagement as a matter of preferred learning styles, this work emphasizes relevance, autonomy, and self-regulation as foundations for sustained participation across diverse learner populations.

Accessibility and Language Adaptations

AI literacy, like computer science literacy more broadly, requires more than minor differentiation layered onto a standardized curriculum. For many students with disabilities, equitable participation may require partial, substantial, or alternative pathways for engaging with AI literacy content, rather than assuming that a single curricular model can be universally adapted. Research on accessibility in technology-enhanced education identifies persistent structural and pedagogical barriers, including instructional materials not designed for accessibility from the outset, misalignment between digital platforms and assistive technologies, and instructional approaches that privilege narrow modes of engagement and representation (Gladhart, 2010). These findings underscore the importance of inclusive design frameworks, such as

Universal Design for Learning, that anticipate learner variability during curriculum development rather than relying on retrofitted accommodations after technologies are already in use.

Language diversity introduces additional considerations for AI literacy education. Technical AI content is often presented primarily in English and assumes familiarity with discipline-specific terminology, which can create barriers for students who are multilingual or learning in a second language. Research on natural language processing and AI systems demonstrates that language models tend to perform unevenly across languages and dialects, reflecting both data imbalances and embedded cultural assumptions (Blodgett et al., 2020; Bender et al., 2021). At the same time, multilingual learners may be particularly well positioned to recognize linguistic bias, cultural misrepresentation, and the limits of AI systems trained predominantly on Anglophone data.

From an educational perspective, language diversity should not be treated solely as a deficit to be remediated, but also as a resource for developing critical AI literacy. Integrating multilingual perspectives into AI literacy instruction can help students examine how language, culture, and power shape AI system design and performance, while supporting more inclusive learning environments. Approaches such as providing multilingual learning materials, allowing students to analyze AI behavior across languages, and explicitly discussing linguistic bias in AI systems can both reduce access barriers and deepen critical engagement with AI as a sociotechnical system (Blodgett et al., 2020).

CONCLUSION: ADVANCING HUMAN-CENTERED AI LITERACY IN HUMAN SERVICES EDUCATION

Artificial intelligence is no longer a speculative or peripheral concern for human services education. As AI-enabled systems increasingly shape the institutional, organizational, and policy contexts in which social workers, counselors, and psychologists are trained and practice, the question is no longer whether AI will influence human services, but how professionals will be prepared to engage with it responsibly. This chapter has argued that AI literacy is a critical component of that preparation, understood not as a narrow technical skill set but as a multidimensional, ethically grounded capacity aligned with the relational foundations and social justice commitments of human services professions.

Central to this argument is the recognition that prevailing approaches to AI literacy have often been insufficient for professions rooted in human judgment, contextual understanding, and ethical responsibility. Much of the existing AI literacy literature emphasizes functional knowledge and tool use, frequently underdeveloping the ethical, critical, and practice-based dimensions that are essential in fields where AI-mediated decisions can have profound consequences for individuals, families, and communities. In response to these limitations, this chapter introduced the Integrated AI Literacy Model for Human Services (IALM-HS) as a conceptual and pedagogical framework designed to address the distinctive needs of social work, counseling, and psychology education.

The IALM-HS advances a normative, rather than empirically prescriptive, model of AI literacy that foregrounds four interdependent domains: technical understanding, critical evaluation, ethical reasoning, and practical application. Taken together, these domains articulate what it means for human services professionals to engage meaningfully with AI systems, moving beyond simple operation toward interpreting outputs, questioning assumptions, assessing appropriateness, and integrating AI into practice in ways that preserve human dignity and professional accountability. Importantly, the model emphasizes that these domains cannot be developed in isolation. Technical understanding without ethical reasoning risks automation bias and uncritical reliance on system outputs; ethical awareness without practical application may remain abstract and disconnected from real-world constraints. Meaningful AI literacy emerges only when these dimensions are cultivated concurrently and situated within professional contexts.

Throughout the chapter, this integrative perspective has been applied across disciplinary, pedagogical, and institutional levels. In social work, AI literacy is inseparable from commitments to equity, transparency, and anti-oppressive practice, particularly as algorithmic systems increasingly influence child welfare, benefits administration, and risk assessment. In counseling and psychology, AI literacy intersects with foundational competencies related to assessment, intervention, and the therapeutic alliance, underscoring the limits of automation in relational and empathic work. Across disciplines, the analysis highlights a shared imperative: AI literacy must be discipline-specific, ethically anchored, and responsive to the lived realities of clients and communities.

The pedagogical strategies examined in this chapter further underscore that developing AI literacy is not a matter of adding discrete content or stand-alone courses to already crowded curricula. Instead, the literature points toward cross-curricular integration, experiential learning, and thoughtfully designed online and hybrid modalities as promising pathways for embedding AI literacy within existing educational structures. When AI concepts are introduced through authentic disciplinary contexts (e.g., case-based learning, supervised simulations, or applied policy analysis), students are better positioned to connect technical knowledge with ethical judgment and professional practice. These approaches also support the development of higher-order competencies, including critical thinking, reflective judgment, and ethical decision-making, which remain central to human services education regardless of technological change.

At the same time, the chapter has emphasized that pedagogical innovation alone is insufficient without sustained faculty development and institutional readiness. Faculty uncertainty around AI integration is best understood not as resistance, but as a reflection of ethical concern, misalignment with professional values, and the absence of established pedagogical frameworks. Supporting faculty capacity therefore requires ongoing professional learning, opportunities for experimentation and reflection, and institutional recognition of the time and labor involved in responsible AI integration. At the institutional level, readiness depends on coordinated strategies that align curriculum design, faculty development, governance, and ethical policy frameworks. Institutions that treat AI adoption as a purely technical upgrade risk fragmented implementation and ethical drift; those that approach it as an educational and organizational transformation are better positioned to support coherent, values-aligned AI literacy initiatives.

The practice-informed examples discussed in this chapter, ranging from AI-supported Motivational Interviewing training to the Allegheny Family Screening Tool, illustrate both the promise and the limits of AI integration in human services contexts. Across these cases, a consistent theme emerges: AI tools are most effective when they function as supports for human judgment rather than substitutes for it. Automated feedback systems, predictive models, and decision-support tools can expand access, scale supervision, and enhance consistency, but they cannot replace relational competence, contextual sensitivity, or ethical reasoning. These examples reinforce the chapter's central claim that AI literacy must equip practitioners to engage with AI as a socio-technical system that reflects human choices, institutional priorities, and societal power structures, and therefore demands ongoing scrutiny and ethical oversight.

Equity and inclusion remain critical considerations throughout this discussion. Digital divides related to access, prior experience, language, and disability shape who is able to participate meaningfully in AI-enhanced education and practice. Addressing these divides requires more than technology provision; it demands inclusive pedagogical design, culturally responsive instruction, and structural supports that recognize learner variability. The application of Universal Design for Learning principles offers one pathway for anticipating and addressing this variability, ensuring that AI literacy education does not inadvertently reproduce the very inequities it seeks to challenge. Moreover, engaging with issues of linguistic bias, cultural representation, and data injustice can transform diversity from a barrier into a resource for critical AI literacy, deepening students' understanding of how AI systems operate within and often reflect broader social hierarchies.

The arguments and evidence presented in this chapter underscore that AI literacy in human services is fundamentally a matter of professional ethics, judgment, and responsibility. Its value lies not in guaranteeing improved efficiency or performance metrics, but in strengthening the capacity of practitioners, educators, and institutions to engage critically and ethically with AI-enabled systems. For students, AI literacy supports adaptability, confidence, and informed decision-making in increasingly AI-mediated practice environments. For faculty, it provides a framework for integrating AI into teaching without compromising disciplinary integrity or relational values. For institutions, it offers a pathway toward responsible, transparent, and equitable AI adoption.

As AI technologies continue to evolve, so too must the educational frameworks that prepare human services professionals to engage with them. The Integrated AI Literacy Model for Human Services is offered as one contribution to this ongoing conversation, providing an organizing framework that invites adaptation, critique, and empirical exploration. Future research will be needed to examine how such models are operationalized in diverse educational contexts, how AI literacy can be meaningfully assessed, and how pedagogical approaches can be refined to support ethical and inclusive practice. What remains clear, however, is that the stakes of AI integration in human services are too high to be left to ad hoc experimentation or purely technical training.

Ultimately, advancing AI literacy in social work, counseling, and psychology is not about keeping pace with technological change for its own sake. It is about ensuring that as AI systems become more influential, the human services professions remain anchored in their core commitments to dignity, equity, relational care, and ethical accountability. By approaching AI literacy as a multidimensional, human-centered endeavor, educators and institutions can help prepare future practitioners not only to work with AI, but to shape its use in ways that support human well-being and social justice in an increasingly automated world.

REFERENCES

Adamakis, M., & Rachiotis, T. (2025). Artificial intelligence in higher education: A state-of-the-art overview of pedagogical integrity, artificial intelligence literacy, and policy integration. *Encyclopedia, 5*(4), 180. DOI: 10.3390/encyclopedia5040180

Ahluwalia, M., Sehgal, S., Lee, G., Agu, E., & Kpodonu, J. (2025). Disparities in artificial intelligence-based tools among diverse minority populations: Biases, barriers, and solutions. *JACC Advances, 4*(5), 101742. DOI: 10.1016/j.jacadv.2025.101742

Ahn, E., Choi, M., Fowler, P., & Song, I. (2025). Artificial intelligence (AI) literacy for social work: Implications for core competencies. *Journal of the Society for Social Work and Research, 16*(1). Advance online publication. DOI: 10.1086/735187

Al-Rantisi, A. M., ElShanti, N. H., & Harb, S. A. (2025). Challenges of using artificial intelligence in social work education. *Social Work Education*, •••, 1–18. DOI: 10.1080/02615479.2025.2483354

Allen, L. K., & Kendeou, P. (2023). ED-AI Lit: An Interdisciplinary Framework for AI Literacy in Education. *Policy Insights from the Behavioral and Brain Sciences, 11*(1), 3–10. DOI: 10.1177/23727322231220339

American Psychological Association. (2025). *Ethical guidance for AI in the professional practice of health service psychology.* https://www.apa.org/topics/artificial-intelligence-machine-learning/ethical-guidance-professional-practice.pdf

Bender, E. M., Gebru, T., McMillan-Major, A., & Shmitchell, S. (2021). On the dangers of stochastic parrots: Can language models be too big? *Proceedings of the 2021 ACM Conference on Fairness, Accountability, and Transparency*, 610–623. https://doi.org/DOI: 10.1145/3442188.3445922

Bewersdorff, A., Nerdel, C., & Zhai, X. (2025). How AI literacy correlates with affective, behavioral, cognitive and contextual variables: A systematic review. *Computers and Education: Artificial Intelligence, 9*. Advance online publication. DOI: 10.1016/j.caeai.2025.100493

Blodgett, S. L., Barocas, S., Daumé, H.III, & Wallach, H. (2020). Language (technology) is power: A critical survey of "bias" in NLP. *ArXiv:2005.14050 [Cs]*. https://arxiv.org/abs/2005.14050

Chouldechova, A., Putnam-Hornstein, E., Benavides-Prado, D., Fialko, O., & Vaithianathan, R. (2018). A case study of algorithm-assisted decision-making in child maltreatment hotline screening. *Proceedings of Machine Learning Research, 81*, 134–148.

Chu, T. S., & Ashraf, M. (2025). Artificial intelligence in curriculum design: A data-driven approach to higher education innovation. *Knowledge (Beverly Hills, Calif.)*, *5*(3), 14. DOI: 10.3390/knowledge5030014

European Commission. (2019). *Ethics guidelines for trustworthy AI*. https://digital-strategy.ec.europa.eu/en/library/ethics-guidelines-trustworthy-ai

European Union. (2024). *Artificial Intelligence Act* (Regulation (EU) 2024/1689). Official Journal of the European Union. https://eur-lex.europa.eu/eli/reg/2024/1689/oj/eng

Gladhart, M. A. (2010). Determining faculty needs for delivering accessible electronically delivered instruction in higher education. *Journal of Postsecondary Education and Disability*, *22*(3), 185–196. https://eric.ed.gov/?id=EJ906692

Hanley, T. (2025). Artificial intelligence and the changing landscape of therapy. *Counselling & Psychotherapy Research*, *25*(4). Advance online publication. DOI: 10.1002/capr.70056

Harizan, S. H. M., & Ally, M. (2025). Artificial intelligence in micro-credentials for open and distance learning: A technologically enhanced systematic review. *Turkish Online Journal of Distance Education*, *26*(3). https://files.eric.ed.gov/fulltext/EJ1479078.pdf

James, P., Lal, J., Liao, A., Magee, L., & Soldatic, K. (2024). Algorithmic decision-making in social work practice and pedagogy: Confronting the competency/critique dilemma. *Social Work Education*, *43*(6), 1552–1569. DOI: 10.1080/02615479.2023.2195425

Kamalov, F., Calonge, D. S., & Gurrib, I. (2023). New era of artificial intelligence in education: Towards a sustainable multifaceted revolution. *Sustainability*, *15*(16), 12451. DOI: 10.3390/su151612451

Kong, S. C., & Zhu, J. (2025). Developing and validating an artificial intelligence ethical awareness scale for secondary and university students: Cultivating ethical awareness through problem-solving with artificial intelligence tools. *Computers and Education: Artificial Intelligence*, *9*, 100447. DOI: 10.1016/j.caeai.2025.100447

Liu, X., Zhang, L., & Wei, X. (2025). Generative artificial intelligence literacy: Scale development and its effect on job performance. *Behavioral Sciences (Basel, Switzerland)*, *15*(6), 811. DOI: 10.3390/bs15060811

Morandini, S., Fraboni, F., De Angelis, M., Puzzo, G., Giusino, D., & Pietrantoni, L. (2023). The impact of artificial intelligence on workers' skills: Upskilling and reskilling in organisations. Informing Science: The International Journal of an Emerging Transdiscipline, 26, 039–068. https://doi.org/DOI: 10.28945/5078

National Association of Social Workers. (2021). *NASW code of ethics*. https://www.socialworkers.org/About/Ethics/Code-of-Ethics

Navasca, R. (2025). Bridging digital and vocational learning: The role of AI in enhancing culturally responsive TLE instruction and pedagogical approaches. *International Journal on Culture. History of Religions*, *7*(SI3), 479–494. DOI: 10.63931/ijchr.v7isi3.398

Okada, A., Sherborne, T., Panselinas, G., & Kolionis, G. (2025). Fostering transversal skills through open schooling supported by the CARE-KNOW-DO pedagogical model and the UNESCO AI competencies framework. *International Journal of Artificial Intelligence in Education*, *35*(4), 1953–1998. DOI: 10.1007/s40593-025-00458-w

Oncioiu, I., & Bularca, A. R. (2025). Artificial intelligence governance in higher education: The role of knowledge-based strategies in fostering legal awareness and ethical artificial intelligence literacy. *Societies (Basel, Switzerland)*, *15*(6), 144. DOI: 10.3390/soc15060144

Rahman, A., Ishak, W. I., Aziz, A., Arif, Z., Salleh, S. M., & Safii, M. (2025). Responsible AI literacy's role in ethical, transparent, and sustainable AI adoption in SMEs: Mediating effects of technology, organization and environment. *Proceedings of the 3rd International Conference on Business, Finance, Management and Economic (BizFAME 2024)*, 196–220. https://doi.org/DOI: 10.2991/978-94-6463-827-1_14

Ruschemeier, H., & Hondrich, L. (2024). Automation bias in public administration - An interdisciplinary perspective from law and psychology. SSRN *Electronic Journal*. https://doi.org/DOI: 10.2139/ssrn.4736646

Saxena, D., & Guha, S. (2024). Algorithmic harms in child welfare: Uncertainties in practice, organization, and street-level decision-making. *ACM Journal on Responsible Computing*, *1*(1), 1–32. DOI: 10.1145/3616473

Schindler, L. A., Burkholder, G. J., Morad, O. A., & Marsh, C. (2017). Computer-based technology and student engagement: A critical review of the literature. *International Journal of Educational Technology in Higher Education*, *14*(1). Advance online publication. DOI: 10.1186/s41239-017-0063-0

Shoval, D. H. (2025). Artificial intelligence in higher education: Bridging or widening the gap for diverse student populations? *Education Sciences*, *15*(5), 637. DOI: 10.3390/educsci15050637

Smith, S. M., Tate, M., Freeman, K., Walsh, A., Ballsun-Stanton, B., & Lane, M. (2025). A university framework for the responsible use of generative AI in research. *Journal of Higher Education Policy and Management*, •••, 1–20. DOI: 10.1080/1360080X.2025.2509187

Song, Y., Weisberg, L. R., Zhang, S., & Tian, X., Kristy Elizabeth Boyer, & Israel, M. (2024). A framework for inclusive AI learning design for diverse learners. *Computers & Education: Artificial Intelligence*, *6*(6), 100212–100212. DOI: 10.1016/j.caeai.2024.100212

Southworth, J., Migliaccio, K., Glover, J., Glover, J., Reed, D., McCarty, C., Brendemuhl, J., & Thomas, A. (2023). Developing a model for AI Across the curriculum: Transforming the higher education landscape via innovation in AI literacy. *Computers and Education: Artificial Intelligence*, *4*(1), 100127. DOI: 10.1016/j.caeai.2023.100127

Tadimalla, S. Y., Cary, J., Hull, G., Register, J., Maxwell, D., Pugalee, D., & Heafner, T. (2025). Comprehensive AI literacy: The case for centering human agency. *ArXiv.org*. https://arxiv.org/abs/2512.16656

Tanana, M., Hallgren, K. A., Imel, Z. E., Atkins, D. C., & Srikumar, V. (2016). A comparison of natural language processing methods for automated coding of motivational interviewing. *Journal of Substance Abuse Treatment*, *65*, 43–50. DOI: 10.1016/j.jsat.2016.01.006

Trianggono, M. M., Prahani, B. K., Zahro, I., Ashadi, F., & Siswono, H. (2025). AI-integrated project-based learning as a pathway to quality education: Enhancing critical and creative thinking in pre-service teachers. *Multidisciplinary Reviews*, *9*(7), 2026308. DOI: 10.31893/multirev.2026308

Tsamados, A., Aggarwal, N., Cowls, J., Morley, J., Roberts, H., Taddeo, M., & Floridi, L. (2021). The ethics of algorithms: Key problems and solutions. *AI & Society*, *37*(1), 215–230. DOI: 10.1007/s00146-021-01154-8

Tsao, J. (2025). Trajectories of AI policy in higher education: Interpretations, discourses, and enactments of students and teachers. *Computers and Education: Artificial Intelligence*, *9*, 100496. DOI: 10.1016/j.caeai.2025.100496

Walter, Y. (2024). Embracing the future of artificial intelligence in the classroom: The relevance of AI literacy, prompt engineering, and critical thinking in modern education. *International Journal of Educational Technology in Higher Education, 21*(1). Advance online publication. DOI: 10.1186/s41239-024-00448-3

Xu, Z., Procko, K., Munje, M., Patterson, K., Sabatini, L., Biswas, J., & Stone, P. (2025). The essentials of AI for life and society: A full-scale AI literacy course accessible to all. *ArXiv.org*. https://www.arxiv.org/abs/2512.04110

Zawacki-Richter, O., Marín, V. I., Bond, M., & Gouverneur, F. (2019). Systematic review of research on artificial intelligence applications in higher education – Where are the educators? *International Journal of Educational Technology in Higher Education, 16*(1). Advance online publication. DOI: 10.1186/s41239-019-0171-0

KEY TERMS AND DEFINITIONS

AI Literacy (Artificial Intelligence Literacy): The ability to understand, critically assess, ethically reason about, and appropriately use AI systems within specific professional contexts, particularly where human judgment and responsibility are central.

Algorithmic Bias: Systematic disadvantages produced by AI systems due to biased data, design choices, or institutional contexts.

Automation Bias: The tendency to defer to algorithmic recommendations without sufficient critical judgment, even when automated outputs conflict with contextual knowledge or professional ethics.

Competency–Critique Dilemma: The educational tension between teaching students to competently use AI systems and preparing them to critically question their limitations, risks, and social consequences.

Critical Evaluation (of AI Systems): The capacity to question AI outputs, assumptions, data sources, and embedded power dynamics in order to determine their appropriateness for a given practice context.

Ethical Reasoning (in AI Use): The application of professional values, moral judgment, and accountability when deciding whether and how AI systems should be used in practice.

Human-Centered Practice: An approach that prioritizes relational engagement, contextual understanding, empathy, and ethical judgment, ensuring AI tools support rather than replace human decision-making.

Integrated AI Literacy Model for Human Services (IALM-HS): A conceptual framework defining AI literacy in human services across four interconnected domains: technical understanding, critical evaluation, ethical reasoning, and practical application.

Responsible AI Integration: The intentional, values-aligned adoption of AI systems guided by transparency, accountability, human oversight, and equity.

Universal Design for Learning (UDL): An inclusive instructional framework that anticipates learner variability by providing multiple ways to engage with, understand, and demonstrate learning.

Chapter 5
Faculty Reflections on Integrating AI:
Successes, Challenges, and Surprises in Social Work and Psychology Education

Sheeba Joseph
https://orcid.org/0000-0003-1302-9825
The Bhopal School of Social Sciences, India

Tanuja Khan
The Bhopal School of Social Sciences, India

ABSTRACT

This study explores faculty reflections on integrating AI in social work and psychology education, focusing on perceived successes, challenges, and surprises, as well as the influence of teaching experience, AI familiarity, and face-to-face teaching. Using a phenomenological qualitative design, data were generated from semi-structured, face-to-face interviews with 16 faculty members. Thematic analysis revealed that AI integration enhanced student engagement, promoted innovative teaching practices, and improved efficiency in instructional tasks. Faculty reported positive surprises, such as increased student creativity and collaboration, alongside challenges, including technical difficulties, ethical concerns, and the learning curve associated with AI tools. Discipline-specific variations were also observed, with social work faculty emphasizing empathy-based simulations and psychology faculty highlighting data-driven insights. The study concludes that AI integration is a dynamic, context-sensitive process that offers pedagogical benefits.

DOI: 10.4018/979-8-3373-4362-4.ch005

INTRODUCTION

Over recent years, artificial intelligence (AI) has emerged as a potent force reshaping educational practice across multiple domains, calling educators to rethink pedagogy, assessment, and the very nature of learning. As tools such as large language models (LLMs), automated feedback systems, chatbots, predictive analytics, and AI-driven simulations become increasingly sophisticated and accessible, instructors must decide not only if they will integrate AI, but how they will do so in a manner consonant with disciplinary values and student needs. In disciplines grounded in human relations, ethics, and psychological understanding such as social work and psychology, this challenge is particularly acute. The tensions between the promise of AI (efficiency, personalization, scalability) and the risks of dehumanization, bias, loss of professional judgment, or ethical compromise require careful navigation by faculty who serve as both innovators and guardians of disciplinary integrity.

In social work education, AI opens up intriguing possibilities. Predictive models may assist in risk assessment, chatbots or virtual clients may simulate client interactions, and automated systems might help manage workflow or provide draft feedback. These affordances can reduce administrative burden, free instructor time, and scaffold student learning (Hodgson et al., 2021). Yet the integration also raises serious concerns: algorithmic bias, threats to confidentiality, erosion of empathy or relational depth, overreliance on "black box" tools, and undermining of professional judgment (Reamer, 2023). Meanwhile, in psychology education, AI offers potential for adaptive learning, automated assessment, simulation of counseling dialogues, and support for research, but also raises issues of validity, interpretability, overdependence, and the risk of diminished critical thinking (Lampou, 2023; Sidiropoulos & Anagnostopoulos, 2024). Although several studies address AI's general impact in education, fewer probe how faculty in social work and psychology actually experience, reflect upon, and respond to AI in their everyday teaching.

The extant literature on AI in education has grown substantially, but much of it emphasizes technology design, student outcomes, or macro-level frameworks, rather than instructors' lived experiences. For instance, Buelvas Parra et al. (2024) provide a comprehensive review of the benefits, challenges, and ethical implications of AI in education, highlighting that while AI can personalize learning and optimize management, it also brings risks of bias, data privacy, and inequity. Lampou (2023) underscores how AI promises to automate tasks and enhance personalized feedback, but cautions about infrastructure constraints and alignment with pedagogical aims. In higher education contexts, a recent systematic review by Ren and Wu (2025) identifies four key themes that characterize effective AI integration strategies: faculty preparedness and AI literacy, the use of AI to support pedagogical innovation, AI as a collaborative learning partner that enhances student engagement, and the intentional design and delivery of learning experiences informed by AI. Alongside proposed competencies and strategies, Ren and Wu (2025) highlight the difficulties of adopting AI-assisted teaching practices. Faculty accounts and empirical studies point to recurring concerns related to novelty-driven engagement, unequal access to technology, technical reliability, and ethical implications. These works are valuable, but they offer less attention to the discipline-specific and relational domains of social work or psychology, and still less to the unexpected outcomes or surprises that faculty encounter during AI implementation.

This study seeks to address that gap by exploring faculty reflections on integrating AI in social work and psychology education, particularly with respect to successes, challenges, and surprises. We treat faculty not merely as implementers of AI, but as sense-makers whose values, experiences, and judgments shape how AI is enacted. By delving into what they consider "success," how they navigate obstacles, and what unexpected or even counterintuitive outcomes emerge, we hope to surface deeper insights into how AI becomes embedded (or resisted) in relational, ethically grounded fields.

Rather than treating AI adoption as a linear or predictive process, this chapter approaches integration as a lived, interpretive experience shaped by professional identity, disciplinary values, and teaching context. A phenomenological lens allows for deeper understanding of how faculty experience success, challenge, and surprise not as outcomes to be measured, but as meanings constructed through practice.

FACULTY-REPORTED EXPERIENCES WITH AI INTEGRATION

Perceived Successes

Prior research on AI in higher education suggests that faculty often describe several areas of perceived success. One of the most cited is efficiency gains, as AI-supported automation of administrative work, grading, and feedback reduces time burdens on faculty, enabling them to focus more on higher-order tasks, such as mentoring, deeper content development, or reflective pedagogy (Dwivedi et al., 2021; Shata & Hartley, 2025). For example, AI-generated feedback on written work helps speed up turnaround times, allowing students to receive more timely responses that support engagement and self-regulated learning (Venter et al., 2024). Another success is personalization, as adaptive tools, predictive analytics, and individual feedback help tailor learning to students' needs, supporting both struggling and advanced learners (Buelvas Parra et al., 2024; Holmes et al., 2019). This is especially valued in psychology education, where attention to individual differences is central to both pedagogy and disciplinary identity (Sidiropoulos & Anagnostopoulos, 2024).

A further advantage frequently reported by faculty is increased student engagement. AI-enabled simulations, virtual clients or chatbots, and adaptive quizzes can make learning more interactive and give students more immediate, hands-on experience. In open and distributed learning contexts, such tools have been shown to help sustain student interest and connect theoretical content to applied learning situations (Yaseen et al., 2025). Faculty also describe AI as fostering pedagogical innovation, noting that experimentation with AI opens up new possibilities for lesson planning, structured critique using AI-generated feedback, and the intentional integration of reflective learning activities. For example, Tsakeni et al. (2025) demonstrate that AI-supported writing tools can scaffold reflective writing and promote metacognitive skill development, particularly when embedded within thoughtfully designed instructional activities.

Successes associated with AI integration are frequently tied to how intentionally these tools are implemented. Prior research suggests that positive outcomes are more likely when faculty design assignments that meaningfully incorporate AI rather than treating it as an add-on, when students receive orientation and guidance in AI use, when expectations and roles are clearly articulated, and when institutional support in the form of policy, infrastructure, and professional development is present (Holmes et al., 2019; Shata & Hartley, 2025). Faculty also report that AI can extend instructional reach—particularly in large classes—by supporting timely, high-quality feedback without diminishing pedagogical engagement (Venter et al., 2024). In social work education specifically, ethically guided applications of AI for data analytics and risk assessment have been described as supporting policy decisions and resource allocation when implemented in partnership with domain experts and grounded in professional values (Ahn et al., 2025). Collectively, these conditions suggest that AI-related successes are most sustainable when supported at both individual and institutional levels rather than relying on isolated faculty initiatives.

Perceived Challenges

Alongside reported successes, faculty reflections strongly emphasize a range of challenges that complicate AI integration in social work, psychology, teacher education, and related disciplines. A primary concern across the literature involves ethical issues, particularly data privacy and confidentiality. Since fields such as social work routinely engage with sensitive personal information, faculty express concern that AI tools may improperly store, process or disclose data, posing risks to clients, students, and communities (Ahn et al., 2025; Reamer, 2023). Closely related are concerns about algorithmic bias and fairness, as many faculty note that AI systems often rely on datasets that unrepresent minoritized or vulnerable populations, potentially producing biased outputs or reinforcing existing inequities (Dwivedi et al., 2021).

Faculty also raise concerns about the potential erosion of relational and empathetic dimensions of teaching and practice. While AI tools may enhance efficiency, they are often viewed as limited in their capacity to account for emotional nuance, cultural context, and professional judgment – capacities that are central to effective practice in psychology and social work. There is apprehension that overreliance on AI may reduce opportunities for students to develop these essential human competencies (Holmes et al., 2019).

Technical and infrastructural challenges are repeatedly noted, including unreliable tools, lack of transparency in AI decision-making processes, errors or hallucinated outputs, limited capacity to handle complex, contextually rich problems, and poor integration with existing learning management systems (Chinoracky & Stalmasekova, 2025). Faculty also describe a growing burden of oversight, as AI-generated outputs often require careful verification, correction, and contextualization – efforts that can offset anticipated time savings if not thoughtfully managed (Kasneci et al., 2023).

Finally, faculty highlight pedagogical challenges related to assignment design, assignment integrity, and student learning. These include concerns about students bypassing meaningful engagement through AI use, maintaining fairness in assessment, fostering critical evaluation of AI outputs, and ensuring that AI integration does not distort curricular priorities or reduce the emphasis on relational and ethical competencies central to professional preparation (Holmes et al., 2019; Dwivedi et al., 2021).

Perceived Surprises

Prior research suggests that a particularly rich and underexamined dimension of AI integration involves unexpected outcomes or "surprises" that emerge during implementation rather than at the planning stage. Studies across higher education report that these surprises span positive, negative, and mixed experiences, often prompting faculty reflection and pedagogical adjustment (Kasneci et al., 2023).

On the positive side, several studies note faculty surprise at the capabilities students demonstrate when engaging with AI tools. Reported outcomes include higher levels of self-regulation, improvements in reflective writing when scaffolded by AI-generated feedback, and creative uses of AI beyond original instructional intentions, such as idea prototyping and iterative refinement with human guidance (Shi et al., 2025). Researchers also describe faculty surprise at how quickly some students adapt to AI tools, even with minimal orientation (Kasneci et al., 2023; Shata & Hartley, 2025). In hybrid and online learning contexts, AI may also help "level the playing field" by supporting students with limited access to office hours, variable learning speeds, or nontraditional schedules, thereby sustaining interaction and continuity when face-to-face engagement is constrained (Rane et al., 2024).

At the same time, the literature highlights negative and mixed surprises associated with AI use. A recurring concern involves the accuracy and quality of AI outputs, including hallucinations, factual errors, and contextually inappropriate suggestions – issues that are particularly pronounced in humanistic and practice-oriented disciplines where nuance, interpretation, and cultural sensitivity are central (Dwivedi et al., 2021; Floridi et al., 2023). Faculty also report being surprised by the additional effort required to verify, edit, and contextualize AI-generated content, noting that these demands can complicate or offset anticipated efficiency gains, particularly during early stages of adoption (Shata & Hartley, 2025).

Further unanticipated challenges documented in the literature include student overreliance on AI for tasks intended to foster originality or critical thinking, necessitating assignment redesign and additional instructional scaffolding (Holmes et al., 2019; Floridi et al., 2023). Researchers also point to emergent ethical dilemmas, such as subtle forms of academic dishonesty, unclear consent around AI use, questions of responsibility for AI-generated errors, and biases that only become visible when tools are applied in specific populations (Reamer, 2023). Finally, several studies note that institutional policies and governance structures often lag behind practice, creating unexpected constraints related to licensing, data governance, or acceptable use (Dwivedi et al., 2021). The literature suggests that surprises cut across levels of familiarity, experience, and instructional context, often reshaping how faculty subsequently interpret both success and challenge. As such, surprises are increasingly framed as part of an adaptive process rather than isolated anomalies (Dwivedi et al., 2021).

CONTEXTUAL FACTORS SHAPING FACULTY EXPERIENCES

Beyond discrete successes and challenges, the literature emphasizes that faculty experiences with AI are shaped by contextual factors related to professional background, technological familiarity, and instructional setting.

Teaching Experience

Prior research suggests that teaching experience – including years of practice, disciplinary background, and prior exposure to educational technology – shapes faculty perspectives on AI integration in important ways. Across multiple studies, faculty with more years of teaching experience often report a combination of greater caution and heightened expectations. They tend to be more attuned to potential risks, more sensitive to shifts in pedagogical norms, and more concerned with preserving core professional values such as empathy, ethics, relational depth, and face-to-face engagement, particularly in disciplines like social work and psychology (Holmes et al., 2019). At the same time, experienced faculty often draw on a rich pedagogical repertoire that can support thoughtful and intentional incorporation of AI, even as established teaching practices may also contribute to resistance or inertia in adopting new tools (Dwivedi et al., 2021).

In contrast, studies frequently describe faculty with fewer years of teaching experience as demonstrating greater flexibility and openness to experimentation with AI technologies. Early-career or junior faculty are often characterized as early adopters, less tethered to traditional lecture-based formats, and more willing to engage in exploratory or "messy" pedagogical innovation (Spathopoulou et al., 2025).

The literature also highlights the role of disciplinary seniority and research background. Faculty with prior experience in AI, data analytics, or educational technology tend to perceive AI integration more positively, reporting greater confidence in evaluating outputs, troubleshooting technical issues, and recognizing pedagogical possibilities (Shata & Hartley, 2025). At the same time, these faculty often articulate more nuanced concerns about unintended consequences, informed by familiarity with prior technological overpromises or ethical challenges documented in both academic and public discourse (Dwivedi et al., 2021).

Importantly, research emphasizes that teaching experience does not operate in isolation but interacts with institutional conditions such as training, policy clarity, and professional culture. Studies suggest that more experienced faculty may require clearer evidence of effectiveness, structured support, and explicit ethical guidance, whereas less experienced faculty may adopt AI more rapidly but benefit from additional scaffolding and mentorship to anticipate challenges (Spathopoulou et al., 2025). Across career stages, faculty development initiatives, mentoring relationships, communities of practice, and peer learning are consistently identified as critical mechanisms for leveraging teaching experience to support effective and ethical AI integration (Holmes et al., 2019).

AI Familiarity

Prior research consistently identifies AI familiarity – defined as faculty comfort, knowledge, and prior experience with AI tools – as a central contextual factor shaping perceptions of AI integration in higher education. Faculty with higher levels of AI familiarity tend to report more positive reflections on AI use, describing greater awareness of potential opportunities as well as a more realistic understanding of limitations and risks (Shata & Hartley, 2025). Familiar faculty are often better positioned to adapt AI tools creatively to pedagogical goals, drawing on prior experimentation in research, educational technology, or technology-mediated teaching contexts.

The literature further suggests that higher familiarity is associated with fewer negative or disruptive surprises during implementation. Faculty with prior exposure to AI report greater capacity to anticipate technical limitations, ethical concerns, or biases and to establish guardrails in advance, such as vetting outputs, training students in responsible use, or critically evaluating AI-generated content (Dwivedi et al., 2021, Ahn et al., 2025). As a result, surprises that do emerge are more likely to be perceived as manageable or instructive rather than destabilizing.

In contrast, lower familiarity is also associated with heightened anxiety during early adoption, including concerns about academic integrity, loss of instructional control, steep learning curves, and uncertainty about how AI tools function or should be governed (Kasneci et al., 2023). As a result, faculty with limited familiarity frequently report higher perceived challenges and more frequent or intense surprises during initial implementation.

Research also indicates that AI familiarity shapes patterns of adoption. Faculty with greater familiarity are more likely to experiment with a wider range of tools, integrate AI more deeply into hybrid or online pedagogies, and move beyond surface-level uses toward more intentional instructional applications (Shata & Hartley, 2025). They are also more likely to advocate for institutional support, professional development, or policy clarification related to AI use. By contrast, faculty with lower familiarity often restrict AI integration to perceived “safe” applications – such as quizzes, automated feedback, or administrative tasks – or defer adoption until they feel more confident or supported.

Importantly, the literature emphasizes that AI familiarity is not static but can be developed over time. Literature consistently highlights the role of faculty development initiatives, peer learning, communities of practice, pilot projects, and reflective experimentation in building familiarity and confidence with AI tools (Holmes et al., 2019). As familiarity increases, faculty report reduced anxiety, greater perceived benefits, and a moderation of many early challenges and negative surprises, underscoring familiarity as a key condition for sustainable and ethical AI integration.

Mode of Teaching

Prior research consistently highlights mode of teaching – including in-person, online, and hybrid formats – as an important contextual factor shaping faculty experiences with AI integration. Across studies, faculty teaching in online and hybrid environments tend to report greater perceived utility of AI tools, particularly for addressing challenges related to distance, time constraints, and learner diversity

(Kasneci et al., 2023; Shata & Hartley, 2025). AI-assisted feedback, chatbots, virtual clients or simulations, automated assessments, and asynchronous learning tools are frequently described as supporting students who cannot attend synchronous sessions, enabling more frequent and timely feedback, and helping sustain interaction when face-to-face contact is limited (Holmes et al., 2019; Kasneci et al., 2023; Venter et al., 2024).

Research suggests that faculty teaching primarily in face-to-face settings often express greater skepticism or caution toward AI integration. Because relational dynamics and immediate human interaction are more salient in in-person classrooms, tools perceived as diminishing spontaneity, emotional responsiveness, or empathic connection are sometimes viewed with concern, particularly in human-centered disciplines such as psychology and social work (Holmes et al., 2019; Ahn et al., 2025). Faculty also raise questions about the authenticity of student participation, academic integrity, and whether AI use may inadvertently reduce meaningful dialogue or embodied engagement in classroom discussions (Kasneci et al., 2023; Shata & Hartley, 2025).

Hybrid modes appear in the literature as occupying an intermediate position, combining affordances and challenges associated with both online and in-person teaching. Faculty teaching in hybrid formats often describe AI as valuable for bridging instructional gaps – for example, by providing asynchronous feedback or supplementary resources while reserving in-person time for relational, experiential, or discussion-based learning (Almusaed et al., 2023). At the same time, studies note that hybrid contexts introduce additional complexity, including increased coordination demands, technical challenges in ensuring seamless integration across modalities, and difficulties maintaining consistent student experiences across online and in-person components (Shata & Hartley, 2025).

SENSITIZING CONCEPTS FOR PHENOMENOLOGICAL INQUIRY

Taken together, the literature on AI in higher education suggests the need for an interpretive framework capable of capturing lived experience, ethical judgment, and contextual nuance. Rather than conceptualizing AI adoption in terms of predictors, outcomes, or linear effects, qualitative scholarship increasingly approaches faculty engagement with AI through sensitizing concepts – thematic lenses that orient inquiry toward how meaning is constructed in practice. These concepts foreground ethics, relationality, trust, and institutional context, aligning closely with phenomenological approaches that privilege experience over causality.

Ethical Responsibility, Professional Values, and Human Judgment

A dominant sensitizing theme in the literature concerns ethical responsibility and the complex moral landscape surrounding AI use in educational contexts. Faculty accounts frequently reflect a tension between optimism about AI's potential to support instructional tasks and concern about risks to academic integrity, fairness, and human agency. Across qualitative studies, educators express apprehension about algorithmic bias, depersonalization of learning, and erosion of critical thinking when AI is introduced without careful oversight (Gealone, 2024; Buele & Llerena-Aguirre, 2025) These ethically inflected concerns underscore the importance of professional development and highlight why AI integration is often experienced not merely as a technical decision but as a values-laden pedagogical choice.

Pedagogical Roles, Relationships, and Professional Identity

Closely related is scholarship examining how AI reshapes pedagogical roles and relationships. Rather than focusing solely on efficiency gains, studies emphasize how faculty interpret AI in relation to their professional identities and teaching philosophies. While some educators frame AI as a supportive "co-intelligence" that enhances instructional workflows, others experience its expansion as a challenge to pedagogical authority, mentorship, and relational depth (Gealone, 2024; Verboom et al., 2025). These divergent interpretations highlight that faculty experience AI integration as a reconfiguration of what it means to teach, care, and engage with students, particularly in disciplines grounded in human-centered practice..

Institutional Context, Trust, and Readiness

The literature also consistently emphasizes the role of institutional context in shaping faculty sense-making. Positive experiences with AI integration are often associated with access to structured professional development, clear policies, and opportunities for collegial dialogue about AI use. In contract, institutional ambiguity or lack of guidance tends to intensify uncertainty, resistance, and ethical concern (Gealone, 2024; Whitbread et al., 2025). Trust and readiness emerge as closely related sensitizing concepts: faculty trust in AI is shaped not only by tool performance but by leadership support, transparency, and alignment with institutional values. Trust functions less as a measurable attribute and more as an interpretive frame through which faculty evaluate risk, responsibility, and professional fit (Lelescu et al., 2025).

Equity, Access, and Integrity in Practice

Finally, scholarship highlights equity and access as cross-cutting concerns in faculty interpretations of AI. Faculty narratives frequently reference uneven access to training, differential digital readiness, and the risk that AI adoption may exacerbate existing inequities in teaching effectiveness or student support. Alongside these concerns are pedagogical tensions related to academic integrity and critical thinking. Educators describe ambivalence about whether AI supports deeper inquiry or inadvertently encourages surface-level engagement, underscoring the paradox that AI can simultaneously enable pedagogical innovation and complicate assessment practices (Gealone, 2024; Whitbread et al., 2025).

Overall, the literature indicates that faculty experiences with AI are shaped by multiple, intersecting interpretive domains: ethical responsibility, pedagogical identity, institutional context, trust and readiness, and equity considerations. These domains function as sensitizing concepts that orient qualitative inquiry toward understanding *how* faculty interpret, negotiate, and make meaning of AI integration in their teaching. Rather than serving as explanatory variables, they provide conceptual lenses that foreground complexity, ambiguity, and lived experience, laying the groundwork for phenomenological investigation.

THEORETICAL BASIS

To support analysis of these sensitizing concepts, the present study draws on multiple theoretical perspectives that illuminate different dimensions of faculty sense-making without reducing experience to prediction or causality. The framework draws conceptually from:

- Technology Acceptance Model (TAM) – Perceived usefulness and ease of use predict acceptance of technology (Venkatesh et al., 2016).
- Diffusion of Innovation Theory (Rogers, 2003) – Faculty adopt innovations based on awareness, persuasion, decision, and confirmation stages influenced by familiarity and experience.
- Transformative Learning Theory (Mezirow, 1997) – Faculty reflections, including surprises, serve as triggers for critical reflection and adaptation.

This multi-theoretical integration helps explain not only whether AI integration succeeds but how educators' cognitive and affective responses interact through experience, context, and reflection.

PHENOMENOLOGICAL RESEARCH DESIGN

Research Purpose

The present study adopts an interpretive phenomenological qualitative research design to explore how faculty in social work and psychology make meaning of integrating artificial intelligence (AI) into their teaching practices. Phenomenology is particularly suited for this research because it emphasizes understanding the lived experiences of individuals and the meaning they assign to these experiences. Faculty perceptions of successes, challenges, and surprises during AI integration are inherently subjective and context-dependent, making a phenomenological approach ideal for capturing these nuanced experiences. The study aims to investigate how faculty experience, interpret, and make sense of AI integration in their teaching practices, providing rich, in-depth insights that extend beyond surface-level observations.

Research Questions

RQ1: How do faculty members in social work and psychology experience and interpret success when integrating AI into their teaching practices?
RQ2: How do faculty experience, understand, and make sense of challenges encountered during AI integration?

Participants

The study involved 16 faculty members, with equal representation from social work (8) and psychology (8) departments. Participants were selected through purposive sampling to ensure that each faculty member had prior experience using AI tools in their teaching. This sampling strategy allows for disciplinary diversity while providing depth in phenomenological inquiry. Inclusion criteria included faculty willingness to participate in face-to-face interviews, and sufficient experience with AI integration to provide informed reflections. The sample was selected to capture variation in teaching experience, AI familiarity, and instructional context, consistent with phenomenological aims of illuminating shared and divergent meanings.

Data Collection

Data was collected through semi-structured, face-to-face interviews, each lasting approximately 40–60 minutes. This method allows for a structured exploration of research questions while maintaining flexibility to probe unexpected insights and follow emerging topics. The semi-structured interview schedule included questions regarding participants' background, teaching experience, AI familiarity, and primary mode of teaching. Core questions focused on perceived successes, challenges, and surprises, as well as reflection on how teaching experience and AI familiarity shaped participants' experiences with AI integration. Additional questions invited reflections on future applications of AI and recommendations for peers. Interviews were audio-recorded with participant consent to ensure accurate transcription.

THEMATIC ANALYSIS WITH INTERPRETATIONS

Data were analyzed using a phenomenological approach focused on identifying shared meanings and experiential themes across participants while attending to contextual variation. Analysis focused not only on identifying recurrent topics but on illuminating how faculty experienced, interpreted, and assigned meaning to AI integration within their professional and pedagogical contexts. Themes were developed to reflect shared experiential meanings rather than discrete categories of behavior, attending to how faculty described emotional responses, ethical judgments, and shifts in teaching identity alongside perceived outcomes.

Theme 1: Experiencing Heightened Student Engagement

Faculty described experiencing heightened student engagement when AI tools were integrated into their teaching, characterizing this engagement as interactive, immersive, and emotionally salient. Rather than viewing engagement solely as increased participation, faculty emphasized changes in how students related to course material and to learning processes more broadly.

In social work education, faculty experienced AI-enabled simulations as creating a safe and structured space for students to practice empathy, ethical reasoning, and decision-making. One participant noted, *"Using AI to simulate client scenarios really helped students practice empathy and decision-making in a controlled environment."* This experience was described as reducing student anxiety while allowing repeated engagement with complex social situations.

Psychology faculty similarly described AI-supported quizzes and predictive models as enhancing curiosity and conceptual engagement. As one participant explained, *"AI quizzes and predictive models made students more curious about behavioral patterns."* Faculty experienced these tools as helping students move from abstract theory to applied understanding.

Across disciplines, faculty interpreted increased engagement as both cognitive and affective, noting heightened curiosity, collaboration, and motivation. Importantly, engagement was experienced not as a byproduct of novelty but as emerging when AI tools were intentionally aligned with pedagogical goals. Faculty reflections suggest that AI reshaped classroom dynamics in ways that supported more student-centered learning while preserving instructor oversight and pedagogical intent.

Theme 2: Experiencing Efficiency and Temporal Relief

Faculty described experiencing efficiency gains through AI integration as a form of *temporal relief*—a felt reduction in time pressure that reshaped how they allocated attention and energy in their teaching roles. Rather than focusing solely on productivity, participants emphasized how automation altered the rhythm of their work and their sense of pedagogical presence.

Across both disciplines, faculty described using AI to automate repetitive administrative and evaluative tasks, including grading of objective assessments, attendance tracking, and preliminary feedback. One participant noted, *"AI grading of objective assignments saved me hours each week, letting me focus more on discussion and mentoring."* Faculty experienced this time savings not simply as convenience, but as enabling a reorientation toward higher-order teaching activities such as mentoring, facilitating dialogue, and designing complex learning experiences.

Rapid AI-generated feedback was particularly salient in faculty accounts. Participants described the immediacy of feedback as supporting students' self-regulated learning and iterative improvement, while also reducing the backlog of grading that often constrains instructor availability. Faculty experienced this immediacy as easing instructional strain and enhancing responsiveness, especially in larger or time-intensive courses.

While both social work and psychology faculty described similar efficiency benefits, their interpretations diverged in emphasis. Social work educators often framed temporal relief in ethical terms, noting that reduced administrative burden allowed greater attentiveness to relational engagement and student support. Psychology faculty more frequently highlighted efficiency as enabling deeper conceptual exploration and discussion of complex material. Across disciplines, faculty stressed that efficiency gains were meaningful only when they supported, rather than supplanted, human judgment and instructional presence.

Importantly, faculty did not experience efficiency as a neutral or purely technical outcome. Instead, temporal relief was described as reshaping professional identity, reducing stress, and creating space for pedagogical creativity. At the same time, participants emphasized the need for balance, expressing concern that overreliance on automation could undermine the relational dimensions of teaching. These reflections suggest that efficiency was experienced as beneficial when AI complemented faculty expertise and pedagogical intent, rather than replacing human engagement.

Theme 3: Reimagining Pedagogical Possibilities

Faculty described experiencing AI integration as opening new pedagogical possibilities, prompting them to rethink how learning activities could be designed, structured, and enacted. Rather than viewing AI solely as a tool for efficiency, participants framed it as expanding what felt pedagogically possible within the constraints of time, curriculum, and instructional format.

Faculty across both disciplines described using AI to generate novel case studies, simulations, and data-informed discussion prompts that would have been difficult or time-consuming to create manually. One psychology faculty member reflected, *"AI helped me create unique case scenarios for my psychology students that I wouldn't have thought of manually."* These experiences were often described as enabling experimentation and creative risk-taking, allowing instructors to explore instructional designs beyond familiar or habitual approaches.

In social work education, faculty experienced AI-supported simulations as particularly valuable for modeling complex social situations and client interactions. These tools allowed instructors to offer experiential learning opportunities while maintaining ethical boundaries and controlled conditions. Psychology faculty, in contrast, emphasized the use of AI to generate datasets, predictive models, or behavioral scenarios that made abstract concepts more concrete and analytically accessible to students.

Across disciplines, faculty interpreted these pedagogical innovations as supporting a more learner-centered orientation, enabling them to adapt instructional materials to student needs, interests, and levels of preparedness. Importantly, innovation was not experienced as purely technical enhancement. Faculty described moments of uncertainty and reflection as they navigated questions about appropriateness, ethical alignment, and instructional purpose. These reflections suggest that reimagining pedagogy through AI involved not only creativity but also careful judgment and recalibration of teaching roles.

Overall, faculty experienced AI as a catalyst for pedagogical imagination rather than a replacement for instructional expertise. The possibilities opened by AI were described as meaningful when they aligned with disciplinary values and learning objectives, reinforcing the view that innovation in teaching emerges through the interplay of technological affordances, professional judgment, and reflective practice.

Theme 4: Experiencing Disruption and Uncertainty

Faculty described experiencing AI integration as marked by moments of disruption and uncertainty, particularly when technical systems failed or behaved unpredictably. These experiences were not limited to inconvenience but were often described as destabilizing, interrupting instructional flow and undermining confidence in AI-supported teaching.

Participants across disciplines reported encountering software crashes, connectivity problems, slow processing speeds, and incompatibility with existing learning platforms. One faculty member reflected, *"Sometimes the AI system crashed mid-class, and I had no way to recover the student data quickly."* Such moments were experienced as stressful and disorienting, particularly when they occurred during live instruction or experiential activities.

In social work education, faculty described technical disruptions as especially problematic when simulations or role-based exercises were interrupted, as these activities depend on continuity and emotional engagement. Psychology faculty similarly reported uncertainty when AI-generated outputs produced errors or unexpected results, requiring immediate judgment calls about whether and how to proceed. In both disciplines, these disruptions heightened faculty awareness of their reliance on technological infrastructure and their responsibility to manage risk in real time.

Faculty experiences of disruption were closely tied to feelings of preparedness and institutional support. Participants with lower prior familiarity with AI described greater uncertainty and hesitation when technical issues arose, whereas those with more experience reported drawing on troubleshooting strategies or contingency plans. Nonetheless, even experienced users described a persistent sense of vulnerability, noting that technical reliability remained largely outside their control.

Overall, faculty experienced technical difficulties not merely as obstacles to be resolved but as moments that exposed the fragility of AI-dependent teaching practices. These experiences underscored the importance of reliable infrastructure, accessible technical support, and institutional readiness. At the same time, they contributed to ongoing recalibration of expectations, shaping how faculty weighed the benefits of AI integration against the risks of disruption in their teaching environments.

Theme 5: Negotiating Ethical Tensions and Responsibility

Faculty described experiencing AI integration as an ongoing process of negotiating ethical tensions and professional responsibility. Ethical considerations were not framed as discrete obstacles but as persistent concerns that shaped how faculty evaluated, limited, and adapted AI use in their teaching.

In social work education, faculty emphasized the importance of preserving student autonomy, empathy, and ethical decision-making. One participant reflected, *"I worry that students might rely too heavily on AI recommendations instead of critical thinking."* While AI-supported simulations were valued for skill development, faculty expressed concern that uncritical reliance on algorithmic guidance could create a false sense of competence or diminish students' capacity for reflective judgment—core elements of client-centered practice.

Psychology faculty similarly articulated ethical unease related to AI's capacity to model behavior without fully capturing human nuance. As one participant noted, *"AI can analyze patterns, but it might miss nuanced human behavior, which is crucial for psychological understanding."* Faculty experienced this limitation as requiring constant pedagogical vigilance, particularly when AI outputs appeared authoritative despite underlying uncertainty or simplification.

Across disciplines, faculty described ethical responsibility as extending beyond content accuracy to include privacy, data governance, and the conditions under which student data were collected, analyzed, or stored. These concerns were often accompanied by uncertainty about institutional policies and accountability, intensifying the moral weight faculty felt when integrating AI into coursework.

Rather than rejecting AI outright, faculty described actively negotiating ethical boundaries through instructional design, explicit discussion of AI limitations, and ongoing reflection with students. Ethical engagement was experienced as inseparable from teaching itself, reinforcing the view that AI integration in human-centered disciplines requires continual attention to professional values, student well-being, and the preservation of human judgment. This theme underscores that ethical responsibility was not peripheral to faculty experiences but central to how AI integration was understood, enacted, and sustained.

DISCUSSION

This study explored faculty reflections on integrating artificial intelligence (AI) in social work and psychology education through a phenomenological lens, foregrounding lived experiences of success, challenge, and surprise. The findings demonstrate that AI integration is not experienced as a uniformly positive or negative innovation, but rather as a complex, context-sensitive process shaped by professional values, teaching context, and reflective sense-making. Faculty narratives revealed that AI simultaneously expanded pedagogical possibilities and raised ethical, relational, and practical concerns, particularly within human-centered disciplines that prioritize empathy, judgment, and relational depth. Collectively, these findings suggest that faculty engagement with AI is best understood not as adoption or resistance, but as an ongoing process of negotiating tensions between technological affordances and deeply held professional values.

Across both social work and psychology, faculty described experiences of enhanced student engagement, temporal relief through improved efficiency, and opportunities for pedagogical innovation as meaningful dimensions of AI integration.

AI-enabled simulations, adaptive quizzes, automated feedback, and data-informed activities were experienced as enriching learning environments and enabled faculty to reallocate time to mentoring, discussion, and higher-order pedagogical work. Importantly, faculty did not describe these successes in purely technical terms. Instead, they interpreted them through discipline-specific pedagogical aims, such as fostering empathy and ethical reasoning in social work or supporting analytical and conceptual understanding in psychology. In this way, perceived success was embedded within broader understandings of what constitutes meaningful learning in professional education.

Faculty experiences were also shaped by contextual lenses, particularly teaching experience, familiarity with AI, and mode of instruction. These factors did not function as predictors of outcomes but as experiential contexts through which AI integration was interpreted. More experienced educators often articulated heightened ethical sensitivity and stronger attachment to relational pedagogy, while less experienced faculty tended to express greater openness to experimentation alongside higher uncertainty. Similarly, faculty with greater AI familiarity described increased confidence and fewer disruptive surprises, whereas those with limited familiarity encountered steeper learning curves and heightened ethical and technical concerns. Mode of teaching further framed these experiences, with online and hybrid contexts amplifying the perceived utility of AI for engagement and feedback, and face-to-face settings foregrounding concerns about relational presence and instructional authenticity. Together, these contextual dimensions shaped how faculty evaluated both the promise and the risk of AI in their teaching.

At the same time, faculty reflections revealed persistent constraints that accompanied AI integration, particularly ethical responsibility, and technical reliability. Ethical concerns were central to faculty sense-making, encompassing apprehensions about student over-reliance on AI, bias in AI algorithmic outputs, data privacy, and the potential erosion of critical thinking and professional judgment. These concerns were not treated as abstract risks but as everyday pedagogical dilemmas requiring ongoing vigilance. Technical challenges – including system instability, software errors, and the additional cognitive and emotional labor involved in monitoring AI outputs – further exposed the limits of automation. Faculty often interpreted these constraints as reminders of the continued necessity of human oversight and judgment, reinforcing the idea that efficiency gains were frequently accompanied by new forms of workload and responsibility.

A particularly salient contribution of this study lies in its illumination of the contradictions embedded in faculty experiences with AI. Faculty frequently described efficiency alongside ethical unease, innovation alongside uncertainty, and increased student engagement alongside concerns about dependency on AI tools. For example, while AI-assisted feedback accelerated grading and improved turnaround time, it also raised questions about assessment authenticity and depth of student learning. Similarly, AI-supported simulations enhanced experiential learning while raising doubts about whether algorithmic representations could adequately capture emotional nuance and contextual complexity. These contradictions underscore that AI integration is not a linear progression toward improvement, but a process marked by tension, ambiguity, and critical self-questioning. From a phenomenological perspective, such discomfort is not incidental but integral to how faculty come to understand and position AI within their pedagogical practice.

Faculty narratives also highlighted the role of surprises – both positive and negative – as pivotal moments in this interpretive process. Unexpected increases in student creativity, collaboration, and self-directed learning were experienced as positive disruptions that challenged existing pedagogical assumptions. Conversely, unanticipated inaccuracies, ethical dilemmas, and student over-reliance on AI prompted reassessment of assignment design, instructional boundaries, and faculty responsibility. These moments of surprise functioned as catalysts for reflection and adaptation, prompting faculty to renegotiate their teaching practices rather than uncritically adopt or reject AI. In this way, faculty learning mirrored the kinds of reflective and transformative learning processes they sought to foster in students.

Overall, this discussion underscores that faculty engagement with AI in social work and psychology education is best understood as a reflective, evolving process rather than a fixed stance toward technological adoption. Success and challenge emerged not as opposing outcomes but as coexisting dimensions of innovation, shaped by context, values, and experience. By centering faculty lived experiences, this study contributes a nuanced understanding of AI integration that honors complexity, foregrounds professional judgment, and recognizes ambiguity as an essential component of pedagogical transformation in human-centered disciplines.

CONCLUSION

This study examined how faculty in social work and psychology experience the integration of artificial intelligence in their teaching, using a phenomenological approach to center lived experience and meaning-making. By foregrounding faculty voices, the study moves beyond generalized claims about AI adoption to illuminate how educators in human-centered disciplines engage with AI in practice.

The findings demonstrate that faculty engagement with AI cannot be reduced to measures of effectiveness, acceptance, or resistance. Instead, AI integration is experienced as a situated and evolving practice shaped by disciplinary values, professional identity, teaching context, and ethical responsibility. Faculty reflections underscore that AI's educational value emerges not from the technology itself but from how it is interpreted, bounded, and enacted within pedagogical relationships.

A key contribution of this study lies in its emphasis on faculty sense-making as central to understanding AI in higher education. By documenting how success, challenge, and surprise coexist in faculty experiences, the study challenges linear or instrumental models of AI adoption and highlights the importance of reflective judgment in navigating educational innovation. This perspective is particularly salient for disciplines such as social work and psychology, where relational depth, ethical reasoning, and human judgment are foundational.

Overall, this study contributes to the growing scholarship on AI in education by offering a nuanced, experience-centered account of faculty engagement with AI. It suggests that meaningful and responsible AI integration requires attention not only to tools and outcomes but also to the professional values, contextual conditions, and interpretive processes through which educators make sense of technological change. By centering faculty lived experience, this work provides a foundation for more ethically grounded, context-sensitive, and human-centered approaches to AI in higher education.

SUGGESTIONS

Drawing on faculty experiences documented in this study, several practical suggestions emerge for supporting meaningful and ethical AI integration in social work and psychology education.

First, faculty development programs should be designed to improve AI familiarity and confidence. Workshops, hands-on training sessions, and continuous professional development initiatives can equip faculty with the necessary skills to use AI tools effectively, thereby reducing anxiety and technical errors. Training should emphasize both pedagogical strategies and ethical considerations, ensuring faculty can implement AI responsibly and align its use with learning objectives. Providing faculty with discipline-specific examples of AI applications can further enhance relevance and thoughtful adoption.

Second, institutions should prioritize technical support and infrastructure development. Reliable software, access to AI platforms, and dedicated IT support are essential to minimize disruptions and maximize the benefits of AI integration. This includes proactive maintenance of AI systems, troubleshooting support during classes, and updates to software that ensure compatibility with existing teaching platforms. Faculty should have easy access to help desks or AI mentors to address technical challenges promptly.

Third, ethical considerations must be embedded into AI integration strategies. Guidelines should be established to ensure student privacy, data security, and responsible use of AI outputs. Faculty should be trained to monitor AI outputs critically, preventing over-reliance or bias in teaching and assessment. Encouraging reflective practice can help faculty identify potential ethical pitfalls and make informed decisions about AI use.

Fourth, AI integration should be context-sensitive and adaptable. The study revealed that teaching experience and mode of instruction (face-to-face) significantly influenced faculty perceptions. Therefore, AI strategies should be flexible, allowing adaptation to faculty expertise, student needs, and teaching contexts. For example, novice faculty may start with small-scale AI activities and gradually expand usage as confidence grows, while experienced faculty can design more complex AI-integrated curricula.

Fifth, ongoing evaluation and feedback mechanisms should be established to monitor AI's impact on learning outcomes and faculty workload. Collecting feedback from both students and faculty can guide iterative improvements, ensuring AI use enhances engagement, innovation, and efficiency without unintended negative consequences. This aligns with the study's findings regarding unexpected outcomes and the need for reflection and adaptation.

Finally, fostering collaborative communities of practice can enhance knowledge sharing among faculty. Peer mentoring, interdisciplinary discussions, and forums for sharing AI experiences can support innovation, reduce challenges, and highlight successful strategies. Collaboration between social work and psychology faculty may be particularly valuable, enabling cross-disciplinary learning while respecting the distinct ethical and pedagogical commitments of each field.

REFERENCES

Ahn, E., Choi, M., Fowler, P., & Song, I. (2025). Artificial intelligence (AI) literacy for social work: Implications for core competencies. *Journal of the Society for Social Work and Research, 16*(1). Advance online publication. DOI: 10.1086/735187

Almusaed, A., Almssad, A., Yitmen, I., & Homod, R. Z. (2023). Enhancing student engagement: Harnessing "AIED"'s power in hybrid education—A review analysis. *Education Sciences, 13*(7), 632. DOI: 10.3390/educsci13070632

Buele, J., & Llerena-Aguirre, L. (2025). Transformations in academic work and faculty perceptions of artificial intelligence in higher education. *Frontiers in Education, 10*. Advance online publication. DOI: 10.3389/feduc.2025.1603763

Buelvas Parra, J. A., Santamaría Escobar, Á. E., & Pertuz Martínez, A. P. (2024). Artificial intelligence in education: Benefits, challenges, and ethical considerations according to scientific evidence. *Journal of International Crisis and Risk Communication Research, 7*(S5). Advance online publication. DOI: 10.63278/jicrcr.vi.606

Chinoracky, R., & Stalmasekova, N. (2025). Ethical problems in the use of artificial intelligence by university educators. *Education Sciences, 15*(10), 1322. DOI: 10.3390/educsci15101322

Dwivedi, Y. K., Hughes, L., Baabdullah, A. M., Ribeiro-Navarrete, S., Giannakis, M., & Metri, B. (2021). Artificial intelligence (AI): Multidisciplinary perspectives on emerging challenges, opportunities, and agenda for research, practice, and policy. *International Journal of Information Management, 57*. Advance online publication. DOI: 10.1016/j.ijinfomgt.2019.08.002

Gealone, D. (2024). Exploring faculty perceptions of AI integration in pedagogical practices at higher education institutions: A qualitative study. *International Journal of Arts. Sciences and Education*, 5(1), 140–147. https://ijase.org/index.php/ijase/article/view/396

Hodgson, D., Goldingay, S., Boddy, J., Nipperess, S., & Watts, L. (2021). Problematising artificial intelligence in social work education: Challenges, issues and possibilities. *British Journal of Social Work, 52*(4). Advance online publication. DOI: 10.1093/bjsw/bcab168

Holmes, W., Bialik, M., & Fadel, C. (2019). *Artificial intelligence in education: Promises and implications for teaching and learning*. Center for Curriculum Redesign.

Kasneci, E., Sessler, K., Küchemann, S., Bannert, M., Dementieva, D., Fischer, F., Gasser, U., Groh, G., Günnemann, S., Hüllermeier, E., Krusche, S., Kutyniok, G., Michaeli, T., Nerdel, C., Pfeffer, J., Poquet, O., Sailer, M., Schmidt, A., Seidel, T., & Stadler, M. (2023). ChatGPT for good? On Opportunities and Challenges of Large Language Models for Education. *Learning and Individual Differences, 103.* Advance online publication. DOI: 10.1016/j.lindif.2023.102274

Lampou, R. (2023). The integration of artificial intelligence in education: Opportunities and challenges. *Review of Artificial Intelligence in Education, 4.* Advance online publication. DOI: 10.37497/rev.artif.intell.educ.v4i00.15

Lelescu, A., Sava, S., Grosseck, G., & Malita, L. (2025). Exploring trust in generative AI for higher education institutions: A systematic literature review focused on educators. *Humanities & Social Sciences Communications.* Advance online publication. DOI: 10.1057/s41599-025-06253-1

Rane, J., Kaya, Ö., Mallick, S. K., & Rane, N. (2024). *Artificial intelligence in education: A SWOT analysis of ChatGPT and its implications for practice and research.* Deep Science Publishing., DOI: 10.70593/978-81-981271-7-4_4

Reamer, F. G. (2023). Artificial intelligence in social work: Emerging ethical issues. *International Journal of Social Work Values and Ethics, 20*(2), 52–71. DOI: 10.55521/10-020-205

Ren, X., & Wu, M. L. (2025). Examining teaching competencies and challenges while integrating artificial intelligence in higher education. *TechTrends, 69,* 519–538. DOI: 10.1007/s11528-025-01055-3

Shata, A., & Hartley, K. (2025). Artificial intelligence and communication technologies in academia: Faculty perceptions and the adoption of generative AI. *International Journal of Educational Technology in Higher Education, 22*(14). Advance online publication. DOI: 10.1186/s41239-025-00511-7

Shi, J., Liu, W., & Hu, K. (2025). Exploring how AI literacy and self-regulated learning relate to student writing performance and well-being in generative AI-supported higher education. *Behavioral Sciences (Basel, Switzerland), 15*(5), 705. DOI: 10.3390/bs15050705 PMID: 40426482

Sidiropoulos, D., & Anagnostopoulos, C.-N. (2024). Applications, challenges and ethical issues of AI and ChatGPT in education. *arXiv preprint.* https://doi.org//arXiv.2402.07907DOI: 10.48550

Spathopoulou, F., Pitychoutis, K. M., & Papakonstantinidis, S. (2025). AI and higher education: Understanding faculty roles in teaching, research, and administration. *Contemporary Educational Technology*, *17*(4), ep600. DOI: 10.30935/cedtech/17406

Tsakeni, M., Nwafor, S. C., Mosia, M., & Egara, F. O. (2025). Mapping the scaffolding of metacognition and learning by AI tools in STEM classrooms: A bibliometric-systematic review approach (2005-2025). *Journal of Intelligence*, *13*(11), 148. DOI: 10.3390/jintelligence13110148 PMID: 41295429

Venkatesh, V., Thong, J. Y., & Xu, X. (2016). Unified theory of acceptance and use of technology: A synthesis and the road ahead. *Journal of the Association for Information Systems*, *17*(5), 328–376. DOI: 10.17705/1jais.00428

Venter, J., Coetzee, S. A., & Schmulian, A. (2024). Exploring the use of artificial intelligence (AI) in the delivery of effective feedback. *Assessment & Evaluation in Higher Education*, *50*(4), 1–21. DOI: 10.1080/02602938.2024.2415649

Verboom, A. D. P. R., Pais, L., Zijlstra, F. R. H., Oswald, F. L., & dos Santos, N. R. (2025). Perceptions of artificial intelligence in academic teaching and research: A qualitative study from AI experts and professors' perspectives. *International Journal of Educational Technology in Higher Education*, *22*(1). Advance online publication. DOI: 10.1186/s41239-025-00546-w

Whitbread, M., Hayes, C., Prabhakar, S., & Upsher, R. (2025). Exploring university staff's perceptions of using generative artificial intelligence at university. *Education Sciences*, *15*(3), 367. DOI: 10.3390/educsci15030367

Yaseen, H., Mohammad, A. S., Ashal, N., Abusaimeh, H., Ali, A., & Sharabati, A.-A. A. (2025). the impact of adaptive learning technologies, personalized feedback, and interactive AI tools on student engagement: The moderating role of digital literacy. *Sustainability*, *17*(3), 1133. DOI: 10.3390/su17031133

KEY TERMS AND DEFINITIONS

Artificial Intelligence (AI): Artificial intelligence refers to the use of computer-based systems and applications that simulate human cognitive functions—such as learning, reasoning, problem-solving, and language processing—to support teaching, learning, assessment, research, and academic administration.

Faculty Reflections: Faculty reflections are systematic, self-reported accounts by teachers describing their experiences, perceptions, emotions, and evaluations of teaching practices, student responses, and institutional support within a specific educational context.

Mode of Teaching: Mode of teaching refers to the method or format through which instruction is delivered, such as face-to-face, online, blended, experiential learning, flipped classroom, or technology-assisted teaching.

Perceived Challenges: Perceived challenges refer to difficulties or barriers experienced by faculty during teaching, including technological issues, student preparedness, ethical concerns, time constraints, or institutional limitations.

Perceived Successes: Perceived successes are faculty-identified positive outcomes of teaching practices, such as improved student understanding, skill development, engagement, or teaching efficiency, based on personal experience rather than objective measurement.

Perceived Surprises: Perceived surprises are unexpected outcomes or experiences encountered by faculty during the teaching process, which may be positive or negative and differ from prior expectations or assumptions.

Phenomenological Research: Phenomenological research is a qualitative research approach that explores and describes individuals' lived experiences and subjective meanings related to a particular phenomenon, as expressed through their personal narratives and reflections.

Psychology Education: Psychology education refers to the academic instruction and training of students in psychological theories, research methods, and applications aimed at understanding human behavior, cognition, emotions, and mental processes.

Social Work Education: Social work education is the structured process of teaching and learning that prepares students with theoretical knowledge, professional values, ethical principles, and practice skills required for social work practice with individuals, families, groups, and communities.

Student Engagement: Student engagement is the degree of students' active involvement in learning activities, demonstrated through participation, interaction, attention, effort, and emotional investment in the teaching–learning process.

Chapter 6
Partnering With AI for Case Study and Simulation-Based Learning in Social Work Education

Rachel Salmon
https://orcid.org/0009-0002-2423-9916
Widener University, USA

Caroline Fitzgerald Campbell
https://orcid.org/0009-0002-8241-5746
Widener University, USA

ABSTRACT

This chapter explores benefits and limitations of using artificial intelligence (AI) in the creation of an Immersive Case Study Environment (ICSE) that supports case study and simulation-based learning across the micro, mezzo, and macro levels of social work practice. It details the planning and collaboration process between an instructional designer and faculty, ethical considerations, pilot applications in various learning formats, early findings, and recommendations for future teaching and research. Key findings from this work include (1) an increased faculty awareness of how immersive case study experiences can lead to customized learning various environments, (2) ways students benefit from a more holistic view of clients and the community, and (3) the need for strategic planning around the adoption of new technology. Ultimately, the use of AI in collaboration with an instructional designer

DOI: 10.4018/979-8-3373-4362-4.ch006

and faculty increased the accessibility of scenario-based learning for resource-limited institutions and provides a more authentic experience aligned with desired learning outcomes.

INTRODUCTION & RATIONALE

The use of case studies to support students in learning clinical skills has been a pedagogical practice for over a century after it was first developed by Harvard University in 1921 (Harvard Business School, 2021). It has since been widely adopted as a teaching strategy in social work, psychology, nursing, and other clinical fields (Penn et al., 2016). Case studies provide realistic examples of issues people face and facilitate learning assessment, analysis, and intervention planning skills. Benefits of case studies and the use of case-based learning include the ability to critically reflect on case components and follow systematic steps in evidence-based analysis of the case and its theoretical connections (Thistlethwaite et al., 2012). Case studies offer exposure to a broader range of client situations and issues than students may encounter in their field practicum (Drisko & Grady, 2018). Additionally, case studies function as part of an active learning cycle by exposing students to unique client experiences without the overwhelming immediacy of live situations, while allowing them to develop and practice skills within the supportive context of the classroom.

However, challenges exist with both the development and utilization of case studies. Penn et al. (2016) describe the time-consuming nature of case study development as one of the biggest obstacles to their use in teaching. A collaborative development process is required to ensure diverse perspectives and identities are represented, skillful narrative storytelling is employed, and significant markers are present that allow students to accurately understand and assess the situation (Popil, 2011). Intentional consideration for when and how case studies are employed in a course and throughout a program's curriculum is essential, and so, too, is evaluating the use of case studies in supporting students to develop important skills and competencies in their social work practice. In response to the desire for more immersive case studies while addressing time and resource constraints, an Immersive Case Study Environment (ICSE) was developed with assistance from artificial intelligence and piloted in a social work program at a small, private university in the Northeast United States. This institution offers a large, online (asynchronous) Master of Social Work (MSW) program and a smaller campus-based MSW program in addition to a BSW and a PhD program.

Over the last decade of its existence, the development of the private university's online program has necessitated close collaboration with the university's Teaching and Learning with Technology department, and subsequent close partnership with a dedicated instructional designer. The instructional designer works with faculty and program administration to ensure the use of best practices in online learning pedagogy and maintain the program's courses in the learning management system. The online MSW program is regularly reviewed by faculty in collaboration with the instructional designer to ensure students receive a high-quality education and engaging experience that prepare them for field experience and their careers. Throughout course review meetings, faculty frequently expressed the need for additional interactivity, especially with the use of case studies.

Faculty have created case scenarios over time, but often faced challenges updating them or creating new ones as the curriculum was revised. A committee of faculty members had previously developed a shared case scenario for use in specific curriculum courses to highlight how different content and skills illuminate aspects of a single case and cultivate diverse skills from social workers in their practice context. For example, in a family practice course, the shared case is explored through a family theory lens, with intervention planning utilizing family theory principles. In a community development course, the same family is examined through a community development and skills lens. While initially effective in examining the same client situation across a variety of course topics, students later expressed frustration with encountering the same case repeatedly across courses. Additionally, students shared in course evaluations that the static nature of the case scenario lacked sufficient depth for sustained engagement in a way that did not reflect the realities of working with clients. The faculty acknowledged this feedback with an intention to develop additional common cases for use across the curriculum but lacked time to collaboratively develop several case studies that could reflect a more dynamic client progression. To implement best practices in the development and piloting of the Immersive Case Study Environment, research on case-based learning, active learning and simulation, and strategies for addressing resource and time constraints were reviewed.

CONCEPTUAL FRAMEWORK

Role of Active Learning

Social work and other helping professions training programs share a central focus in learning skills and interventions that are grounded in theory, knowledge, and ethics. Howell (2021) describes how active learning and other practices, such as the flipped classroom, increase student engagement and that reflection skills are best learned in experiential practice. Active learning, characterized by Bloom's taxonomy (1956), is a framework encompassing various pedagogies that employ diverse activities, experiences, and techniques beyond traditional lectures (Martella & Schneider, 2024). These activities include role-playing, affective experiences, case studies, problem-based learning, and peer-to-peer discussions (Martella & Schneider, 2024). Bloom's taxonomy of learning (1956) identifies the need for learners to engage in increasingly higher orders of cognitive skills ranging from remembering and understanding to analyzing and evaluating concepts. Readings, videos, and class discussions often facilitate remembering and understanding, whereas role-plays and interactive case scenarios support experiential application, a higher-order skill on the taxonomical scale which enables students to analyze and evaluate interactions, theoretical approaches, and their effectiveness.

Active learning in social work education is also supported by learning science theories, including Cognitive Load Theory, which highlights the limits of working memory when learners engage with complex and emotionally charged material (Sweller et al., 2019). Across counseling, social work, and other disciplines, learning clinical skills requires students to attend to a combination of theoretical frameworks, professional ethics, relationship dynamics, self-awareness of emotions, and decision-making processes that shape work with clients. This multiplicity of demands can easily overwhelm developing practitioners when learning relies primarily on direct teaching of concepts through lecture and skills in practicum settings. In contrast, active learning strategies such as case-based discussion, guided role-play, and structured reflection can help students manage cognitive load by breaking complex clinical processes into more accessible, practice-based components. When instruction is scaffolded, students can move from observation and understanding of concepts in the work toward increasingly complex application. In this way, learners are better able to integrate knowledge and skill rather than become cognitively overloaded. These conditions create a strong foundation for simulation-based learning, which builds upon active learning principles while increasing exposure to realistic and complex scenarios in ways that more closely resemble clinical practice.

Use of Simulation in Social Work Education

The Council on Social Work Education (CSWE), which serves as the accrediting body of social work educational programs in the United States, identifies extensive practicum experiences as the "signature pedagogy" of social work education. The goal of field practicum experiences is to expose students to a full range of issues and presentations; however, in practice, many placement sites focus on a narrower set of populations. Simulation has been found to be an effective strategy in social work education, allowing for scaffolding clinical skills with a wider range of specialized cases and exposure to interprofessional collaboration (Kourgiantakis et al., 2020). Simulation-based learning moves a step beyond experiential approaches by offering structured, immersive opportunities for students to apply skills, make decisions, and reflect on their responses within realistic clinical scenarios.

In experiential learning theory, simulation aligns with the cycle of experience, reflection, conceptualization, and application and transfer of learning that follows the processes of how clinicians learn in practice (Kolb, 1984). It also moves through higher orders of cognitive skills identified in Bloom's Taxonomy (1956), focusing on idea generation, analysis of authentic situations, reflexivity, and professional judgement. Research in social work education demonstrates that simulation can support student self-efficacy, self-awareness, and perceived competence in a safe environment across both in-person and online formats, helping students feel more prepared for field placement (Asakura & Bogo, 2021; Baker & Jenney, 2023; Kourgiantakis et al., 2020; Rogers & MacCormac, 2025). Simulations also prepare students for the added cognitive load associated with managing the dual demands of clinical encounters, including their own emotions and reactions when working with clients, allowing time to reflect on their own responses as they simultaneously work through ethical and clinical decision-making (Jefferies et al., 2025).

In social work education programs, competencies are defined by the CSWE. Student achievement of CSWE competencies is most often measured in the field practicum evaluation, completed by a supervising social worker, but also measured through assessment embedded within the curriculum by faculty. Using simulation can measure learning outcomes more effectively than traditional written assessments by aligning the evaluation of skill application with CSWE competencies (Bogo et al., 2011). For example, students demonstrate competencies related to ethical and professional behavior by showing evidence of their ethical decision making, explaining their rationale, and maintaining professional boundaries in simulated practice. Other competencies, such as engagement and assessment, can be observed when students demonstrate empathy, attunement, and collaboration during simulated client interactions and carry out integrated biopsychosocial assessments in complex scenarios. Clinical interventions can be evaluated based on how students choose, apply, and explain interventions that address client needs. In this way, faculty can directly evaluate skills in application in the classroom.

A scoping review of research on virtual simulation in social work education completed by Baker and Jenney (2023) highlighted that as a complement to field education, the signature pedagogy identified by the CSWE, simulation offers the means for students to demonstrate competency in preparation for successful field placement. They also recognized that while simulation offers a flexible and scalable approach to expanding students' exposure to diverse client presentations and provides the safety, structure, and reflection necessary for meaningful clinical learning, many institutions lack the time and financial resources to implement it effectively.

Artificial Intelligence Integration in Response to Higher Education Needs

Implementing high-quality simulations can be a challenge with limited faculty time, institution resources, and the need for diverse, well-developed case materials (Baker & Jenney, 2023). To address resource limitations, higher education institutions have begun using artificial intelligence (AI) large language models (LLMs) to assist with the development of educational content. Torun and Şanal (2025) identified multiple benefits of AI in higher education – including course material preparation, increased customization to support diverse learners, and greater content diversity – based on interviews with university faculty and students. They determined that most benefits are reliant on responsible integration and awareness of usage and advise that a critical first step in beneficial utilization of AI is improving awareness and literacy amongst both faculty and students.

In response to heightened availability of AI and its potential benefits, learning management systems are working to integrate their own AI services directly into their platforms. Mzwri and Turcsányi-Szabo (2025) explored the use of an AI platform integrated directly into the Canvas learning management system that was able to access and pull results from assessments, and direct students to specific course content within Canvas courses. Their results indicated benefits related to supporting students and improving learning outcomes while also streamlining administrative tasks, thus reducing teacher workloads.

To specifically focus on increasing levels of engagement, institutions have begun utilizing AI platforms to assist with the development of simulation-based learning activities, taking advantage of their ability to rapidly create content. For an institution that utilized ChatGPT 3.5 for simulation-based learning in the medical field, the large language model's adaptability and efficiency proved valuable for creating simulation content (Zheng et al., 2024). Zheng and colleagues experienced an increase in their ability to generate interactive learning material, personalize content for learners, and improve the efficiency with which content can be created for simulation-based learning.

As some academic institutions and individual faculty members are open to exploring and integrating the use of AI in their teaching, others have varied perceptions of AI and its use in an academic setting. The adoption of new technologies has been studied at length, with the Technology Acceptance Model developed by Davis (1989) highlighting how differences in adoption are shaped by perceived usefulness and perceived ease of use. These varying perceptions and their impact on technology adoption are still being seen. A study surveying both faculty and staff at a higher education institution highlighted the varying perspectives, with some finding AI to be a "disruptive educational technology" and others seeing benefits to personalized learning support and research and analysis (Damiano, et al., 2024). Damiano et al. (2024)'s survey results also identified concerns related to potential plagiarism and student accountability, although multiple students indicated that "they would not use ChatGPT to plagiarize but believed others would," raising questions about whether such concerns reflect actual behavior or perceived risk. The perception around artificial intelligence and its use in education, just as with other new technologies, is a consideration that cannot be ignored.

Ethical and Justice Considerations

As the use of AI in education and simulation-based learning content development grows, research on its use is still limited, with several considerations to address. Even without the use of AI, there are existing concerns regarding ethical simulation-based learning related to authenticity, representation, and potential harm to students belonging to marginalized communities (Asakura, 2024). The inclusion of AI introduces new ethical considerations regarding biases, necessitating validation methods to reduce bias in AI-generated output (Lazcoz & Miguel, 2025). These considerations will likely persist or intensify, especially with regard to image and video generation, as AI-generated visuals of human beings are prone to bias related to race and gender. Research using artificial intelligence for simulations specifically with an affective component to demonstrate situation-based emotions showed benefits to student learning but required significant validation measures to ensure minimal bias or generalizations (Dai & Ke, 2022).

Artificial intelligence also poses a complex environmental impact due to the substantial energy required to train and operate generative AI platforms. This energy consumption raises concerns about both the carbon and water footprints, as data center cooling, electricity generation, and server manufacturing contribute to increased water consumption as AI demand grows (Li et al., 2025). While assessments on the environmental impact of AI and large language models have occurred since their inception, many lack comprehensiveness, complicating efforts to understand the extent of their impacts (Berthelot et al., 2025). The CSWE identified environmental justice as an integral part of two competencies in professional social work, with a specific focus on how environmental justice concerns impact human rights and inform policy practice (Cashwell, 2024). Still, there remains limited guidance on the ways in which this can be integrated throughout social work curricula. Further frameworks are needed to provide a lens for how to clearly evaluate the benefits and potential harm that AI use may have for social and environmental justice issues.

Artificial intelligence offers substantial potential, although as growth continues, researchers and educators must remain diligent in addressing limitations and ethical considerations. These implications were heavily considered in the planning and use of

AI for content creation in the ICSE to ensure efficiency in prompting and put a plan for faculty review of content in place to avoid harm to marginalized communities.

Scalability Considerations

Acknowledging future teaching and scalability considerations, the use of AI for content development compared to faculty written cases or standardized patients offers benefits and challenges. Faculty-written cases are widely used as a teaching tool, and use of role plays with these cases supports development of clinical skills in both assessment and intervention. Benefits of these case studies are that they are often grounded in specific theory and practice purposes aligned with curricular content focus, and that the faculty member has a familiarity with the case over time and can adapt details based on current practice. However, a limitation of these types of case studies is that they rely on assessment of past, static situations that do not change or evolve in response to clinical intervention or in-the-moment clinical judgment. These case studies are often individually focused and cannot always represent the power dynamics, full range of sociopolitical factors, and relational dynamics that shape everyday practice (Kourgiantakis et al., 2020). Standardized clients have also been used for simulation in clinical skills training as they provide emotionally responsive and real-time interaction that support the development of skills in relational connection, emotional attunement, and clinical decision-making guided by ethics (Bogo et al., 2011; Logie et al., 2013). A challenge of using standardized clients is often the time and resource intensive capacity needed.

In contrast, AI-based simulations may offer greater consistency and scalability and create space for ongoing skills rehearsal across a range of scenarios, but they also carry the risk of oversimplifying responses, recreating implicit biases, and prioritizing cognitive decision making over self-reflective and attuned clinical practice (Crawford, 2021). Given that social work and counseling professions are based in the development of a therapeutic relationship as the vehicle for all change, these nuanced skills in relationship development must always be at the forefront, whether that is given a pedagogical choice of AI integrated design, or more traditional tools for learning. Given both the benefits and potential cautions, AI simulations are best understood not as replacements for human-centered pedagogies, but as complementary tools that can expand access to practice opportunities when intentionally embedded within reflective, relational, and values-driven social work education.

While AI can support the creativity and diversity of case materials, responsibility for clinical judgment, ethical decision-making, supervision, evaluation of student competence, and relational processes must remain under the guidance of clinical professionals, or in higher education contexts, faculty. Positioning AI as a useful teaching support and organizational tool, rather than a source of clinical or evaluative guidance, helps ensure that innovation enhances the relational, ethical, and supervisory foundations shared across social work, counseling, and psychology training.

ICSE DESIGN AND DEVELOPMENT

Exploring Existing Methods and Practices

With an understanding of best practices in the use of case studies and simulation, the instructional designer explored potential methods to expand the use of case studies. Criteria for consideration included the ability to increase interactivity and realism without increasing cognitive load, the necessary financial and human resources, the capacity for customization, and scalability. The instructional designer sought out existing examples of interactive case studies to examine work by other learning institutions and how they were balancing the need for more engagement with limited resources. Examples included utilizing website design to organize complex case studies with clickable navigation to different information related to the case, creating video scenarios with embedded questions or prompts, developing case studies with interactive elements using eLearning authoring software, role playing with standardized patients (either in person or through video conference), and purchasing licenses for a virtual reality case simulation platform. Each existing option was reviewed based on previously identified criteria. The financial resources required to create video scenarios, employ standardized patients, or purchase licenses for a virtual simulation platform all required from $10,000 to $50,000 or more, making those options challenging. In contrast, website-based case studies lacked the desired level of interactivity.

The instructional designer proposed the use of Articulate Storyline, one of many eLearning authoring tools used to create interactive online learning experiences, to the directors of the online and on-campus MSW programs. This software utilizes a slide-based interface similar to Microsoft PowerPoint, but offers custom interactions, branching scenarios, and advanced quizzing features in a web accessible format. The instructional designer had previous experience using Articulate Storyline to create interactive learning activities and knew the software's capabilities. Using Articulate Storyline required dedicated time but offered full customization and options for scalability. An existing license held by the university was available, incurring no additional financial costs, although it is normally an annual subscription of approximately $900-1200, depending on subscription plan. To reduce the time required to develop new or expanded case study content, the use of AI to assist with planning and developing case study and simulation content was discussed. Based on the review of research and existing work at other higher education institutions, a plan was put into place to partner with AI to assist with content creation with appropriate content review and vetting, then utilize Articulate Storyline to develop the ICSE.

New Content Development

To prepare for content development, the instructional designer and social work faculty discussed case types, families, and situations that would enable students to evaluate and assess clients, achieve course learning objectives, meet CSWE competencies, and prepare for field experiences. Other considerations included ensuring demographic and experiential diversity, opportunities to apply trauma-informed and culturally responsive practices, and the incorporation of social work practice at the individual, family, group, organizational, and community levels. The decision to utilize AI to support content creation created opportunities to expand the case studies beyond the existing faculty-written cases; however, it was imperative that AI remain a support rather than a replacement and not dictate how students navigate simulated case situations.

Articulate Storyline provided a means of building an interactive platform for students to navigate through different screens and interact with clickable content, allowing for larger amounts of information to be presented in an organized way to reduce cognitive load. The instructional designer suggested that, in addition to developing specific case studies of individuals or families (micro level of social work practice), AI could be utilized to assist in the development of an entire community (mezzo level of social work practice), immersing students in the clients' living, working, and schooling environments and available resources. This opened the door to including the micro, mezzo, and macro levels of social work practice and a more immersive and holistic experience.

Lacking significant experience utilizing AI for case studies, the instructional designer initially kept the content development strategy loosely defined until an initial case was tested, avoiding assumptions about output quality and appropriateness. A free OpenAI ChatGPT 4.0 account was utilized for AI-generated content. Work was done in a single saved thread of prompts, ensuring the ability to reference previous prompts and responses for consistency.

Here is the first prompt used:

"Provide details about a family that can act as a case study to be used in a Master of Social Work program. Provide enough information so that students can analyze the family situation using different social work theories, identify potential interventions, and apply trauma-informed principles."

ChatGPT's output included a family of four from Guatemala, undocumented residents facing immigration challenges, adjustment to the United States, fears of eviction and deportation, recent job loss, financial instability, alcoholism, depression, anxiety, a history of abuse, medical issues, and academic struggles among the children. The case information was organized into sections:

- Family Members: *Information on each family member, including name, age, gender, employment or academic status, and school or community involvement*
- Family Background & Strengths: *A history of past challenges, current situation, family values, and strengths*
- Current Challenges: *An explanation of the family's current challenges, including perspectives from different family members, their impact, and the reason for initial social work referral.*
- Social Work Analysis & Intervention Strategies: *A list of applicable social work theories and potential interventions students could suggest, based on working with a specific family member or the entire family.*
- Discussion Questions for MSW Students: *Suggested questions for use as case-related discussion prompts.*

The output was reviewed by a social work faculty member and the instructional designer to identify whether the case and its details met identified needs, and how adjustments to prompting could improve the output. It was determined that the case provided cultural diversity compared to existing cases, although the family's challenges were more extensive than desired and included multiple stereotypes associated with immigrant families. Additional prompting of ChatGPT was used to retain specific details – including family member identities and demographics, challenges related to acclimating to the United States, the children's experiences of stress, anxiety, and academic struggles, and employment challenges – while requesting the removal of other elements. The removal of the elements of alcoholism, history of abuse, depression, and medical issues alleviated the intensity of the challenges faced by the family and reduced redundancy with other existing cases. To monitor changes in ChatGPT's output, individual prompt adjustments were made to analyze differences. With each individual prompt, ChatGPT produced a revised version of the entire output. Through continued prompting, ChatGPT produced a case that met identified needs with appropriate content.

Using multiple prompts in the initial case study was less efficient but ultimately proved successful in demonstrating how ChatGPT manages changes and adjusts output. This process provided insight into how adjusting the first prompt could yield better results earlier, enhancing efficiency going forward. For subsequent case studies, prompts to ChatGPT included more specific details to avoid redundancies, ensure specific coursework needs were addressed, and request diversity in challenges and situations.

Requests for additional case study examples included the following:

- "Provide a case study that is appropriate for use in an MSW program that includes a married couple with no children, who are doing well financially, but struggling with infertility and the strain on their marriage it is causing."
- "Provide a case study that is appropriate for use in an MSW program that includes a family with multiple children where the mother is struggling to take care of children while also being the primary caregiver for her own mother who refuses to move into an assisted living facility. Include additional details related to the children that add complexity to the situation but avoid overlapping challenges faced in other case studies created in this thread."
- "Provide a case study that is appropriate for use in an MSW program that includes a single adult who is non-binary and works either an evening or overnight job that is causing issues with sleep as well as maintaining friendships and other relationships. Include relevant details and ensure this case is diverse from other cases created in this thread."
- "Provide a case study that is appropriate for use in an MSW program that includes a three-generation household that is culturally diverse from other cases in this thread. Include challenges faced by the grandparent around losing independence, challenges faced related to becoming caregivers to parents and children simultaneously and create other challenges that this family could face that are realistic but also do not have too much overlap with other cases created in this thread."

Added specificity in the prompts to ChatGPT allowed for more efficient prompting, improving the rate at which quality content could be created. However, no cases were used based on the initial prompt alone. Some cases required more changes than others, but all AI-generated cases needed some modification. Minor changes included adjustments in ages to avoid cases with similarly aged children, changing names, or altering places of employment and were done manually rather than generating new output from AI. Larger changes included requesting that children face distinct challenges, as multiple cases involved children with school-related anxiety. These changes required additional prompting from AI as the changes affected multiple aspects of the case.

To explore ChatGPT's capabilities for expanded case details, referral paperwork for social work or counseling, mental health questionnaires (e.g., depression and anxiety screeners, biopsychosocial assessments), and a transcript of a potential intake meeting were requested for one case study. ChatGPT was able to quickly create samples of referrals, questionnaire results, and an intake screening transcript. The material was reviewed by social work faculty to determine validity and appropriateness for the associated case study material. The referrals and questionnaire results were deemed appropriate, although the transcript required additional prompting and manual adjustments to be appropriate for student use.

Expanding Existing Content

In addition to developing new case studies, existing case studies for the program were uploaded to ChatGPT with prompts requesting additional information about the family and situation consistent with what was developed in the new cases. ChatGPT produced a more expansive family history, additional details about current challenges, potential social work theories to apply, and relevant questionnaire results. The output for the first existing case study included unwanted changes to the original details of the family and their situation. Due to these cases already being developed and agreed upon by social work faculty, the integrity of the family situation in these cases needed to remain unchanged. For subsequent case studies uploaded to ChatGPT, the prompt was modified to request no alteration of details about the family or situation, only to expand and provide additional information. This process provided a consistent experience between the newly developed and existing case studies.

Once a desirable number of case studies were completed, ChatGPT was utilized to experiment with developing a fictitious community for the clients of the case studies. The development of an entire community, including demographics, strengths and challenges, and available resources, would allow the case study experience to become more immersive and allow for the application of macro level social work concepts and frameworks to cases.

The following prompt was used:

"Create a fictitious community for an interactive platform where the individuals and families from each of the cases within this prompt thread could realistically live. Include population statistics as well as comprehensive information around the following: demographics (race/ethnicity/income/religion/etc.), housing availability with breakdown of price ranges, community resources available that are typically seen in a town of the identified size, strengths and challenges of the community, along with any other relevant information you find necessary."

ChatGPT quickly provided information for a fictitious town called Greenwood Heights with a population of 20,000, including:

- A detailed percentage breakdown of the town's population by race, ethnicity, languages spoken, and religion

- An outline of community resources and their offerings in the town, including schools, health care facilities, a community center, a library, places of worship, police and fire stations, public transportation, and outreach programs
- Recommendations for the number of grocery stores, restaurants, and other food services suitable for a town of this size
- Recommendations for available community programs for youth, teens, adults, and seniors.

A social work faculty member specializing in group, organizational, and community level social work practice was consulted to review the output from ChatGPT related to the fictitious town. They were asked to consider the content included in the output as well as specific course assignments to determine if the inclusion of the town information would be beneficial for students. The faculty member expressed enthusiasm about incorporating macro level concepts into case studies and offered suggestions for additional content. Macro level concepts included community organizations, program development, and types of advocacy and intervention with larger systems such as organizations and institutions. The MSW program's Organization and Program Development course includes assignments that require assessing community organizations, the populations they serve, and unmet needs. With expanded details about the town's community center, this course could utilize the ICSE across multiple assignments. Additional prompting to ChatGPT generated information about the community center's programming and organizational structure including employees, funding, and history.

All output from AI was saved in text documents and stored in a shared cloud-based drive for access, so cases could be reviewed or uploaded to an AI platform for revisions if needed. The set of cases and community information were built into the Articulate Storyline software by the instructional designer over six months, completed in addition to their regular work and projects, creating an interactive platform for students to explore the town and its residents. The first draft of the ICSE included a clickable menu of demographic information, an interactive map to see the housing and public transportation layout, clickable icons to represent buildings and resources within the town, and a resident map linking to specific case studies. The ICSE would allow learners to not only review case studies but navigate and explore the community those clients live in and view their proximity to resources and public transportation.

To prevent the adoption of the ICSE from becoming a barrier to learning, significant consideration was given to user experience and accessibility. The Web Content Accessibility Guidelines (WCAG) and Articulate Storyline's built in accessibility checker were referenced to ensure accessibility standards were met, creating an equitable learning experience. The role of perceived usefulness and ease of use in technology acceptance, as identified in the Technology Acceptance Model (Davis, 1989), was considered throughout the design and incorporated into ICSE testing and feedback collection to support successful adoption.

FACULTY REVIEW AND CHANGE MANAGEMENT

Review Process

The instructional designer and social work faculty collaborated throughout development to review and validate content, though this focused on individual cases. Upon completion of the first draft of the ICSE, full-time social work faculty were recruited to test and review its content prior to distribution to all faculty or implementation in courses. Seven faculty volunteered to participate, at which point they were given access to the ICSE to review, attended an informational meeting with the instructional designer, and provided feedback on the content and their experience using the ICSE.

Transparency with faculty around the use of AI was a priority. During the informational meeting, faculty were informed that the cases included in the ICSE were a combination of cases newly created by ChatGPT and existing cases expanded by ChatGPT. The instructional designer explained that leveraging AI for content development allowed for additional customization to accommodate faculty, course, and student needs. The rationale behind utilizing AI, the strategy of its use and potential concerns were discussed, and it was noted that while the content had already been reviewed by some faculty members, a more comprehensive review was needed. Faculty were asked to review the details of the cases and provide feedback, focusing on appropriateness, diversity, and avoiding harm to students in marginalized groups. After reviewing the ICSE, faculty members discussed their feedback individually with the instructional designer to ensure clarity and confidence in how necessary content updates would be made.

Faculty Feedback

Feedback from faculty was predominantly positive after an in-depth review of the case content, although many were focused more on feelings of excitement around the immersive nature of the ICSE rather than the content itself. In future reviews of cases for appropriateness, providing content in text form will be considered to avoid distraction. Collecting feedback via meeting rather than a form or survey allowed for focusing the conversation on the analysis of case study content. All seven faculty members were satisfied with the level of diversity and none of them identified obvious evidence of any potential harm to students in marginalized communities. Some faculty members suggested and assisted with minor modifications to cases to either increase diversity in the experiences or to create more consistency within a case based on their knowledge of specific situations. One faculty member identified that no clients were working shift work and requested that an adjustment be made to one client's employment situation. Another faculty member requested a change in how a client responded to a family challenge to better align with behavior manifestations of their specific diagnosis.

Due to the importance of collecting meaningful feedback on case content and their appropriateness, general feedback related to user experience was not requested until content-related feedback had been collected and implemented. A common question that arose was related to what else was possible with the ICSE. The instructional designer discussed what was possible within the Articulate Storyline software as well as what type of content could be developed with the use of AI, emphasizing that not all content that could be developed by AI should be used in this type of activity. Two faculty members asked about utilizing AI to create images. The instructional designer referenced research by Cordero et al. (2025) on bias in AI-generated images as the rationale for not using AI-generated visuals in the cases, which faculty understood. A second faculty member asked about the use of maps in the ICSE. They commented that the maps used were static images with icons on them, asking if it was possible to allow students to zoom and pan around the community, using platforms such as Google Maps as an example. The instructor designer indicated that currently, the software and technology being used would not allow for this but they would continue to explore possibilities for increasing interactivity specifically with community maps. All other requests by faculty were either able to be incorporated or were retained for a future iteration after running the pilot.

Two faculty members requested additional information be added to the ICSE with consideration for their specific course and assignments, which were both able to be completed prior to the pilot. One requested including restaurants and bars to incorporate a recovering alcoholic's prior favorite location and proximity to alcohol access into a case study. The second requested an assisted living facility for work with older adults and their caregivers. A request was also made for the development of cases within the mental health clinic in the community. These cases would be specifically from the perspective of a clinician rather than the client, offering opportunities for students to identify ethical issues in the handling of a situation, identify signs of burnout, or assist a clinician through an intake meeting with prompts to ask the client. To properly dedicate the appropriate time to that idea and the necessary content, it was decided to further develop a plan to implement those cases in a later iteration of the ICSE.

After all content-related feedback had been addressed, overall functionality and user experience of the ICSE was discussed amongst the instructional designer and faculty members. With the extensive amount of information provided in the ICSE, the ability to easily navigate the activity was a priority. Faculty members were able to provide helpful feedback around the way information was presented to students and many expressed feelings of excitement around the ability to provide students with a more interactive learning experience.

Faculty Perspectives on Artificial Intelligence

Feedback during faculty review suggested that faculty perspectives on the use of AI to build case study content varied considerably. Two faculty members indicated that they felt reservations about the activity during the informational meeting when the use of AI was brought up, although the transparency with the process for content development and review eased some of those reservations. One faculty member indicated they were "not completely against the use of AI" but were concerned about the students and other faculty who are against using AI and how they would feel about the activity incorporating its use. In considering this feedback, Zhai's (2024) comprehensive framework on initial perceptions, learning processes, and the integration of AI into teaching practices provided a useful lens for understanding variation in faculty comfort with the ICSE. The framework identifies four roles – "Observer, Adopter, Collaborator, and Innovator" – that reflect differing levels of acceptance and engagement with AI in pedagogy (Zhai, 2024, p 2). These categories helped clarify how faculty might be supported at different stages of comfort and identify pathways for increasing meaningful classroom use of the ICSE.

Four of the seven faculty members included in the review process were open to its use and comfortable with the result, especially with their knowledge of the content review process. One faculty member who had consulted on the community information, indicated wanting to use AI to enhance assignments using the expanded information that would be available to students. The instructional designer shared recommendations for how to prompt AI efficiently for the faculty member to test.

Their prompt to ChatGPT is as follows:

"Create a discussion forum that focuses on a case study for an organization. Students are hired as consultants to help Greenwood Heights Community Center. The leadership team has determined they need an assessment of the current progress of the organization, and support in strategic planning for next steps in their growth, as well as determining what kind of funding they should begin to consider supporting that growth."

Initial output generated by ChatGPT provided a potential discussion topic but lacked specific objectives or program evaluation tools. Additional prompting generated appropriate necessary background knowledge of program evaluation covered in previous topics of the course. Subsequent prompts for the Community Center case directed AI to create specific tasks for discussion forum instructions, including identifying one funding opportunity, conducting a mini strategic analysis using a SWOT framework (Strengths, Weakness, Opportunities, Threats), and prompting students to develop one goal with objectives, a theory of change, outcome evaluation, and trauma-informed care principles. This improved the specificity of the assignment and integration of course content, showing promise for the use of AI to create assignments that are focused on measurable outcomes closely connected with the course content.

All faculty reviewing the ICSE were asked to share any aspects of the activity or process that made them feel more comfortable with AI being utilized to prepare for this potential obstacle. Faculty comfort with AI use was the strongest when they understood the extensive review process. Six of the seven faculty members indicated that the level of review the cases underwent made them feel comfortable with AI being used. Three faculty members suggested that if case content had not gone through any review, they would not be interested in using the ICSE. This feedback on the perception of using AI for case study content influenced the communication plan for the full release of the ICSE. Disclosure of AI use would include that all content developed by AI went through rigorous review by multiple social work faculty members and explain that all client information included in AI prompts was fictional.

PILOT IMPLEMENTATION: APPLYING THE CONCEPTUAL FRAMEWORK IN PRACTICE

Aligned with the body of knowledge on clinical learning from theory and practice, the ICSE was piloted to investigate how AI-aided, simulation-supported learning could function across different teaching formats. After faculty review, the ICSE was piloted in two 14-week graduate-level social work courses taught by the same instructor to maintain a consistent teaching approach and communication style. One course was delivered online in an asynchronous format (Organization and Program Development; n = 12), while the second was in-person (Social Work Practice with Families; n = 13). The courses were chosen intentionally for their different teaching methods and levels of practice to examine the ICSE's perceived usefulness, ease of use, and instructional flexibility. These considerations were linked to the Technology Acceptance Model and previous discussions about adoption and engagement. In both courses, students received an initial introduction to the ICSE through a video demonstration or in-class walkthrough. Students used the tool to complete one case-based assignment and then filled out an anonymous survey reflecting on their experience.

Pilot Course 1: Organization and Program Development (Macro Practice Context)

The Organization and Program Development course, offered asynchronously, focused on leadership, organizational assessment, program planning, evaluation, and systems-level social work practice. Students identified an organization—often related to their field placement or professional experience—and applied the course concepts through discussion and applied assignments. The ICSE was introduced in the first week with a video demonstration, providing time for students to become familiar with it. The ICSE served as the main simulation tool for engaging with an imagined community organization, Greenwood Heights Community Center. The community center reflected real-world organizational complexity by offering layered access to information, including publicly available organizational data and more detailed content related to structure, funding, trauma-informed practice, and evaluation processes. Some information was intentionally left incomplete to mirror authentic organizational conditions, requiring students to assess, infer, and question—skills important in macro social work practice.

To place the organization within its ecological context, students explored a GIS-based community map within the ICSE, which included demographic, socioeconomic, and cultural data such as age, income, race, language, employment, and household composition. This approach supported prior literature that highlighted experiential learning and cognitive scaffolding by allowing students to connect organizational analysis with community context instead of relying solely on abstract descriptions. Toward the end of the course, students used their accumulated skills to consult the organization in three areas: organizational assessment, strategic planning questions, and potential funding pathways. They shared their analyses through written or video discussion posts and collaborated with peers as co-consultants, reinforcing collaborative learning and reflective practice.

Pilot Course 2: Clinical Family Practice (Micro Practice Context)

The Clinical Family Practice course, offered in-person, emphasized foundational family therapy models while also addressing diversity, intersectionality, and sociocultural context. This course already included experiential methods such as role play and case discussion, making it suitable for exploring how the ICSE could enhance simulation-based learning. Starting in Week 2, students used the ICSE to investigate community-level resources like housing, schools, and healthcare. They also examined how family location and neighborhood context connect with access to services. A specific family case scenario was consistently used over multiple weeks, allowing students to apply different theoretical and assessment lenses that aligned with the weekly course content.

The ICSE provided a reliable but adaptable case environment that included family background, presenting concerns, and occasionally documentation including intake notes or standardized assessments. This setup allowed students to practice assessment, engagement, and intervention planning while navigating both the available information and gaps in the family narrative, similar to real clinical work. As the course continued, students worked through multiple family scenarios to practice specific skills (such as assessment, genogram and ecomap creation, and intervention planning) before integrating these skills in role plays. Peers provided feedback on clinical approaches, cultural considerations, and engagement strategies, supporting reflective learning and skill differentiation discussed earlier in the literature.

Modality-Specific Adaptations and Instructional Flexibility

In both courses, the ICSE showed flexibility in supporting learning across different teaching methods. In the on-campus clinical course, the tool acted as a shared simulation space that supported live role plays done later and group discussions. In an asynchronous setting, the ICSE enabled an opportunity for case analysis through discussion forums, written consultation tasks, and video assignments. Potential adaptations, like live video conferencing simulations, recorded role plays, or small group exercises, show how AI-supported simulation can enhance experiential learning while being responsive to faculty workload and course design. These specific uses reflect earlier discussions on perceived usefulness and ease of use, demonstrating how the ICSE aligns with both educational goals and practical constraints in higher education.

Outcomes and Lessons Learned

The instructor observed that the students' ability to toggle between the documentation, initial client information, and neighborhood or family resources created an organic flow of information. This dynamic use of the online perceived as more engaging than reading and discussing text-based case studies and supported students' ability to layer information in ways that enhanced assessment skills and overall comprehension. Rubrics aligned to practice behaviors, such as managing ethical dilemmas in a simulated session, provided measurable evidence of professional competence. Anecdotally, students shared they hoped for even more background information about the case studies, showing the limitation of any one case scenario. However, often in social services, clinicians deal with families that may have limited ability to articulate their experiences, either due to trauma, lack of trust in the system, or missing information for themselves. Students were encouraged in these moments to view gaps in information as an important part of the work with families.

Student Feedback

Students were surveyed to collect feedback on their experience using the ICSE, their perceptions of ease of use and usefulness, and the quality of content and organization, taking into consideration the Technology Acceptance Model (Davis, 1989). Specifically, students were asked to complete an online survey in which they rated their comfort navigating the ICSE, the clarity and organization of the content, whether the ICSE supported successful assignment completion, and whether it improved their ability to make decisions related to client care or organizational practice, using a 5-point Likert scale. Students were also asked to provide open-ended feedback on their overall experience using the ICSE and provide any suggestions for further enhancements.

Participants were asked to rate their experience navigating the ICSE site ranging on a scale from Extremely Comfortable to Not Comfortable. Most participants reported that the ICSE was easy to use, with 84.6% of respondents indicating being either extremely comfortable or mostly comfortable navigating the ICSE and that the content was clear and organized. When asked about ability to successfully complete their assignment, all respondents answered either strongly agree, agree, or neutral, with no respondents indicating that they were unsuccessful on their assignments due to the ICSE. 76.9% of respondents indicated that they believed using the ICSE improved their ability to make decisions regarding client care or in program development processes with the community-based organization, although it is acknowledged that this perception is likely based on limited experience in the social services field.

Open ended feedback provided by students was specific and contributed to the understanding the ICSE's range of use and potential improvements. Multiple students expressed that they preferred utilizing the ICSE for case studies over reading text, highlighting the level of detail and the holistic view of the client gained from seeing their community and access to resources. One student stated, "it felt more real to be able to direct a client specifically to the community center's support meetings with a day and time instead of using a general statement to find a meeting." Another student stated that they "appreciated the level of detail in the web of relationships, seeing a client in a case employed at a place in the community." Common themes of other comments included liking the documentation included with cases, the number of cases and their diversity being useful, and feeling that ICSE was more applicable or closer to real world situations than reading case studies in text.

Areas of improvement were also identified, and suggestions were made by student participants. Twenty percent of respondents indicated being either somewhat comfortable or not comfortable navigating the ICSE. Due to the anonymity of the survey, more specific details could not be obtained regarding the rationale or specific issues faced, making it unclear whether there were issues that could be addressed or if more instruction on using the ICSE was required. Going forward in feedback collection, when students indicate being either somewhat or not comfortable navigating the ICSE, the survey will prompt for additional open-ended questioning to gain more insight into any challenges. Suggestions made by students included adding more statistics related to challenges faced by the community, incorporating additional details specific to evaluation and applying intervention strategies, and bringing in documentation for all families instead of only some.

Survey results were reviewed by the instructional designer and faculty participating in the pilot to identify strengths, challenges, and a plan for improvements prior to further implementation. Results around ease of use were promising, although additional means of providing directions will be included to improve feedback related to usability, especially in asynchronous courses where faculty explanation is more limited. Student suggestions around including more documentation will be discussed with additional social work faculty to ensure adding documentation does not interfere with existing assignments that might require students to complete their own documentation as part of the assignment. The additional statistics recommended will be implemented into the ICSE prior to the next course session. Feedback collection will continue as more courses incorporate the ICSE.

IMPLICATIONS AND FUTURE DIRECTIONS

Limitations

The use of AI in the development of the ICSE allowed for more efficiency in creating content as well as increased diversity in case scenarios. However, faculty time remained a limitation for faculty members reviewing content and providing feedback. Faculty indicated that it was easier to review content than to create it themselves, although many admitted that it was still difficult to dedicate time to complete the review.

A limitation of the pilot was that the ICSE was not tested in two identical courses in both on-ground and online formats, but rather two different courses with varying areas of focus: one being program and organization development, and the other centered on clinical practice with families. Additionally, the instructor noted that in the asynchronous format, students were provided a choice of using the ICSE or a field practicum organization, slightly limiting its use and the discussion related to ICSE content. In the final integration discussion assignment, students were asked to play the role of a social work consultant and use program evaluation skills to advise the organization's development. In this use of the ICSE, the instructor identified a need for additional information to be built into the case scenario over time so that they could adequately highlight this as an example in weekly videos throughout the semester. The instructor noted that understanding the community organization case scenario's depth required students to navigate effectively through the ICSE's embedded tabs. Students reported that pre-recorded videos were less interactive, and found that if they missed a step initially, they found some difficulty in getting back to the page they needed with relevant case information. In future classes, the instructor plans to hold a live video session to guide the class through the case scenario, allowing students to pose live questions in response to practice navigating the ICSE. The development and use of the ICSE demonstrated potential for increasing active and experiential learning and engagement for the social work classroom.

Future Research

Future research areas include the continuation of a formal evaluation process of the ICSE in online asynchronous and on-campus classrooms, as well as in courses beyond the organizational and clinical family practice courses piloted. Exploring the relationship between increased competency mastery after using the ICSE compared to traditional teaching methods will be essential. It will be important to explore differences in levels of competency and behavioral outcome mastery in clinical practice domains – such as assessment, case conceptualization, intervention planning, and evaluation (CSWE EPAS, 2022) – between courses using the ICSE and those relying on more traditional teaching approaches that prioritize discussion and written formats.

Future Teaching and Scalability

Future teaching recommendations include examining and developing opportunities for a range of instructors across the social work curriculum to utilize the ICSE to incorporate varied perspectives on the effectiveness of the case study process. Supporting instructors in some level of learning AI prompting could create case scenarios that continue to reflect the aims of each unique classroom. Continued feedback from social work faculty to increase familiarity with the types of assignments that could be used with the ICSE will drive updates and improvements to further tailor content to specific learning aims and competencies. It will also be important to review ICSE content on a regular schedule informed by feedback and curriculum revisions. Saved text versions of ChatGPT output from the case development process can be reused by uploading them to an AI platform, if needed, to support updates or revisions to cases.

Designing a customized ICSE with AI assistance requires careful planning to determine community and case study content, knowledge of effective AI prompting, access to an eLearning authoring tool, and personnel with the skills to use it. In higher education institutions where an authoring tool or specialized support is not available, partnering with AI for content development can still enhance case study experiences and provide a more holistic approach to learning.

With consideration for future interdisciplinary use, the ICSE was presented at a university-hosted professional development session for faculty across disciplines focused on innovation in teaching and learning. Faculty members from different disciplines including biology and nursing requested follow up meetings to discuss how a similar Immersive Case Study Environment model could be incorporated at either a course or program level. There are significant opportunities to continue expanding this work, in both research and teaching, to improve the student learning experience and skill development.

REFERENCES

Asakura, K. (2024). Toward a critical approach to simulation-based social work education: Guidelines for designing simulated client case scenarios. *Journal of Social Work Education*, *60*(1), 102–114.

Asakura, K., & Bogo, M. (2021). Editorial: The use of simulation in advancing clinical social work education and practice. *Clinical Social Work*, *49*, 111–116.

Baker, E., & Jenney, A. (2023). Virtual simulations to train social works for competency-based learning: A scoping review. *Journal of Social Work Education*, *59*(1), 8–31.

Berthelot, A., Caron, E., Jay, M., & Lefèvre, L. (2025, July). Understanding the environmental impact of generative AI services. *Communications of the ACM*, *68*(7), 46–53.

Bogo, M., Regehr, C., Katz, E., Logie, C., & Mylopoulos, M. (2011). Developing a tool for assessing students' reflections on their practice. *Social Work Education*, *30*(02), 186–194.

Cashwell, S. (2024). Bringing environmental justice to the practice setting: Putting the environment in Person-in-Environment. *Journal of Human Rights and Social Work*, •••, 1–8.

Cordero, D., Zhao, Y., Diaz, P., & Weiss, G. M. (2025). Unveiling bias: Analyzing race and gender disparities in AI-generated imagery. *2025 IEEE 49th Annual Computers, Software, and Applications Conference (COMPSAC), Computers, Software, and Applications Conference (COMPSAC), 2025 IEEE 49th Annual, COMPSAC*, 318–323. https://doi.org/DOI: 10.1109/COMPSAC65507.2025.00051

Council on Social Work Education. (2022). Educational policy and accreditation standards (EPAS:6, 7, 8 AND 9:).

Crawford, K. (2021). *The atlas of AI: Power, politics, and the planetary costs of artificial intelligence*. Yale University Press.

Dai, C., & Ke, F. (2022). Educational applications of artificial intelligence in simulation-based learning: A systematic mapping review. *Computers and Education: Artificial Intelligence*, *3*. Advance online publication. DOI: 10.1016/j.caeai.2022.100087

Damiano, A. D., Lauría, E. J. M., Sarmiento, C., & Zhao, N. (2024). Early perceptions of teaching and learning using generative AI in higher education. *Journal of Educational Technology, 52*(3), 346–375.

Davis, F. D. (1989). Perceived usefulness, perceived ease of use, and user acceptance of information technology. *Management Information Systems Quarterly, 13*(3), 319–340.

Drisko, J., & Grady, M. D. (2018). Teaching evidence-based practice using cases in social work education. Families in Society, 99(3), 269-282. https://doi.org/ (Original work published 2018)DOI: 10.1177/1044389418785331

Harvard Business School. (2021). Case Method: 100 Years. Harvard Business School. https://www.hbs.edu/case-method-100

Howell, R. A. (2021). Engaging students in education for sustainable development: The benefits of active learning, reflective practices and flipped classroom pedagogies. *Journal of Cleaner Production, 325*, 129318.

Jefferies, G., Fox, M., Dodds, L., & Davis, C. (2025). A theoretical framework for understanding the importance of implementing simulation in social work education. *Social Work Education, 44*(2), 354–367.

Kolb, D. A. (1984). *Experiential learning: experience as the source of learning and development.* Prentice-Hall.

Kourgiantakis, T., Sewell, K. M., Hu, R., Logan, J., & Bogo, M. (2020). Simulation in social work education: A scoping review. *Research on Social Work Practice, 30*(4), 433–450.

Lazcoz, G., & de Miguel, I. (2025). Is more data always better? On alternative policies to mitigate bias in Artifical Intelligence health systems. *Bioethics, 39*, 414–424.

Li, P., Yang, J., Islam, M. A., & Ren, S. (2025). Making AI less "thirsty": Uncovering and addressing the secret water footprint of AI models. *Communications of the ACM, 68*(7), 54–61.

Logie, C., Bogo, M., Regehr, C., & Regehr, G. (2013). A critical appraisal of the use of standardized client simulations in social work education. *Journal of Social Work Education, 49*(1), 66–80.

Martella, A. M., & Schneider, D. W. (2024). A reflection on the current state of active learning research. *The Journal of Scholarship of Teaching and Learning, 24*(3), 119–136.

Mzwri, K., & Turcsányi-Szabo, M. (2025). Bridging LMS and generative AI: Dynamic course content integration (DCCI) for enhancing student satisfaction and engagement via the ask ME assistant. *Journal of Computers in Education*. Advance online publication. DOI: 10.1007/s40692-025-00367-w

Penn, M. L., Currie, C. S. M., Hoad, K. A., & O'Brien, F. A. (2016). The use of case studies in OR teaching. *Higher Education Pedagogies*, *1*(1), 16–25. DOI: 10.1080/23752696.2015.1134201

Popil, I. (2011). Promotion of critical thinking by using case studies as teaching method. *Nurse Education Today*, *31*(2), 204–207. DOI: 10.1016/j.nedt.2010.06.002

Rogers, L., & MacCormac, A. (2025). Finding a balance: Using a pre-post test to evaluate the effectiveness of scenario-based learning using a blended approach among undergraduate nursing students. *Nurse Education Today*, *147*. Advance online publication. DOI: 10.1016/j.nedt.2025.106573

Sweller, J., Van Merriënboer, J. J., & Paas, F. (2019). Cognitive architecture and instructional design: 20 years later. *Educational Psychology Review*, *31*(2), 261–292.

Thistlethwaite, J. E., Davies, D., Ekeocha, S., Kidd, J. M., & MacDougall, C., Matthews, Purkis, J., & Clay, D. (2012). The effectiveness of case-based learning in health professional education. A BEME systematic review: BEME Guide No. 23. *Medical Teacher*, *34*(6), e421–e444. DOI: 10.3109/0142159X.2012.680939

Torun, F., & Şanal, S. O. (2025). The perspectives of academicians and students regarding the use of generative artificial intelligence in higher education. [IJTE]. *International Journal of Technology in Education*, *8*(1), 65–87.

Zhai, X. (2024). Transforming teachers' roles and agencies in the era of generative AI: Perceptions, acceptance, knowledge, and practices. *Journal of Science Education and Technology*, •••, 1–11.

Zheng, K., Shen, Z., Chen, Z., Che, C., & Zhu, H. (2024). Application of AI-empowered scenario-based simulation teaching mode in cardiovascular disease education. *BMC Medical Education*, *24*, 1003–1013.

KEY TERMS AND DEFINITIONS

Artificial Intelligence (AI): computer system that capable of performing tasks typically associated with human intelligence

Instructional Designer: professionals responsible for creating engaging learning experiences and applying best practices in pedagogy based on evidence-based practices

Large Language Model: an advanced artificial intelligence system trained on massive amounts of text and datasets enabling text generation, translation, and question answering

Macro Level of Social Work Practice: one of three levels of social work practice, focusing on work with the local, national, and global structures and institutions in the wider social environment that affect individuals, groups, and communities including legislative, funding, and large-scale change work

Mezzo Level of Social Work Practice: one of three levels of social work practice, typically focusing on the group dynamics and relationships in larger groupings such as schools, organizations, and other groupings of individuals, allowing a social worker to work to change larger systems through this group focus

Micro Level of Social Work Practice: one of three levels of social work practice in the profession, describing work with individuals and families, which is seen as the small unit of an overall systems approach in social work

Scenario-Based Learning: an active and experiential learning method designed to immerse students in realistic situations to build decision-making skills

Simulation: instructional scenarios to mimic a real-world situation, allowing students to participate in a controlled setting

Chapter 7
Reimagining Social Work Assessment in the Age of AI

David Keegan
https://orcid.org/0009-0000-1903-2895
Excelsia University College, Australia

Bonny Cotter
Excelsia University College, Australia

ABSTRACT

The rapid emergence of generative artificial intelligence (AI) has prompted significant debate within social work education regarding its ethical integration into teaching and assessment. Drawing on a case study from a Master of Social Work program in Australia, the authors describe an assessment redesign that incorporated generative AI tools to scaffold, rather than replace, professional reasoning. Findings from two cohorts reveal mixed responses from students and educators, highlighting benefits such as improved efficiency and skill development alongside concerns about authenticity and academic integrity. The chapter opens with a summary of current perspectives on the role of AI in social work and concludes with practical recommendations for educators, stressing the importance of clear purpose, rubric adjustments, technical readiness, and alignment with ethical codes. Integrating AI into social work education offers opportunities for preparing graduates for technologically integrated practice while preserving core values of empathy, critical thinking, and accountability.

DOI: 10.4018/979-8-3373-4362-4.ch007

INTRODUCTION

Social work is a profession built on the quality of human engagement. Various digital technologies have been edging into the realm of social work since the turn of the 21st century with developments in personal computing, mobile phone technology, social media, and the internet (Babaeva et al., 2023; Kominkiewicz & O'Neil, 2025). Even more so have these technologies become a greater part of tertiary education, leading to reduced face-to-face time and a demand for online learning opportunities (Goldingay et al., 2020; Mooney et al., 2024). However, until recently, technology applications in social work were largely restricted to administrative tools to support efficiency such as keeping case records, secure storage of information, communication efficiency, and to support research.

The COVID-19 pandemic arguably acted as a catalyst for wider adoption of technologies, particularly in the health sector, with accelerated adoption of technologies that facilitated interaction between social worker and client due to the inability to meet in person (Barbosa da Silva et al., 2024). In late 2022, ChatGPT was released to the world (Kamoun et al., 2024) and, whilst the term 'Artificial Intelligence' had been around since the 1950s, the release of ChatGPT made the term more commonplace. It also brought with it the ability for a machine to complete tasks in natural language that were previously considered only possible by a human (Hodgson et al., 2023).

Definitions of AI are varied, and the term is often used to refer to a range of different technologies ranging from machine learning software to Large Language Models (LLMs) and algorithmic decision-making tools. For the sake of simplicity we will use a basic definition of Artificial Intelligence (AI) as referring to machines or programs that perform tasks usually associated with humans (Goldkind, 2021). It needs to be acknowledged that AI is present in many forms of technology that we use daily such as mobile phones, computers, cars and some home devices, making it already part of our everyday lives. However, much of what this chapter focuses on is generative AI which essentially uses a large volume of data and statistical prediction to determine appropriate categorization and responses to a particular set of inputs (Báez et al., 2025; Feuerriegel et al., 2024).

In this chapter we seek to explore the role of social work tertiary educators in responding to the emergence of this technology within a context where there remains no consensus on how and if AI should be integrated into social work practice. We will first explore some of the arguments for and against the integration of AI in tertiary social work education and present an AI literacy focused approach to the integration of AI in assessments. We will then outline our experiences as a result of experimenting with the integration of AI into one assessment in a skills-based unit of a Master of Social Work (Qualifying) program in Australia. We finish with reflections and advice for those seeking to do the same.

ASSESSMENT AND AI LITERACY

AI has the potential to transform the role of social work and the way we engage with clients and each other (Al-Rantisi et al., 2024; Asakura et al., 2020; Boetto, 2025), and therefore social work educators will need to rethink the way they do assessment (Hodgson et al., 2023). Some scholars argue that assessments need to be categorized into 'AI-proof' assessments and 'non-AI-proof' assessments such as the Liu and Bridgeman (2023) two-lane approach. In this approach 'lane 1' is for assessments that are secure or eliminate the potential use of AI. These primarily include in-person oral or skills-based demonstrations. In 'lane 2', AI is permitted and there are no restrictions; however, students are advised on appropriate tools to use based on the characteristics of the assessment. Whilst this approach clearly sets out a methodology that 'secures' assessments that target course level essential skills and knowledge from the use of AI, there is critique about this approach with some suggesting the need for a middle 'lane' where AI is encouraged but with some rules or limits attached (Curtis, 2025).

The two-lane approach seems to be growing in popularity with educational institutions as they seek to reconcile various higher education and industry accreditation requirements which demand evidence of authentic learning. This is reasonable given that traditional assessment approaches in social work, such as essays and written reflections, are easily generated or assisted by AI. The two-lane approach also helps institutions to clearly differentiate learning that is AI assisted and that which is genuinely produced by the student alone. However, we argue that approaches like this reinforce the idea that the use of AI in learning can or should be 'controlled' rather than recognizing the need to also teach skills and knowledge that will help graduates to ethically navigate AI in the workforce once they graduate. Whilst the two-lane approach technically seeks to develop student competency in the use of AI tools, there is a risk that institutions will focus more on the control aspects and less on the resources needed to support the development of student competency in the use of AI technologies. Human services organisations are already adopting AI tools. Social work students need to have the requisite skills and knowledge to determine the appropriate ethical use cases, and social work educational institutions have a responsibility to prepare students for this scenario with hopes that they may positively shape if, how, and when AI may be used. This is even more so critical given the nature of social work as a helping profession for those who are psychologically, socially, spiritually, and physically vulnerable.

Rather than a focus on secured and non-secured assessments, we have instead taken an AI literacy approach which emphasizes the need for educators to equip students with the necessary knowledge, skills, and mindset to be able to critically evaluate and utilize the potential of AI whilst also learning to collaborate with others to ensure benefit for the broader social good (Kong et al., 2025; Long & Magerko, 2020). This approach shifts the focus from controlling AI to exploring the opportunities for AI to scaffold skills and knowledge development. Simultaneously, this approach aims to introduce AI elements to the classroom and assessments in order to provide opportunities to model appropriate uses of AI whilst also developing an understanding of its limits and risks.

Importantly, we propose that a social work view of AI literacy requires not just a simple functional awareness of AI applications and how to use them appropriately, but also a structural and systemic lens that recognizes the potential impact on the broader social and environmental good and the role of institutional accountability in achieving this. In other words, we need graduates that are able to recognize and exercise their individual responsibilities whilst also ensuring that organisations, governments, and corporations are accountable to the broader social good with regards to things like environmental impact (Guest et al., 2025), the reproduction of dominant colonial discourse (Russ-Smith & Lazarus, 2025), and the social and political disruption resulting from misinformation (Flenady & Sparrow, 2025; Guest et al., 2025).

These issues also spill over into the educational context with risks including the authenticity of student work (Corbin et al., 2025; Ivanov, 2023), the ability of students to find and discern accurate information (Flenady & Sparrow, 2025), the threat to critical and analytical thinking (Darwin et al., 2024; Zhou et al., 2024), and the potential outsourcing of knowledge creation to AI (Hodgson et al., 2023). Social work has traditionally been taught in a face-to-face context given its strong emphasis on relational skills and the development of critically diverse perspectives on social wellbeing and justice (Hodgson et al., 2022). Whilst technology has been slowly creeping into the delivery of social work education through online learning (Goldingay et al., 2020), the addition of freely available AI tools along with neoliberal drivers to deliver more with less, means that there are real challenges to the delivery of authentic learning in social work education. One particular challenge that is compounded by the advancements in AI, is to resist the further removal of the human from social work education and practice.

At a minimum, we are of the view that social workers need a baseline literacy or competency in AI so that they can make informed choices about it in their education and as they enter the workforce. Goldkind (2021) supports this and argues for an approach to social work education where students are taught to understand the 'algorithm' by exploring how and where AI is used and what the associated risks are. She further argues for social work and computer science collaborations to ensure that social justice and ethics are embedded in the future of these technologies. The rulebook has not yet been written for the use of AI in social work or many other professions, and therefore we believe that a literacy approach will prepare students to navigate the ambiguity that currently exists and enable them to be active agents in shaping how AI is integrated into social work. It logically follows that teachers must also be provided with the time and resources to adequately develop their own digital and AI literacy (Al-Rantisi et al., 2024).

AI literacy should ultimately sit within a broader commitment to digital literacy within educational institutions, meaning that for AI literacy to be a successful strategy it must be positioned within a broader commitment to developing general digital awareness and capabilities including facilitating equitable access to technology. For example, Sadiku and Musa (2021) describe digital literacy as a set of technical, cognitive, social, and emotional competencies that enable individuals to navigate digital life. This includes the development of capabilities in relation to digital identities, device access and usage, digital communication skills, digital security, and digital rights. In this context, AI literacy should be part of a broader commitment to develop digital capabilities that enable students to understand and exercise their rights and responsibilities.

Annapureddy et al. (2025) provide a useful starting point for describing what a baseline AI literacy looks like in practice. They offer twelve competencies that aim to provide individuals with the general skills and knowledge needed for ethical uptake of AI. The following table includes an abbreviated summary of the 12 competencies:

Table 1. AI competency model (Annapureddy et al., 2025)

	COMPETENCY	BASIC DESCRIPTION
1	Basic AI Literacy	Baseline understanding of AI concepts
2	Knowledge of generative AI models	Basic understanding of generative AI and its functions
3	Knowledge of the capacity and limitations of generative AI tools	Ability to assess capabilities and constraints
4	Skills to use generative AI tools	Practical skills to use generative AI in various contexts
5	Ability to detect AI-generated content	Discernment in relation to AI produced content
6	Ability to assess the output of generative AI tools	Skills to critically assess AI outputs
7	Skill in prompting generative AI tools (prompt engineering)	Ability to tailor and adapt AI outputs to specific needs
8	Ability to program and fine-tune generative models	Technical skills to customize AI tools for specific contexts
9	Knowledge of the contexts where generative AI is used	Ability to assess appropriateness of AI in differing contexts
10	Knowledge of the ethical implications	Understanding of ethics and what responsible use looks like
11	Knowledge of the legal aspects	Ensure individuals operate within the law
12	Ability to continuously learn	Mindset of curiosity and continuous learning as the technology advances.

These skills and knowledge have value within the educational context as well as within professional practice. For example, if students are better able to detect AI-generated content and develop a continuous learning mindset, then perhaps they will be better at critically evaluating content and the motivations behind it. If they understand the risks of certain AI applications in context, perhaps they will take a more cautious approach to how and when they utilize AI tools.

Guest et al. (2025) argue that social workers must also adopt a critical approach to AI which actively questions the discourses surrounding AI, considers the impact of AI on the environment, the exploitation of labour in poor countries used to train AI models, the impact of misinformation and disinformation on social cohesion and political stability, and the potential for AI to further exclude marginalized communities that do not fit normative profiling. Therefore, AI literacy should be more than just mere technological capability and should also include moral and ethical obligations of both individuals and institutions. Further work is needed to develop AI literacy models that bring attention to the impact of individual or industry-based use of AI on the broader social good. However, we do already have core theoretical frameworks and ethical guidelines that underpin the social work profession, and these can arguably guide students and educators in the absence of structured guidelines and with regards to the more macro obligations. The emerging ethical issues surrounding AI already provide a potentially useful case study base for educators seeking to teach these theoretical frameworks in action by exploring theoretical perspectives on different use cases and media perspectives.

In summary, we propose that AI is a technology that brings new ways of working and has the capacity to enhance the work of social workers, yet it also brings significant ethical challenges. Given that it is new and has significant potential for harm, we must teach students the appropriate knowledge and skills to discern appropriate and inappropriate uses. At an individual level, ethical challenges exist in relation to informed consent, overreliance on AI-generated dictation, and use of automated assessment information. At a social level, it is increasingly difficult to discern truth, and AI development is dominated by some of the world's richest people who are arguably motivated by profit rather than social benefit. Social workers will encounter the individual and social impacts of AI and must not become part of the problem by blindly adopting technology that they do not understand. Social workers are also integral to raising the voices of the marginalized and oppressed and therefore must not become complicit in silencing these voices through AI tools that fail to acknowledge the uniqueness of the individual. Therefore, AI literacy in social work education is critical as the use of AI becomes more commonplace in our society.

WHY IS AI RELEVANT TO SOCIAL WORK?

Social work is a profession characterized by a broad practice framework that includes clinical and practical interventions to support individual needs as well as a focus on addressing structural and systemic factors that lead to oppression and marginalization such as rights, equity, consumer participation, and the fair distribution of resources (Keegan & Farwa, 2025; Watts & Hodgson, 2019). Social work therefore draws from a range of disciplines with a primary focus on psychological and sociological theorists to develop a worldview of individuals that are inherently socially linked through structures and norms that govern day-to-day life. In addition to learning a range of intervention skills, social workers must develop a strong foundational understanding of the conditions that create and/or maintain marginalization, oppression, and exclusion.

The social work discipline is centred around the pursuit of social justice, which encompasses equitable and fair access to resources, advancing human rights, and ensuring consumer participation in decision-making (Watts & Hodgson, 2019). Social workers seek to influence and change policies and practices that lead to oppression, such as those related to gender, class, ethnicity, race, age, education, and wealth. They believe that power, access to resources, and rights are not equally distributed. They seek to unveil the conditions within society that create oppression and marginalisation whilst also critiquing the typical individualised explanations of social problems and solutions (Allan et al., 2020; Healy, 2022). Furthermore, social work has a diverse and broad scope of practice, spanning roles within allied health and a range of direct practice settings through to policy, advocacy, and community development.

Social work is therefore both a micro and macro profession that seeks to intervene to assist both individual and systemic needs. In this context, AI has many potential applications that include administrative tools, predictive analysis and assessment tools, self-help tools, and tools that support creativity and planning.

Critical theory plays a key role in the foundational knowledge of social work as it encourages a focus on how the 'othering' of certain people is embedded in social and political structures via discourses that maintain the status quo of the dominant class, usually driven by white, western ideologies (Healy, 2022). This is established through the development of critical thinking and challenging the values and assumptions we bring to the profession. It also involves learning to consider multiple perspectives and to position the role of social worker as a facilitator of social justice (Watts & Hodgson, 2019).

Western democracies tend to be dominated by Neoliberal ideologies that position the responsibility for social problems onto individuals and seek to commodify social work into a series of transactional interventions (Johnstone et al., 2022). Whilst this paradigm has been around for some time in the social work profession, developments in AI have generated new enthusiasm for the potential that AI brings to creating added efficiency and responding to more people in an industry that is experiencing growing demand (James et al., 2024; Keegan & Farwa, 2025). However, without critique and appropriate skill development, these technologies are likely to perpetuate oppression by boxing people into statistical categories, applying standardized assessment and intervention strategies, and overlooking intersectional complexities.

The issues that lead to structural oppression are intersectional, meaning that many people experience multiple forms of simultaneous oppression leading to a compounded effect (Hill Collins, 2019). Humans are therefore unable to be reduced to a formula and no two individual experiences, needs, or intervention requirements are identical. However, as generative AI tools rely on predictable patterns and the use of data that is primarily made up of normative or dominant populations, the reliance on such technology is likely to further marginalize those in our society who do not fit into the dominant norms or diagnostic criteria. Hence, AI-dependent responses to human needs are unlikely to be reliable and will become increasingly impersonal. Qualified and competent social workers must therefore remain central to the delivery of human services rather than being replaced.

James et al. (2024) highlight the importance for social workers to resist AI as a form of algorithmic decision-making that predetermines the role of the social worker and instead argue for social workers to take a proactive role in shaping how and why AI is used in the professional context. They maintain that it is important for social workers to shape rather than be shaped by AI. Furthermore, they support the idea that social workers need to develop AI literacy in order to become familiar with the capabilities and risks of using AI in various contexts.

There is a growing body of critical literature in relation to the risks of AI. As previously mentioned, Guest et al. (2025) issue a call to resist and ban AI due to the harms it causes and the unresolved ethics in relation to the data it uses. These authors highlight significant environmental impacts, the lack of ethical governance, and misleading narratives about the safety and capability of AI as core reasons why a more critical approach to AI is needed. However, they do acknowledge the need to teach the public about AI whilst actively resisting its unquestioned adoption within educational settings. This is in part because of the neoliberal narratives that currently surround AI and its tendency to present as more capable and safer than it is. Social workers have historically played a key role in highlighting such risks and advising on inclusive and ethical approaches.

We agree on the need for a critical lens on the adoption of AI but argue, as Kong et al. (2025) and Goldkind (2021) do, that teaching students to understand, recognize, and use AI ethically will enable them to critically evaluate and analyse the development of AI within our industry and to collectively shape the broader societal response to it. The challenge for educators is to ensure that social work students obtain and understand the core social work theories, professional values, ethics, and the principles of social justice that are central to social work whilst enabling students to effectively navigate the emerging implications of new AI technologies in this space.

ASSESSMENT DESIGN

Powell and Forsyth (2024) argue that authentic assessment requires the educator to focus on how the student is being prepared for current and future social change. They argue that generative AI can play a role in augmenting or scaffolding the learning and assessment experience and does not require that we depart from traditional pedagogical wisdom in relation to assessment. Central to all good assessment is a clear understanding of what is being assessed and how it relates to the unit learning outcomes. If AI is viewed as a tool or part of the assessment strategy, then it is possible for assessments to remain valid and ensure authentic learning if they are well designed with AI in mind. Following the same logic outlined for students, if educators are AI literate, they can better understand the various applications of AI and make informed decisions about the skills and knowledge that students may need as they graduate. This of course requires engagement with industry in order to understand how it is being used and the ethical challenges that are presenting.

Central to our argument is that it is not our role as educators to determine if AI is appropriate or not in the context of social work. Rather, our role is to educate prospective social workers about this technology in a way that prepares them for potential use cases and a full understanding of the risks, opportunities, and challenges that come with this technology. This includes being prepared for a world that is more technologically integrated and where motivations are likely driven by neoliberal principles of efficiency and predictability and potentially a dehumanization of our profession. Furthermore, Reamer (2023) validates the approach of using AI as a scaffold rather than a shortcut and encourages assessments which incorporate the use of AI in their design whilst still preserving academic integrity. Assessment therefore becomes a tool to help students become familiar with the technology and to critically evaluate it in the safety of the classroom.

However, this approach does not resolve all of the issues that educators face with AI. For example, AI makes it easy for students to obtain summaries of literature or create generalist answers to theoretical concepts, enabling students to avoid spending time reading and thinking through academic literature to develop deeper learning (Hodgson et al., 2022). Multilingual students are able to use translation tools which create a positive effect on their ability to absorb information but limit their command of the spoken language in which they need to operate upon graduation (Wang et al., 2023). Furthermore, AI lacks transparency in how it produces and sources information, leading to difficulties in discerning truth or authorship of some sources (Liu, 2021; Saidin et al., 2025), and not all students have equal access to the latest technologies (Darwin et al., 2024). Opinions are mixed about whether AI limits or enhances creativity and whether it supports critical thinking with distinguishing factors primarily relating to how AI is used and scaffolded within education (Darwin et al., 2024; Hodgson et al., 2022; Zhou et al., 2024). Kamoun et al. (2024) highlight that students and educators do not necessarily have the same knowledge, attitudes, and perceptions of AI. This can lead to misunderstandings in what constitutes plagiarism or inappropriate uses of AI. The logic behind an AI literacy approach is that students will be better aligned with educator and industry expectations of ethical uses.

In summary, we are not arguing that scaffolding AI into assessment will solve all issues related to authentic assessment or resolve ongoing threats that AI poses to social work. Educators will need to keep adapting as technologies further develop and it is important that the core foundations of social work pedagogy are not undermined in the process.

SOCIAL WORK INDUSTRY STANDARDS

It is important to also acknowledge that social work education is externally accredited by professional accrediting authorities in most Western countries, and therefore the roles of professional associations and external authorities must be recognized. However, in the UK (Social Work England, 2021), US (Council on Social Work Education, 2022), and Australia (Australian Association of Social Workers, 2024), the respective social work accreditation standards do not explicitly mention – at the time of writing – artificial intelligence in their core accreditation documents but each does mention a requirement for some form of digital or technological use competency. The US standards go the furthest in specifying that students are proficient in the ethical use of technologies in social work practice.

In the EU there is not one single accrediting body, but there is now the EU AI Act which regulates the use of AI in the EU (Future of Life Institute, 2025) and seeks to set accountabilities in the creation and use of AI. In an article reviewing US and Canadian social work accreditation documents, Dali and Caidi (2023) argue that standards in relation to ethical technology use in social work are not keeping up with real developments in practice and ethical use of newer technology remains a bonus skill rather than a core one in accreditation documentation. This seems to be the case in the Australian and UK context also by evidence of the limited reference to technology or AI in ethical and accreditation documentation.

The debate on AI in social work is therefore still in its youth, and guidance on ethical governance and integration with accreditation is limited. Social work educators are operating with limited guidance outside of existing practice standards and ethical frameworks. These will develop over time and educators have an opportunity to be at the forefront of shaping these at an industry level. In the absence of structured guidance, educators can draw upon existing frameworks such as the

International Human Rights Declaration (Saidin et al., 2025) and the US Standards for Technology Use in Social Work (National Association of Social Workers, 2017).

CASE STUDY – INTEGRATION OF AI INTO A SOCIAL WORK ASSESSMENT

The following case study outlines our experiences in trying to pursue an AI literacy approach through the introduction of generative AI into a final year skills unit in the Master of Social Work (Qualifying) program. We have laid it out in sections describing the context and reflections on teacher and student experiences followed by tips that outline our lessons learned for anyone wishing to try this approach for themselves. This case study is not offered as a 'best practice' approach but rather as a reflection on an experiment and the learnings from it.

The Context

Taking an AI literacy approach and recognizing that many students were already using AI tools, we decided to experiment with formally including the use of an AI tool in an assessment task. A final year skills unit was selected that has a focus on case formulation and intervention planning. This unit is part of the Master of Social Work (Qualifying) program at Excelsia University College, which is an entry level postgraduate program for admission to the social work profession in Australia.

The students were primarily international students who were not native English speakers. Whilst not always the case, it was reasonably common for these students to utilize AI tools to assist with the clarity and structure of their academic writing. However, it was not clear which tools were being used and what understanding these students had about the risks and opportunities associated with generative AI. These students were also not consistently declaring AI use in their work.

Excelsia University College is a non-profit, private, tertiary education institution located in Western Sydney with a cohort of approximately 150 students per intake. Like most educational institutions, it has been grappling with how to strike the right balance between adapting educational practices to accommodate AI whilst maintaining academic integrity. Excelsia's policies on AI therefore walk a fine line between encouraging innovation in the use of AI whilst also seeking to set clear limits with a strong focus on academic integrity and meeting regulatory requirements. Therefore, at an institutional level, there was a permissive environment to experiment with structured AI tasks within assessments as long as academic integrity was maintained and learning outcomes were met.

It was important that we had a clear goal in mind that would give the use of AI purpose and teach new skills whilst also not taking away the need for students to exercise creativity and critical thinking (Hodgson et al., 2023; Ivanov, 2023). It was also important that AI was used as a scaffold rather than a shortcut (Reamer, 2023), so we sought to incorporate AI tools as part of a larger sequence of tasks whilst still preserving academic integrity. Additionally, we wanted to model ethical application of AI and reinforce the principles that AI must never become a substitute for human originality, reasoning, and professional judgment.

In this second-year social work skills unit, 'Skills and Models of Intervention in Social Work Practice', students are introduced to foundational and evidence-based practice approaches, including trauma-informed practice, crisis intervention, motivational interviewing, risk and safety assessment, and narrative therapy methods. These approaches are applied to various direct practice settings including with individuals, families, and groups. A key assessment task within the unit involves students developing and working with a fictitious client profile over the course of the semester. In the initial weeks, students collaborate in pairs to simulate an intake interview, during which students generate a client profile for their colleague. They are explicitly instructed not to use personal experiences or real-life stories and are provided with structured guidelines to support ethical and professional engagement. Students have scope to determine the specific details of the case and its complexity.

Students must take notes during the simulated intake interview that they will then use to help them formulate the case report. The client profile must reflect an understanding of trauma and its impacts, and incorporate a range of intersecting challenges such as mental health conditions, disability, developmental disorders, socio-economic disadvantage, poverty, unemployment, financial insecurity, experiences of abuse, isolation, suicidal ideation, intergenerational trauma, post-traumatic stress, grief and loss, relationship difficulties, school-related issues, family and domestic violence, homelessness, and the effects of injury or accident. Students may embellish the initial scenario as appropriate to meet the requirements of the assessment.

The students assume the role of a social worker in a community-based organisation and are asked to prepare a brief client report summarizing the information collected in the intake interview. They are instructed to include a description of the agency and referral context, background and history of the client, observations from the interview, and a summary of the support provided along with an initial case plan outlining next steps.

It is at this point that we decided to introduce a generative AI tool (in this case, CoPilot or ChatGPT) to help them organise their handwritten or typed notes into a professional report. Students were required to submit their original notes along with their case report in order to help assessors validate authenticity.

Students were provided with guidance about how to use the AI tools during class times via advice on prompting and reviewing generated content. This aimed to build confidence and competence in using these tools appropriately and gave an opportunity for tutors to outline ethics in relation to content accuracy, inherent bias, and the ethical management of confidential data. A pre-recorded video was also developed to support students with understanding how to appropriately prompt these tools to fulfill the assessment requirements. Our initial approach did not include broader AI literacy training.

To complement the report, students were also required to construct a genogram and eco-map for their fictitious client to create a visual representation of the client's relationships, systems, and support networks. Examples and guidance were provided in tutorial classes, and the completed diagrams were embedded within the final assessment document.

Students were guided to input their client notes into either ChatGPT or Co-Pilot without names or other identifying information in order to protect client confidentiality. Even though the client data was fictitious, we felt it important to include this as part of the approach. Students then prompted the AI to produce a summary report with recommended headings. Next, students needed to review and edit the report to ensure it was logical, included comprehensive information, and met assessment requirements. Finally, students submitted their final report along with the notes from their initial interview.

The Teaching Experience

It was an important expectation of the assessment that students demonstrate a clear and coherent link between their original client notes and the final generated report. The report must accurately reflect the information gathered during the intake interview and show evidence of review and refinement. It should be apparent that the original data was sufficiently detailed to support the creation of a well-articulated and realistic client report. Where this was not the case, gaps in the report often emerged, resulting in inconsistencies or implausible content. These issues typically indicated that students had not adequately reviewed or critically evaluated the quality of the AI-generated output.

The unit has several classes with multiple tutors. Some tutors were familiar with using AI and others were not. We found that those who were more familiar were more readily able to embrace the assessment whereas those who were not familiar, or who were less in favour of adopting the technology, were more resistant to its inclusion in this assessment. All tutors had previously taught the unit and were familiar with its content but were not necessarily familiar with using AI tools in their work or within an academic assessment. Some support and guidance was offered to tutors but, on reflection, more could have been done to also support their knowledge of AI and comfort with the validity of the assessment.

Concerns remained for some teachers in relation to the authenticity of the assessment and whether the use of GenAI contributed to deskilling students. This tension was exacerbated by the lack of industry leadership and guidance on the appropriate use and ethics associated with GenAI. However, this was offset by a preference by sessional staff to bring the use of AI into full view rather than trying to eliminate it or have students using it covertly. Most teachers therefore took an open-minded approach to the assessment.

A potential downside is that marking these assessments did take a little longer than previous course iterations. Reference needed to be made to the original notes to ensure authenticity whereas the original version required just the reviewing of the content of the final report. This did not seem to be significant for tutors as they saw value in trying something new and were committed to the assurance of learning that came from this extra step. However, appropriate remuneration of time for marking is an important consideration.

Some teachers were unsure about whether the use of AI would make it harder to assess student capability because of AI potentially filling in knowledge gaps or generating ideas for the student. The assessment design tried to account for this by requiring students to review and add to the information that was formatted or generated by AI. It was also not the only form of assessment in this unit, and the assessment was worth only 30% of total marks.

The assessment rubric was adjusted to account for some basic contributions by the AI tools to the student work including emphasizing comprehensiveness and fit for purpose format and recommendations. The student results still produced a reasonable distribution of final products, and teachers indicated that the level of student analysis and effort was still apparent in their work. Students who put more effort into fleshing out the case study and considering appropriate recommendations tended to do better. This was also recognized by the students in their feedback:

> *"It was the quickest assessment I have done thanks to the use of AI. I thought I would get a high distinction due to its effectiveness, but I was impressed with the feedback I got as the tutor didn't agree with some recommendations, and I agreed with her point later on." (Feedback from a student participant)*

The Student Experience

The assessment was implemented over two consecutive semesters in 2025 and, as part of course review, general feedback was collected from students about their experiences of including AI in the assessment. Ethics approval (STA-25-PD-DK-004) was obtained from Excelsia University College for a basic anonymous survey which gathered information about prior use of AI tools, their feelings about this assessment, and their views about the suitability and usefulness of the assessment.

A total of fifty-two responses were obtained out of a cohort of approximately three hundred students. Eighty-two percent of respondents were aged between 26-35 years old. All respondents were under the age of 45, and 71% identified as female with the remainder identifying as male. Thirty-five percent of the cohort were from the first semester and 65% were from the second.

When asked how often participants normally used artificial intelligence tools like ChatGPT or Copilot, 49% indicated that they use these sometimes with 32% of participants using these tools more than two times per week. Eighteen percent indicated that they rarely used these tools and 0% indicated not using AI tools at all. Only 10% of participants indicated that they had previously been encouraged by a teacher to use AI in an assessment and 27% were not sure. Sixty-nine percent of participants indicated that they had previously used AI to help them complete an assessment in other subjects.

When asked about feelings before and after the assessments, most students indicated feeling anxious, nervous, and unsure before starting the assessment with only a small proportion of students selecting that they felt excited and happy. After completing the assessment, this reversed with the majority indicating that they felt happy and excited and a small proportion selecting anxious and nervous.

Therefore, all participants had some level of familiarity with using AI tools and had some familiarity with using AI in the context of assessment but at relatively low levels. For many it seemed to be the first time it had formally been introduced to an assessment. It seems that initially, some students expressed hesitation about using generative AI tools but, after completing the assessment, they felt more comfortable about it.

Teachers identified that some students voiced concerns that their assessments would return high rates of AI detection and therefore create a risk of breaching the academic integrity or AI use policy. The student apprehensions potentially reflected prior experiences with more punitive approaches to AI use in academic settings, where the focus is on detection rather than ethical and supervised integration.

Students were also asked to respond to statements on a 5-point Likert scale from strongly disagree to strongly agree. Most students agreed that the assessment helped them learn new skills, was easy to understand, and helped them learn about the ethical use of AI. However, a small proportion of students deviated from the majority by indicating that they found the assessment hard to understand and complete and that they did not feel comfortable using AI in the assessment. It is possible that these students were among the small proportion of students that had less exposure to AI prior to the assessment and would benefit from more literacy training. One student also made the following comment which may help further illustrate these responses:

"I haven't had much help using CoPilot [sic] as I sought out the assessment with my tutor's guidance. I haven't used CoPilot [sic] before and it would've killed more time figuring out how to use it. It would be helpful to students if a training session/seminar is held to understand the ethical use of AI and how it can be used as tool, instead of using it as a source of knowledge." (Feedback from a student participant)

Overall Reflections

We have used this assessment twice now over two cohorts of students with a similar approach used each time. Overall, the standard of assessments was quite varied. Some students embraced the task, demonstrating thoughtful use of AI tools, careful review of their output, and strong linkage between their initial intake notes and the final report. Others submitted adequate reports but failed to ensure consistency or realism, often due to insufficient review or weak connection to the original data. This highlighted a key learning outcome that while AI can support professional practice, it cannot replace core interpersonal, analytical, and critical thinking skills.

This simple modification to the assessment did not seem to significantly mask the level of student competency in the core assessment skills that were being tested in this assessment. Students still needed to collect useful inputs in order to create a meaningful and comprehensive report. It reinforced the idea that students must remain the owners and managers of the data and that AI should be integrated as a tool to support execution. Students had to also ensure that they took responsibility for the accuracy and format of the data.

Whilst effort was put into guiding students on the ethics of using GenAI, further instruction is needed in relation to outlining best practices with regard to client consent where AI is used. As AI tools become more integrated into professional settings, clients may need to be informed that such technologies are used to organise and process data—even when the data may be de-identified. The need for robust data governance, transparency, and privacy protections will remain essential, and may become even more critical as digital tools evolve (Boetto, 2025; Keegan & Farwa, 2025).

We had assumed that students had general literacy skills in relation to AI. On reflection, this may not have been the case with some students commenting that they would like more training and some students not sufficiently scrutinising the output from the AI tool. Our conclusion is that more basic AI literacy training, such as that outlined earlier in this chapter, is needed in order to support students to best utilize GenAI tools.

The decision to allow students to frame their own scenario gave the students freedom to imagine a suitable case scenario; however, it tended to limit the complexity of the scenario. Students who did not sufficiently embellish their scenario tended to have weaker final reports as there was limited depth of analysis that could be tested. In the future, we are considering having the teachers role play a set scenario that includes issues of bias, power, and intersectionality to enable a richer assessment and require students to engage more complex skills and draw on theoretical frameworks. GenAI tools will less naturally do this without specific prompting, and students will likely have to add this analysis rather than rely on AI alone. We also identified a need to review the weighting of skills in the rubric to account for student versus AI capabilities.

There were also a wide variety of report formats in the submissions as we did not provide enough explicit instruction in relation to this. Some students elaborated on the outputs from AI and others retained the abbreviated version of GenAI text with dot points or bold headings with brief summary text. Providing more explicit instructions on the format of the report may make the expectations clearer and create a more uniform approach.

CONCLUSION

The assessment task was framed to demonstrate how AI could be used professionally and responsibly – not as a substitute for clinical reasoning or interpersonal engagement, but as a support tool for documentation, organisation, and reflective practice. Students were required to critically review AI-generated output, ensure alignment with original client notes, and maintain professional standards of clarity, realism, and ethical integrity. This aligns with the assertion that social workers must remain accountable for all professional decisions and that AI is best applied in an augmentative role (James et al., 2024; Reamer, 2023). Professional standards echo this expectation, with the AASW Practice Standards (AASW, 2023) requiring social workers to act in accordance with the values, principles and guidelines of the AASW Code of Ethics 2020, including 'being accountable for the quality of our practice, the decisions we make, and our professional actions'.

AI should enhance, rather than replace the empathy and critical thinking at the heart of social work. It requires thoughtful implementation, guided by trauma-informed and anti-oppressive principles, with purposeful attention given to the risks associated with algorithmic bias, lack of transparency, reduced direct human engagement, and inequitable access.

Incorporating AI into assessment tasks serves a dual purpose: it prepares students for real-world practice where such tools may be present, and it fosters ethical literacy around their use. Students learn to manage data responsibly, critique outputs, and understand the boundaries of AI's role in professional settings. This is not about creating shortcuts; rather, it is about cultivating digital competence alongside ethical awareness.

Yet unease remains. As educators we must continue to ask: are we shaping the future of practice, or being shaped by it? Perhaps the answer lies in our willingness to lead the conversations and embed ethical frameworks into our teaching, again ensuring that human skills – such as empathy, judgment, and deep relationship – remain central even as the tools around us evolve.

So, the integration of generative AI into social work education presents both pedagogical opportunities and ethical dilemmas. As educators, we have a responsibility to equip social work students, tomorrow's practitioners, with the awareness, skills, and confidence needed for hybrid practice (Goldkind, 2021). If we can make AI and digital literacy central to social work education, then perhaps we will create a future generation of social workers who are prepared to navigate the opportunities and the challenges that it brings.

TIPS FOR THE INTEGRATION OF AI INTO SOCIAL WORK ASSESSMENT

We have put together a list of tips for social work educators who want to integrate generative AI into their assessments. These tips reflect our learning from this case study and our reading on the topic.

1. **Clarify the Purpose** – Consider why you want to include AI tools in the assessment and what function or skills you want students to learn or demonstrate as a result of its integration. Is the introduction of AI teaching something important? How does this assessment relate to others across the course? In particular, we recommend avoiding the substitution of human judgment or under-emphasising the application of professional knowledge, ethics, or theory. These are easy for AI to mimic but undermine the student's opportunity to obtain deep learning through reading and analysis.
2. **Adjust the Rubric** – AI makes some traditional tasks easier; therefore, rubrics need to be adjusted to reflect this. For example, the quality of writing and accuracy of referencing should perhaps be weighted higher than previous expectations. Furthermore, as with all assessment, the rubric needs to clearly target the skills and knowledge that you are trying to assess. This may include requiring students to provide evidence of scrutinizing AI outputs or of prompts that were used to generate the content. This should link back to your purpose and what is most important to be assessed. We therefore recommend taking the time to reflect on the rubric and how it is weighted, considering the role of AI versus the role of

the student in the assessment. In this particular assessment, we have moved to more highly weight critical engagement and analysis of content to reach a pass mark, with higher marks awarded for greater complexity of analysis and use of literature and theory to support arguments. It is likely that the skills being assessed or the threshold to be reached will need to be adjusted in some way when accounting for AI in an assessment.

3. **Ensure Technical Readiness** – Do not assume that your students or your teachers know how to use AI tools correctly or ethically in the context of social work. Allocate time to teach basic skills related to the tools that you are recommending including functionality, prompting, limitations, and use cases. Make space in the unit to practice the skills that you want students to use. AI literacy training at a course and staff training level would be ideal and should focus on skills, knowledge, and mindset.
4. **Give Clear Instructions** – As with all assessments, clear instructions help to outline the purpose and expectations of the student. Moderating and testing these with others may help to identify blind spots. Clearly explain what is permitted and what is not in relation to the use of the AI tool you are focusing on.
5. **Build Student Confidence** – We found it useful to provide a quick demonstration video and also supplied students with examples of effective prompts that they could use to generate the outputs needed. We reinforced the idea of Copilot as a support tool rather than a shortcut. Make time within classes for students to practice and learn from mistakes. It may also be useful to clarify how the assessment relates to and fits within the scope of your institutional AI policy.
6. **Link to Code of Ethics** – An important component of developing AI literacy is the development of ethical consciousness in relation to an individual's use of AI. The industry Code of Ethics will always remain paramount and includes the need for students to consider how the principles of confidentiality, transparency, and accountability are applied to the use of AI tools.
7. **Create Space to Explore Questions** – When trying new things, it is important to create safe spaces for questions and experimentation. This should be considered for both students and teaching staff and may include sessions to ask questions, seek feedback, and discuss anxieties. Teachers may also need similar support through internal mentoring from teaching and learning experts.
8. **Prepare Teachers** – Naturally, the teaching staff must believe in the authenticity of the assessment and feel confident to teach and assess the associated skills and knowledge. Therefore, it is critical to engage teaching staff in discussions about the motives for incorporating AI and ideally to include them in the assessment design so that there is support and capability. They must also have the opportunity to be trained in AI literacy and to practice with the tools if they are to be able

to teach this to students. This requires investment from institutions in training, mentoring, and access to a variety of AI tools relevant to their discipline.

9. **Include Reflection** – As with all teaching and learning activities, feedback and evaluation are important aspects of continuous improvement. It is important to try something, learn from it, and adapt the task for each cohort. It is also important for students to reflect on the experience and what they learned about the use of AI through the process. These reflections further help students to explore the pros and cons of engaging AI in the professional context.
10. **Review Policies on AI that Focus on Detection and Control** – When undertaking the assessment, there was a tension for some teachers between detection of inappropriate use of AI and assessment of the skills being demonstrated and assessed regardless of the AI use. In this example, the important skill was the ability to analyse a case scenario and present it in a short report format with recommendations for intervention. The use of AI was expected, and students still had to appropriately reference it in accordance with 7th edition APA referencing requirements. Our view is that policies should focus on the establishment of clear assessment design and with instructions that outline what is permitted. Academic integrity principles are still essential but are not as simple as they were pre-AI where issues of integrity focused more on copying the work of others. Resources need to be invested to support teachers to design and implement best practice assessments rather than simply police AI use. This cannot be achieved without effective training in AI literacy for staff and students and without the space to innovate.
11. **Consider Workload and Resource Implications** – Setting up an assessment like this for the first time will likely require additional workload hours for assessment design and for teacher and student support. This will ensure a well thought out assessment design and that students are not disadvantaged if they are not familiar with using AI tools. Tutors may also need training and support to be confident in the authenticity and reliability of the assessment and to ensure consistency in grading. Furthermore, some forms of assessment may be needed that cannot be graded in a typical timeframe or may require in person activities with two assessors. A rethinking of traditional assessment grading allocations may be needed, particularly in relationally-focused professions like social work.
12. **Engage in Course Level Planning** – Course level planning is needed to ensure that AI literacy is embedded across the program and that assessments are appropriately varied to assess required learning outcomes through mixed methods of assessment. Not every assessment needs to or should include AI. The incorporation of AI competencies into assessment strategy is necessary, though, for at least a portion of assessments. This should be integrated into regular course

review cycles and will need to be resourced with training and adequate policy reform.

REFERENCES

AASW Practice Standards. (2023). https://my.aasw.asn.au/file-asset/0699g000001T7hsAAC

Al-Rantisi, A. M., ElShanti, N. H., & Harb, S. A. (2024). Challenges of using artificial intelligence in social work education. *Social Work Education*, 1–18. DOI: 10.1080/02615479.2025.2483354

Allan, J., Briskman, L., & Pease, B. (2020). *Critical social work: Theories and practices for a socially just world* (Routledge, T.Francis Group, Ed.; 2nd ed.).

Annapureddy, R., Fornaroli, A., & Gatica-Perez, D. (2025). Generative AI literacy: Twelve defining competencies. *Digit. Gov.: Res. Pract.*, *6*(1), 13. Advance online publication. DOI: 10.1145/3685680

Asakura, K., Occhiuto, K., Todd, S., Leithead, C., & Clapperton, R. (2020). A call to action on artificial intelligence and social work education: Lessons learned from a simulation project using natural language processing. *Journal of Teaching in Social Work*, *40*(5), 501–518. DOI: 10.1080/08841233.2020.1813234

Australian Association of Social Workers. (2024). *Australian social work education and accreditation standards*. Retrieved 29th December 2025 from https://aasw-media.s3.ap-southeast-4.amazonaws.com/wp-content/uploads/2025/10/00.-AASW-ASWEAS-2024.pdf

Babaeva, A., Samerkhanova, E., Guseva, L., Shmeleva, N., & Gromov, B. (2023). Social work in the digital age. *E3S Web of Conferences, 381*, 1023. DOI: 10.1051/e3sconf/202338101023

Báez, J. C., Bjugstad, A., Park, T. K., Jones, J. L., Bidwell, L. N., Sage, M., & Hitchcock, L. I. (2025). Social work educators innovating with generative AI: An exploratory study. *Journal of Social Work Education*, 1–16. DOI: 10.1080/10437797.2024.2411170

Barbosa da Silva, J., Espinal, M., Garcia-Saiso, S., Fitzgerald, J., Marti, M., Bascolo, E., Haddad, A. E., & D'Agostino, M. (2024). A digital transformation for primary health care. *Bulletin of the World Health Organization, 102*(1), 2–2A. DOI: 10.2471/BLT.23.290726

Boetto, H. (2025). Artificial intelligence in social work: An EPIC model for practice. *Australian Social Work*, 1–14. DOI: 10.1080/0312407X.2025.2488345

Corbin, T., Walton, J., Bannister, P., & Deranty, J.-P. (2025). On the essay in a time of GenAI. *Educational Philosophy and Theory*, 1–13. DOI: 10.1080/00131857.2025.2572802

Council on Social Work Education. (2022). *Educational policy and accreditation standards for baccalaureate and master's social work programs.* Retrieved 29th December 2025 from https://www.cswe.org/getmedia/bb5d8afe-7680-42dc-a332-a6e6103f4998/2022-Educational-Policy-and-Accreditation-Standards-(EPAS).pdf

Curtis, G. J. (2025). The two-lane road to hell is paved with good intentions: Why an all-or-none approach to generative AI, integrity, and assessment is insupportable. *Higher Education Research & Development*, 1–8. DOI: 10.1080/07294360.2025.2476516

Dali, K., & Caidi, N. (2023). Social work education for the digital age: Insight from information science. *Social Work Education, 42*(5), 663–693. DOI: 10.1080/02615479.2022.2057942

Darwin, Rusdin, D., Mukminatien, N., Suryati, N., Laksmi, E. D., & Marzuki. (2024). Critical thinking in the AI era: An exploration of EFL students' perceptions, benefits, and limitations. *Cogent Education, 11*(1). Advance online publication. DOI: 10.1080/2331186X.2023.2290342

Feuerriegel, S., Hartmann, J., Janiesch, C., & Zschech, P. (2024). Generative AI. *Business & Information Systems Engineering*, *66*(1), 111–126. DOI: 10.1007/s12599-023-00834-7

Flenady, G., & Sparrow, R. (2025). Cut the bullshit: Why GenAI systems are neither collaborators nor tutors. *Teaching in Higher Education*, 1–10. DOI: 10.1080/13562517.2025.2497263

Future of Life Institute. (2025). *EU Artificial Intelligence Act.* Retrieved 29th December 2025 from https://artificialintelligenceact.eu

Goldingay, S., Hodgson, D., Boddy, J., Nipperess, S., & Watts, L. (2020). Online and blended social work education in Aotearia New Zealand and Australia negotiating the tensions. *Advances in Social Work & Welfare Education*, *21*(2), 62–74.

Goldkind, L. (2021). Social work and artificial intelligence: Into the matrix. *Social Work*, *66*(4), 372–374. DOI: 10.1093/sw/swab028

Guest, O., Suarez, M., Müller, B., van Meerkerk, E., Oude Groote Beverborg, A., de Haan, R., Reyes Elizondo, A., Blokpoel, M., Scharfenberg, N., Kleinherenbrink, A., Camerino, I., Woensdregt, M., Monett, D., Brown, J., Avraamidou, L., Alenda-Demoutiez, J., Hermans, F., & van Rooij, I. (2025). Against the uncritical adoption of 'AI' technologies in academia. *Zenodo.* https://doi.org/https://doi.org/10.5281/zenodo.17065099

Healy, K. (2022). *Social work theories in context* (3rd ed.). Bloomsbury.

Hill Collins, P. (2019). *Intersectionality as critical social theory*. Duke University Press.

Hodgson, D., Goldingay, S., Boddy, J., Nipperess, S., & Watts, L. (2022). Problematising artificial intelligence in social work education: Challenges, issues and possibilities. *British Journal of Social Work, 52*(4), 1878–1895. DOI: 10.1093/bjsw/bcab168

Hodgson, D., Watts, L., & Gair, S. (2023). Artificial intelligence and implications for the Australian Social Work Journal. *Australian Social Work, 76*(4), 425–427. DOI: 10.1080/0312407X.2023.2247833

Ivanov, S. (2023). The dark side of artificial intelligence in higher education. *Service Industries Journal, 43*(15-16), 1055–1082. DOI: 10.1080/02642069.2023.2258799

James, P., Lal, J., Liao, A., Magee, L., & Soldatic, K. (2024). Algorithmic decision-making in social work practice and pedagogy: Confronting the competency/critique dilemma. *Social Work Education, 43*(6), 1552–1569. DOI: 10.1080/02615479.2023.2195425

Johnstone, M., Catrina, B., & Ross, N. (2022). The McDonaldization of social work: A critical analysis of mental health care services using the Choice and Partnership Approach (CAPA) in Canada. *Journal of Progressive Human Services, 33*(3), 223–243. DOI: 10.1080/10428232.2022.2050117

Kamoun, F., Ayeb, W. E., Jabri, I., Sifi, S., & Iqbal, F. (2024). Exploring students' and faculty's knowledge, attitudes, and perceptions towards ChatGPT: A cross-sectional empirical study. *Journal of Information Technology Education*, 23.

Keegan, D. J., & Farwa, A. (2025). Human Services 2.0: Navigating ethics, innovation, and applications of AI in human services. In Ahmed, E., Babar, A. R., Samad, A., Ahmed, R. I., & Beydoun, G. (Eds.), *Strengthening Human Relations in Organizations With AI* (pp. 247–272). IGI Global., DOI: 10.4018/979-8-3693-6507-6.ch010

Kominkiewicz, F., & O'Neil, M. (2025). The application of artificial intelligence to social work education and practice. In *Encyclopedia of Social Work*. NASW Press and Oxford University Press.

Kong, S.-C., Korte, S.-M., Burton, S., Keskitalo, P., Turunen, T., Smith, D., Wang, L., Lee, J. C.-K., & Beaton, M. C. (2025). Artificial Intelligence (AI) literacy – An argument for AI literacy in education. *Innovations in Education and Teaching International*, *62*(2), 477–483. DOI: 10.1080/14703297.2024.2332744

Liu, B. (2021). In AI we trust? Effects of agency locus and transparency on uncertainty reduction in human–AI interaction. *Journal of Computer-Mediated Communication*, *26*(6), 384–402. https://doi.org/https://doi.org/10.1093/jcmc/zmab013

Liu, D., & Bridgeman, A. (2023). *What to do about assessments if we can't out-design or out-run AI?* University of Sydney. Retrieved 11th November 2025 from https://educational-innovation.sydney.edu.au/teaching@sydney/what-to-do-about-assessments-if-we-cant-out-design-or-out-run-ai/

Long, D., & Magerko, B. (2020). *What is AI literacy? Competencies and design considerations* Proceedings of the 2020 CHI Conference on Human Factors in Computing Systems, Honolulu, HI, USA. DOI: 10.1145/3313831.3376727

Mooney, L., Cummings, C., Koller, J. M., Dunkle, J., & Bobadilla, T. (2024). Perspectives of social work faculty/staff and students about online learning and practicum education. *Journal of Teaching in Social Work*, *44*(5), 462–475. DOI: 10.1080/08841233.2024.2408170

National Association of Social Workers. (2017). *Standards for technology in social work practice*. https://www.socialworkers.org/Practice/NASW-Practice-Standards-Guidelines/Standards-for-Technology-in-Social-Work-Practice

Powell, S., & Forsyth, R. (2024). Generative AI and the implications for authentic assessment. In *Using generative ai effectively in higher education* (1st ed.). Routledge., DOI: 10.4324/9781003482918-15

Reamer, F. (2023). Artificial intelligence in social work: Emerging ethical issues. *International Journal of Social Work Values and Ethics*, *20*, 52–71. https://doi.org/10.55521/10-020-205

Russ-Smith, J., & Lazarus, M. (2025). *The AI (R)evolution*. Monash University. DOI: 10.26180/27274938.v5

Sadiku, M. N. O., & Musa, S. M. (2021). Digital Intelligence. In Sadiku, M. N. O., & Musa, S. M. (Eds.), *A primer on multiple intelligences* (pp. 163–174). Springer International Publishing., DOI: 10.1007/978-3-030-77584-1_13

Saidin, S. S., Ahmad, N., & Aziz, S. (2025). Ethical governance of artificial intelligence in organizations: Challenges and strategies. In Ahmed, E., Babar, A. R., Samad, A., Ahmed, R. I., & Beydoun, G. (Eds.), *Strengthening human relations in organizations with AI* (pp. 59–82). IGI Global., DOI: 10.4018/979-8-3693-6507-6.ch003

Social Work England. (2021). *Qualifying education and training standards 2021.* Retrieved 29th December 2025 from https://www.socialworkengland.org.uk/media/3423/1227_socialworkengland_standards_drft_qual_ed_training_standards_2021.pdf

Wang, T., Lund, B. D., Marengo, A., Pagano, A., Mannuru, N. R., Teel, Z. A., & Pange, J. (2023). Exploring the potential impact of artificial intelligence (AI) on international students in higher education: Generative AI, chatbots, analytics, and international student success. *Applied Sciences (Basel, Switzerland)*, *13*(11), 6716. DOI: 10.3390/app13116716

Watts, L., & Hodgson, D. (2019). *Social justice theory and practice for social work: Critical and philosophical perspectives* (1st ed.). Springer Nature., DOI: 10.1007/978-981-13-3621-8

Zhou, X., Teng, D., & Al-Samarraie, H. (2024). The mediating role of generative AI self-regulation on students' critical thinking and problem-solving. *Education Sciences*, *14*(12), 1302. DOI: 10.3390/educsci14121302

ADDITIONAL READING

Beckingham, S., Lawrence, J., Powell, S., & Hartley, P. (Eds.). (2024). Using generative AI effectively in higher education: sustainable and ethical practices for learning, teaching and assessment (1st ed.). Routledge, Taylor & Francis Group. DOI: 10.4324/9781003482918

Corbin, T., Walton, J., Bannister, P., & Deranty, J.-P. (2025). On the essay in a time of GenAI. *Educational Philosophy and Theory*, 1–13. DOI: 10.1080/00131857.2025.2572802

KEY TERMS AND DEFINITIONS

AI Literacy: A set of specific knowledge and skills required to use AI effectively and safely.

Artificial Intelligence (AI): Technology that is able to perform tasks usually limited to humans.

Assessment: The process of testing capabilities in specific skills and knowledge related to unit learning outcomes.

Digital Literacy: A set of specific knowledge and skills required to use digital technologies effectively and safely.

Generative Artificial Intelligence (GenAI): Technology that is able to generate new text in response to user prompts and drawing from large volumes of data to predict an appropriate response.

Rubric: A set of criteria that guide the allocation of marks for a specific assessment.

Social Work: A helping profession focused on the pursuit of social justice.

Chapter 8
Designing and Assessing AI-Enabled Programs in the Helping Professions:
Leadership, Learning Design, and Accreditation

Jenifer Norton
https://orcid.org/0009-0007-8900-6247
Moravian University, USA

ABSTRACT

This chapter examines artificial intelligence integration at the program level in social work, counseling, and psychology education, arguing that ethical and effective adoption requires more than isolated course-level experimentation. Drawing on the author's experience as a program director and learning designer, it positions AI as educational infrastructure that can support assessment planning, accreditation alignment, and sustainable course development when governed by professional values and human judgment. The chapter explores AI-supported curriculum and rubric alignment, online learning design workflows, and collaboration with subject matter experts, while addressing ethical tensions related to transparency, equity, faculty workload, and the limits of automation. It offers a leadership-oriented framework for responsible, program-level AI governance in the helping professions.

DOI: 10.4018/979-8-3373-4362-4.ch008

INTRODUCTION: WHY PROGRAM-LEVEL AI INTEGRATION MATTERS NOW

Programs, not tools, are the ethical unit of artificial intelligence integration in the helping professions. Much of the current discourse in higher education focuses on tool-specific capabilities such as generating feedback, simulating practice scenarios, automating grading, or personalizing learning pathways (e.g., Lee & Moore, 2024; Zhao, 2024). Within social work, counseling, and psychology education, this focus often triggers necessary ethical questions regarding bias, empathy, relational practice, and professional judgment (Masters, 2023; Reamer, 2023; Shoemaker et al., 2025). These conversations are essential. Yet, taken alone, they risk obscuring a more fundamental reality: AI does not enter professional education as an isolated instructional aid. It enters through programs, including curricula, assessment systems, accreditation processes, and institutional accountability structures.

As a program director involved in assessment, and as a learning designer building and sustaining online programs at scale, I encounter AI not as a classroom novelty but as an infrastructural reality. Decisions about AI use rarely remain confined to a single assignment. Instead, they reverberate across program learning outcomes, accreditation narratives, licensure alignment, and faculty governance. This observation aligns with broader scholarship emphasizing that educational technologies reshape institutional practices and power relations, not merely instructional techniques (Marshall et al., 2024; Timotheou et al., 2023). The ethical risks and opportunities of AI, therefore, cannot be adequately addressed at the level of individual tools or isolated pedagogical experiments. They must be examined at the level where responsibility is ultimately held: the academic program.

Ethical and effective AI integration in the helping professions requires intentional program-level leadership and governance. While faculty autonomy and pedagogical creativity are critical, they are insufficient to ensure that AI use aligns with professional values, accreditation standards, and public trust. Uncoordinated, bottom-up innovation often exacerbates inequities, increases faculty burden, and produces uneven learning experiences (Schophuizen & Kalz, 2020; Selwyn, 2022). In professional education, these risks are amplified by the high-stakes consequences of program-level decisions, which shape graduates' readiness for ethical and competent practice (Reamer, 2023).

Leaders in social work, counseling, and psychology are navigating complex pressures. Students are already using generative AI in ways that outpace institutional policy (Chan, 2023; Kasneci et al., 2023; Moorhouse et al., 2023). Faculty vary widely in AI familiarity, comfort, and ethical orientation (Kim et al., 2025). Accrediting bodies are beginning to ask implicit, if not yet explicit, questions about authorship, assessment validity, and learning evidence in AI-mediated environments, especially in online contexts (Berridge et al., 2025; Rodriguez et al., 2024). At the same time, programs face intensifying demands to document outcomes, close assessment loops, and demonstrate continuous quality improvement, all within constrained staffing and resources (Banta & Blaich, 2010; Laundon & Grant-Smith, 2023; Singer-Freeman & Robinson, 2020). AI is often positioned as a potential solution to these pressures. However, without clear governance, it can easily obscure accountability. The central concern here is how programs can design structures that make ethical use more likely over time.

From this vantage point, AI is a form of educational infrastructure. Like learning management systems, assessment platforms, or field education databases, AI reshapes how work is done and how decisions are justified (Adamakis & Rachiotis, 2025; Salido et al., 2025). Treating AI as infrastructure brings vital questions to the fore: Who decides how it is used? For what purposes? With what safeguards?

This chapter examines these questions through two interrelated lenses. The first is programmatic assessment and accreditation in the helping professions, with particular attention to social work education accreditation, online program review, institutional assessment cycles, and alignment with external licensure expectations. Drawing on direct experience with assessment planning, data aggregation, and accreditation documentation, the chapter explores how AI can support – yet also complicate – program-level assessment processes. Prior work on assessment in professional education underscores both the promise of analytics-informed decision-making and the dangers of decontextualized data use, particularly when assessment results inform high-stakes judgments (Isaacs, 2021; Slade & Prinsloo, 2013). These tensions are magnified when AI is introduced into assessment workflows.

The second lens is learning design, especially in the context of developing online psychology programs with limited design resources and varied subject matter expert engagement. Here, the chapter examines how AI can function as a course design partner – supporting alignment, coherence, and scalability – without displacing disciplinary expertise or homogenizing professional voice. This discussion builds on learning design scholarship emphasizing intentionality, alignment, and the relational dimensions of curriculum development (Campbell et al., 2007; Dickens et al., 2025). Particular attention is paid to the distinction between AI use during course development and AI use during course delivery, a distinction that carries significant ethical and pedagogical implications for students and faculty alike (Reiss, 2021; Williams, 2024).

I maintain a balanced posture toward risk. AI is neither an inevitable solution nor an existential threat; it is a powerful, imperfect tool whose value depends on the structures within which it is embedded. Ethical gravity is sustained by grounding all discussions in the core commitments of the helping professions: relational accountability, respect for human dignity, equity, transparency, and responsibility to the public (American Counseling Association, 2014; American Psychological Association, 2017; National Association of Social Workers, 2021).

Preview: Three Lessons That Shape the Chapter

To orient the reader, this chapter is built upon three foundational lessons derived from practice:

- Treat AI as infrastructure, not authority.
- Differentiate AI use by role and developmental readiness.
- Make boundaries auditable through governance trails rather than "vibes."

The chapter proceeds by situating the program director as an ethical steward, examining AI-supported assessment, and offering strategies for accreditation and learning design governance. To reduce repetition throughout these sections, the following matrix serves as the primary "map" for role-differentiated boundaries.

Table 1. Role-differentiated AI use in helping-professions programs (functions × boundaries)

Role	Course Design & Build	Assessment Planning & Rubrics	Accreditation/ Assessment Documentation	Instruction & Feedback (in-course)	Student Work (learning artifacts)
Program Director	**Permitted** (governance + alignment checks)	**Permitted** (guardrails, validity, equity prompts)	**Permitted** (drafting *with disclosure* + human verification)	**Constrained** (avoid "hidden automation")	**Excluded** (no AI judgment of readiness/fitness)
Learning Designer	**Permitted** (workflow acceleration, alignment, UDL checks)	**Permitted** (rubric drafting support; SME review)	**Constrained** (summaries only after evidence is secured)	**Constrained** (templates/ structures; no substitution for teaching)	**Excluded** (no evaluation of sensitive reflective/ relational tasks)
Faculty/ SME	**Permitted** (review/revision; voice + ethics)	**Permitted** (rubric language drafts; human scoring)	**Constrained** (narratives with oversight)	**Constrained** (transparent, student-facing boundaries)	**Constrained/ Excluded** depending on task (see rubric criterion below)
Students	**Constrained** (AI literacy practice, critique tasks)	**Excluded** (no AI-generated evidence for high-stakes competence)	**Excluded**	**Constrained** (use only when assigned/allowed + documented)	**Constrained/ Excluded** for reflective, relational, and gatekeeping evidence

Table 1 illustrates how AI use must be differentiated by role, function, and ethical boundary. Rather than asking whether AI is "allowed" or "disallowed" in general, program-level stewardship requires specifying who may use AI, for what purposes, and under what constraints. The remainder of this chapter elaborates how this role differentiation shapes learning design, assessment, accreditation, and governance decisions.

THE PROGRAM DIRECTOR AS ETHICAL STEWARD OF AI INTEGRATION

In professional education, program directors occupy a distinctive role. They are simultaneously responsible for curricular coherence, assessment integrity, accreditation compliance, and student readiness for practice. When AI enters this ecosystem, it does not merely add an instructional option; it reshapes the conditions under which these responsibilities are met. Therefore, AI integration is a leadership challenge that calls for ethical stewardship rather than technical management.

Much of the existing literature on AI in higher education frames responsibility at either the individual faculty level (e.g., instructional decisions, assessment design) or the institutional level (e.g., policy, infrastructure, procurement). Program leadership sits between these layers, translating institutional expectations into pedagogical practice while safeguarding disciplinary values and professional standards. In the helping professions, where programs function as gatekeepers to the field, this intermediary role carries significant weight (Reamer, 2023). Program directors are not merely implementers of policy. They are stewards of professional formation.

Beyond Compliance: Stewardship Versus Surveillance

One of the most immediate risks of AI integration is a drift toward surveillance. As concerns about authorship and assessment validity grow, programs may feel pressured to adopt restrictive policies or detection tools. While well-intentioned, these approaches often undermine trust and conflict with the relational, anti-oppressive values central to the helping professions (Berridge et al., 2025; Giray et al., 2025).

Ethical stewardship offers an alternative. Rather than asking how to control AI, stewardship asks how its use can be shaped to support learning, equity, and accountability. This shift mirrors broader critiques of technocratic governance in education, which caution against treating complex human practices as problems to be solved through monitoring and automation (Potgieter, 2020; Selwyn, 2014; Williamson, 2017). Stewardship requires a clearer articulation of boundaries than compliance alone. It demands that leaders engage faculty in dialogue about why certain uses of AI align with professional goals while others do not.

Program-Level Decision Making: Setting the Guardrails

A central task for program directors is determining which AI decisions must be made at the program level and which should remain with individual instructors. Unexamined decentralization leads to fragmented practices that undermine equity, assessment coherence, and accreditation narratives.

Program-level decisions are necessary where consistency is required, such as minimum standards for transparency and the alignment of learning outcomes with AI-supported assessments. Table 1 provides the necessary guardrails for these decisions, differentiating between a student's evidence of competence (excluded) and a director's administrative drafting (permitted). Without shared frameworks in these areas, programs risk presenting incoherent or even contradictory accounts of learning and assessment to external reviewers (Ahn et al., 2025; Rodriguez et al., 2024; Watts, 2025).

At the same time, excessive centralization can erode faculty agency and stifle pedagogical innovation. Research on technology-enhanced learning consistently highlights the importance of instructor judgment and contextual adaptation (Prieto et al., 2011). Ethical stewardship, therefore, involves holding a productive tension: establishing guardrails that protect professional standards while preserving space for discretion. This balance is critical in interdisciplinary programs spanning social work, counseling, and psychology, where epistemological traditions and pedagogical norms may differ. Program directors must navigate these differences without defaulting to the lowest common denominator or imposing uniformity where it is neither feasible nor desirable.

Faculty Agency, Consent, and Workload

AI integration also raises questions about faculty labor. As institutions promote AI for efficiency or innovation, faculty may experience adoption as an implicit mandate. A report from the American Association of University Professors (2025) notes that educators are often marginal in institutional AI initiatives, despite being directly affected by their implementation. Program directors must recognize faculty consent and workload as ethical issues. Stewardship requires centering faculty perspectives and acknowledging that AI adoption entails significant cognitive and temporal labor.

This includes recognizing conscientious objection as a legitimate stance. Not all faculty should embrace AI in the same ways or at the same pace. Furthermore, while AI is often framed as a labor-saving tool, it frequently redistributes rather than reduces work. Reviewing AI-generated content, verifying outputs, and redesigning assessments require time and expertise (Alsharefeen, 2025; Nicola-Richmond et al., 2025). Program leaders must be attentive to how these demands accumulate, particularly for faculty with heavy service or mentoring responsibilities.

Box 1. Vignette: Navigating the "Detection vs. Literacy" Divide

In a large Master of Social Work (MSW) program, the Director faced a growing divide among the social work faculty. One group, concerned about the "devaluation of the degree," advocated for mandatory AI detection software and a "human-only" writing policy for all core clinical courses. They argued that if a student used AI to draft a social history or a treatment plan, the program could no longer vouch for that student's clinical empathy or critical thinking.

A second group, focused on digital equity and workforce readiness, argued that banning AI would disadvantage students from underrepresented backgrounds and leave graduates unprepared for an AI-augmented landscape. They proposed an "AI-Literacy" model where students were taught to use AI for case brainstorming while documenting their prompts and critiques.

The Director recognized that neither a total ban nor an unguided "open door" policy fulfilled her role as an ethical steward. Drawing on the functions and boundaries in Table 1, they convened a series of "values-alignment" sessions. Rather than debating the tools, the faculty mapped the "non-negotiables" of the MSW curriculum. They agreed that while AI could be used to draft a community advocacy letter (workflow acceleration), it was excluded from reflective journals, where the learning process itself was the outcome. By centering the purpose of the task rather than the detection of the tool, the Director moved the program from a culture of suspicion to one of transparent, role-differentiated governance.

Program Leadership at the Intersection of Ethics, Assessment, and Trust

Ultimately, a director's role in AI integration is inseparable from questions of trust among faculty, students, and the public. In the helping professions, this trust is foundational. Graduates are entrusted with the well-being of individuals, families, and communities, and programs are responsible for certifying their readiness for that work (Croaker et al., 2017; Foster & McAdams, 2009).

AI complicates traditional markers of trust by obscuring creative processes and introducing probabilistic outputs into high-stakes contexts. Program directors cannot resolve these tensions alone, but they can convene conversations and model ethical deliberation. By framing AI integration as a collective responsibility rather than a technical fix, leaders ensure that innovation serves, rather than supplants, the moral commitments of professional education.

In this sense, ethical stewardship is not an additional task; it is a reframing of program leadership. It involves navigating uncertainty and making principled decisions where no solution is without risk. AI makes this work more visible, but it does not change its ethical core.

Key Takeaways: Ethical Stewardship and Programmatic Trust

- **Transition from Compliance to Deliberation:** Move beyond surveillance and detection tools. Instead, focus on how AI can support professional values and encourage a culture of disclosure, treating AI use as a professional judgment call rather than a policy violation.
- **Define Non-Negotiables and Guardrails:** Use the role-differentiated boundaries in Table 1 to identify where AI use is excluded. By clearly defining tasks that must remain "human-only" (e.g., clinical self-reflection and relational skills), directors protect the program's gatekeeping role and the integrity of professional certification.
- **Prioritize Professional Formation:** Center the relational and human elements of social work, counseling, and psychology that AI cannot replicate. Ensure that AI integration serves the development of a student's professional identity rather than replacing the "use of self" that defines the helping professions.
- **Protect Faculty Agency and Acknowledge Labor:** Treat faculty hesitation as a source of ethical insight. Recognize that AI adoption is a choice and that it often increases cognitive and temporal workload through required human verification and assessment redesign.

AI AND PROGRAMMATIC ASSESSMENT IN THE HELPING PROFESSIONS

Assessment in social work, counseling, and psychology serves multiple, sometimes competing purposes: supporting student learning, demonstrating accountability to accrediting bodies, informing curricular improvement, and certifying readiness for professional practice. These functions operate at different levels, from individual assignments to program-wide learning outcomes, and they rely on interpretive judgment as much as technical measurement. Integrating AI into these processes offers new forms of analytic support while raising questions about validity and equity.

This section examines AI's role in programmatic assessment, distinguishing it from course-level grading or feedback. Rather than asking how AI can assess students, the focus here is on how AI helps programs learn from evidence and where clear ethical boundaries must be drawn.

From Course-Level Assessment to Program-Level Evidence

A persistent challenge is the gap between course-level evaluation and program-level evidence. Faculty routinely collect rich information about student learning through assignments, discussions, simulations, and field evaluations. Yet translating this information into coherent programmatic evidence that can support continuous improvement and satisfy accreditation requirements often proves difficult (Ewell, 2009; Kuh et al., 2015). Data are dispersed across courses, formats, and platforms, and the labor of aggregation and interpretation frequently falls on a small number of faculty or administrators.

AI appears, at first glance, to offer a solution. Natural language processing, pattern recognition, and data synthesis tools promise to reduce this mechanical burden by identifying trends across student work and mapping learning outcomes to assessments. However, programmatic assessment is a meaning-making process requiring contextual understanding of curriculum design, student populations, and professional expectations (Schuwirth & van der Vleuten, 2020). AI-generated summaries or trend analyses can obscure nuance or inadvertently privilege what is most easily quantified (Peters & Chin-Yee, 2025). For helping professions programs, where assessment involves complex constructs like ethical reasoning, relational competence, and reflective capacity, this risk is acute. The challenge is using AI as infrastructure without displacing human judgment.

Supporting the Assessment Cycle: Design and Alignment

AI adds the most value when integrated into the upstream stages of the assessment cycle: planning, design, and alignment. It functions as a synthesis partner, helping surface possibilities that faculty then critically examine. One of the most productive uses of AI is translating broad competencies into observable performance indicators. The following example (Table 2) shows how AI was used to brainstorm more measurable criteria for a Psychology Program Learning Outcome (PLO):

Table 2. "Before and after" rubric refinement (psychology)

Element	Before (Human Draft)	After (AI-Assisted & Faculty-Verified)
PLO	"Students will demonstrate cultural humility in practice."	Same
Criterion	"Shows respect for diverse client backgrounds and perspectives."	"Identifies specific intersections of identity (e.g., race, class, gender) and describes how these factors influence the therapeutic alliance."
Why It Improved	The "Before" version was too vague for consistent faculty scoring.	The "After" version provides a concrete "look-for" that is easier to measure across different clinical case studies.

Consistent with the boundaries in Table 1, this AI use is permitted for program directors and learning designers during the "Assessment Planning" phase. However, for security and ethics, AI tools are never used to handle raw student data. In this case, program-level assessment was intentionally built within the learning management system using tools such as Canvas Outcomes, allowing data collection, aggregation, and reporting to occur within a secure, FERPA-compliant environment.

Equity, Bias, and the Interpretation of Assessment Data

Equity is central to assessment. Data are never neutral; they reflect curriculum design choices, instructional contexts, institutional structures, and the social positions of students. For this reason, equity-conscious assessment requires interpretive judgment, contextual knowledge, and ethical responsibility, capacities that cannot be delegated to automated systems.

While AI is often promoted as a means of identifying patterns or disparities in educational data, the use of AI for assessment data analysis carries significant ethical and practical risks. Systems trained on historical data may reproduce existing inequities, particularly when those inequities are embedded in assessment practices or institutional contexts (Barocas & Selbst, 2016; Obermeyer et al., 2019). Moreover, analytic outputs – especially when abstracted from lived educational contexts – risk encouraging deficit-oriented interpretations that locate problems in students rather than in curriculum design, instructional support, or structural barriers.

For these reasons, the program described here deliberately chose not to use AI for the analysis or interpretation of assessment data. Instead, assessment evidence is reviewed through collaborative, human-led processes. This approach reflects a core ethical commitment: equity work in professional education must remain accountable to human interpretation, particularly when assessment findings inform curricular decisions, resource allocation, or judgments about student readiness.

This governance choice also supports transparency. Accrediting bodies expect programs to explain how findings were generated and interpreted. Human-centered assessment processes – grounded in documented rubrics, faculty deliberation, and clear decision trails – are more readily explainable and defensible than opaque analytic systems.

Box 2. Vignette: The "Assessment Revitalization" Project

A Counseling Program Director was preparing for a mid-cycle accreditation review. The program had plenty of data, but it was "messy" – a collection of varied assignments across twelve different sections of a practicum course. Faculty were exhausted by the prospect of manually mapping these assignments to the new 2024 CACREP standards.

The Director used an AI tool as a "mapping assistant." They provided the tool with the program's existing syllabi and the new accreditation standards, asking it to identify where specific competencies were being assessed. The AI surfaced a significant gap: while "Crisis Intervention" was mentioned in lectures, it was never formally assessed in the clinical rubrics.

This allowed the Director to lead a faculty meeting focused on *curriculum design* rather than *data entry*. The AI did not make the decision to change the curriculum; it merely made the misalignment visible. By focusing AI on the "infrastructure" of the assessment plan, the program saved dozens of hours of administrative labor while keeping the high-stakes evaluation of student clinical skills entirely in the hands of the faculty supervisors.

Guardrails: What Should Not Be Automated

Perhaps the most important decisions concern what artificial intelligence should not do. In the helping professions, certain judgments are too consequential to delegate. These include determinations of professional readiness, fitness for practice, and ethical competence.

As established in Table 1, student learning artifacts remain an excluded domain for AI judgment. While AI can help draft a rubric, it cannot "score" a student's empathy or cultural responsiveness. Delegating these judgments risks narrowing the competencies that distinguish our professions. Program leaders must articulate these boundaries clearly to protect the program from mission drift.

Key Takeaways: AI-Supported Assessment

- **Focus on Upstream Design:** Use AI to refine rubric language and curriculum maps (as seen in Table 2) rather than to evaluate student work.
- **Maintain Data Sovereignty:** Keep student data within FERPA-compliant LMS environments; do not feed raw student work into generative AI for "grading."

- **Prioritize Human Interpretation:** Reserve the analysis of assessment trends for human-led, equity-conscious dialogue. AI should help tell the story, not write the conclusion.
- **Defend Professional Readiness:** Ensure that all certifications of clinical competence and "fitness for practice" are based on faculty-validated evidence, as per the "Excluded" boundaries in Table 1.

ACCREDITATION, LICENSURE, AND AI: NAVIGATING PRESENT AND FUTURE EXPECTATIONS

Accreditation and licensure occupy a distinctive place in the helping professions. Unlike many academic disciplines, social work, counseling, and psychology education are explicitly tied to public protection, professional gatekeeping, and the legal recognition of practice. Accreditation is a social contract affirming a program's responsibility to prepare graduates who are ethically, cognitively, and relationally equipped for professional work. As artificial intelligence becomes embedded in educational processes, this contract is increasingly tested.

To date, many accrediting bodies have not issued detailed or prescriptive guidance on the use of AI in education. However, existing accreditation standards already emphasize core concerns (e.g., academic integrity, validity of assessment evidence, transparency of instructional practices, consistency across delivery modalities, and accountability for student learning) that are directly implicated by AI-enabled practices (American Counseling Association, 2026; Reamer, 2019). Proactive, values-driven leadership is less about anticipating new rules and more about ensuring that AI integration remains legible, defensible, and aligned with these existing responsibilities.

Accreditation as Professional Accountability

Accrediting bodies evaluate whether programs can demonstrate learning in credible, defensible ways. Accreditation review is not concerned solely with whether data can be processed quickly, but with how learning outcomes are defined, how assessment methods align with those outcomes, and how results are interpreted and used to inform improvement (Banta & Blaich, 2011). Processes that obscure these relationships, even if they appear efficient, undermine the spirit of accreditation. As noted in Table 1, while the handling of assessment data remains a human-led process to preserve security and judgment, the Program Director may use AI for accreditation/assessment documentation. This is a permitted function when used for drafting narratives, provided there is clear disclosure and human verification.

AI's role is situated upstream and downstream of assessment evidence. Upstream, it supports the development of outcomes-aligned rubrics. Downstream, it assists with drafting narratives that articulate the program's assessment story for internal review or self-studies. In both cases, AI functions as a support for human communication, not as a substitute for professional judgment, interpretation, or accountability.

Box 3. Vignette: The Governance Trail

A Social Work Program Director was writing the "Continuous Improvement" section of a self-study. They had used AI to help synthesize three years of faculty meeting minutes where AI policy was debated. Instead of hiding this, the Director created a "Governance Trail" appendix.

This appendix documented the program's decision-making process, including the dates of faculty votes, the specific ethical guardrails adopted, and the rationale for why certain clinical tasks remained AI-free. By documenting the "why" behind their AI use, the program demonstrated high-level professional oversight. During the site visit, the reviewers noted that this transparency actually increased their confidence in the program's integrity, as it showed the leadership was actively managing the technology rather than ignoring it.

Preparing for Future Accreditation and Licensure Scrutiny

Licensing boards rely on accredited programs to certify that graduates are ready for safe practice. If AI-supported instruction raises questions about whether competencies were authentically demonstrated, programs may face challenges from employers and regulators. In this context, a conservative approach to high-stakes AI use is an expression of professional responsibility. Programs should focus on three lessons to "future-proof" their accreditation status:

1. **Treat AI as infrastructure, not authority:** Use AI to build better maps and reports, but never to make final judgments on student readiness.
2. **Differentiate AI use by role:** Ensure that the boundaries established in Table 1 are clearly communicated to all stakeholders.
3. **Make boundaries auditable:** Shift from "vibes-based" policy to documented "governance trails" that show human oversight in action.

To maintain transparency, programs can include a disclosure statement in their accreditation materials. The following example illustrates how to acknowledge AI support while asserting human authorship:

Box 4. Disclosure of AI Support in Documentation

Portions of the narrative in Standard 4 (Assessment of Student Learning) were drafted with the assistance of generative AI. This tool was used to synthesize internal faculty reports and summarize established assessment workflows. All AI-generated drafts were reviewed, edited, and verified for accuracy by the Program Director and the Assessment Committee. The final evaluative judgments, interpretations of data, and plans for curricular improvement represent the original work and professional authority of the faculty.

Key Takeaways: Accreditation and Trust

- **Own the Narrative:** Use AI as a drafting partner for complex reports, but ensure the "voice" and final responsibility remain human (as specified in Table 1).
- **Prioritize Transparency:** Document the use of AI in your self-studies. Transparency is a professional ethic that builds trust with reviewers and the public.
- **Link AI to Existing Standards:** Frame your AI governance in terms of "Validity," "Integrity," and "Equity," concepts that accreditors already value and understand.
- **Protect the Public Contract:** Ensure that licensure-critical skills, such as ethical decision-making and relational competence, are never assessed by AI, maintaining the program's role as a reliable gatekeeper.

AI AS LEARNING DESIGN INFRASTRUCTURE IN ONLINE PSYCHOLOGY PROGRAMS

For many programs, discussions of AI focus on student-facing tools. Far less attention is paid to the role AI can play before a course ever opens, during the labor-intensive work of course design. In online psychology programs serving adult learners and working professionals, this design work is foundational. Course quality and alignment with professional competencies are largely determined long before instruction begins.

This section examines AI as learning design infrastructure. Drawing on the development of a custom generative AI system trained on institutional mission and student characteristics, I illustrate how AI can function as a mediating infrastructure. It supports scale and consistency while preserving human expertise.

Designing at Scale: Reinvesting Time into Quality

Programs often operate under constrained resources where a single instructional designer may be responsible for building multiple courses simultaneously. Traditional development timelines of 10 to 12 weeks per course are often unsustainable. The risk is not only burnout but inconsistency, as courses developed under pressure may diverge in structure or workload expectations.

AI can help address this tension when approached as infrastructure. In the case examined here, a custom GPT was trained on institutional goals and established course design documents. This allowed development timelines to be reduced to approximately six weeks. Importantly, this timeline was not driven by automation alone. Instead, it was a reallocation of human effort. Less time was spent drafting from scratch, and more time was devoted to review, revision, and pedagogical judgment.

Efficiency gains are ethically meaningful only when they reinvest time into higher-order work. As noted in Table 1, AI use in course design and build is permitted for learning designers to support workflow acceleration and Universal Design for Learning (UDL) checks. AI-supported scale becomes problematic when speed replaces deliberation; it becomes valuable when speed enables deeper engagement where it matters most.

AI in Learning Design Workflows: A Before and After Comparison

Central to this redesigned workflow was the use of AI to support a structured process grounded in best practices. The custom GPT was trained using course context documents and build documents developed through years of instructional design experience. These documents encoded not only content expectations, but assumptions about adult learners, cognitive load, accessibility, and alignment with learning outcomes.

The initial phase involved feeding the AI with the basic course concepts and materials that SMEs had developed independently. From this input, the system generated a course discovery and context document – a blueprint articulating course purpose, learning outcomes, student needs, assessment philosophy, and instructional approach. This document was then reviewed and revised by the SMEs, ensuring disciplinary accuracy and conceptual integrity.

Once this shared blueprint was established, AI was used to generate draft course modules aligned with the agreed-upon structure and outcomes. This approach shifted module development from an open-ended creative task to a guided refinement process. Learning outcomes were drafted and refined with explicit attention to program competencies, assessments were aligned systematically, and consistency across courses in a multi-course sequence was maintained.

The value of this workflow lies in the coherence it enables. Courses developed through this process share a common pedagogical logic and workload rhythm. For adult learners navigating online programs alongside work and family responsibilities, such consistency is a form of equity (Chick et al., 2025).

The following example (Table 3) illustrates how AI-assisted design, mediated by a learning designer, improves the coherence of a typical psychology course module:

Table 3. Measurable improvements in course alignment

Feature	Before (SME-Only Draft)	After (AI-Assisted and Designer-Mediated)
Module Structure	9 loosely related activities and readings.	4 scaffolded activities explicitly mapped to a single outcome.
Alignment	Unclear link between the discussion prompt and the final case study.	Direct scaffolding where the discussion drafts a portion of the case study.
Student Workload	Heavy and unpredictable, varying by 5 to 10 hours per week.	Predictable workload rhythm with standardized "time-on-task" estimates.
Accessibility	Basic text-based materials only.	Inclusion of UDL checks, such as alternative format suggestions and clear signposting.

Working With Subject Matter Experts

Collaboration with SMEs is indispensable but challenging. SMEs bring deep disciplinary knowledge but may have limited familiarity with online pedagogy. Over time, a pattern emerged in our workflow. When SMEs interacted directly with the AI, cognitive load increased and attention sometimes shifted away from pedagogical questions. In some instances, SMEs responded to AI-generated ideas by over-expanding modules, inadvertently increasing content density beyond what was appropriate for the student population.

In response, the workflow was redesigned. The instructional designer now assumes primary responsibility for interacting with the AI to generate draft materials. The designer uses the AI to trim, consolidate, or sequence activities to support a steady pace. SMEs then engage as reviewers and revisers, focusing their expertise on accuracy, application, and disciplinary voice. This shift allows SMEs to contribute where their expertise is most valuable: evaluating whether examples resonate with professional practice and whether activities support authentic application.

Key Takeaways: Learning Design Infrastructure

- **Use AI to Enhance Coherence:** Focus AI application on the "infrastructure" of the course, such as alignment mapping and workload balancing, rather than just content generation.
- **Redefine the SME Role:** Position the SME as the final authority and "voice" of the course while the learning designer uses AI to manage the technical build and pedagogical structure.
- **Reinvest Efficiency Gains:** Ensure that shortened development timelines result in more time for human-led ethical reviews and UDL improvements.
- **Maintain Role Boundaries:** Adhere to the permissions in Table 1, ensuring that while designers use AI for "build" tasks, the final disciplinary integrity remains with the faculty experts.

ETHICAL GOVERNANCE OF AI AT THE PROGRAM LEVEL

Ethical commitments to transparency and accountability do not implement themselves. For programs in social work, counseling, and psychology, these values must be translated into deliberate governance decisions. This section examines how programs operationalize ethics through transparency, structured decision-making, and intentional limits on data use.

Transparency That Students Can Understand

Transparency is a foundational ethical requirement in the helping professions, particularly where power differentials exist (American Counseling Association, 2014; American Psychological Association, 2017; National Association of Social Workers, 2021). At the program level, this begins with explicit communication about where AI is used and, crucially, where it is not. Making these distinctions visible prevents misunderstanding and supports informed participation by students and faculty alike.

Avoiding "hidden infrastructures" is essential. When AI quietly shapes curriculum design o, assessment framing without acknowledgment, it undermines trust. Transparency does not require technical disclosure algorithms. Instead, it requires clarity of purpose, scope, and oversight. Programs should be able to explain, in accessible language, why AI is used in specific contexts and who remains responsible for decisions influenced by its outputs.

Trust, in this sense, is not a one-time disclosure but an ongoing relational practice. Programs that communicate proactively about AI use – rather than reacting defensively or retroactively – are better positioned to maintain confidence among students, faculty, and external stakeholders. In professional education, where graduates' competence has real-world consequences, this trust is inseparable from ethical practice.

To move from abstract policy to practice, programs can adopt the following artifacts to operationalize the boundaries established in Table 1:

Box 5.

Artifact A: Brief AI Literacy Assignment (Psychology/Counseling)

Assignment: Critique an AI-Generated Case Conceptualization Task: Students are provided a short client vignette and an AI-generated conceptualization that is intentionally "culturally thin" or overly pathologizing.

- **Graded Requirement:** Identify five specific limitations regarding bias, missing context, or cultural humility. Students then rewrite the conceptualization using a trauma-informed lens.
- **Learning Outcome:** This exercise builds the "epistemic humility" required to use AI as an object of critique rather than an authority.

Artifact B: Course-Level Policy Excerpt

AI Use in This Course: You may use generative AI only for brainstorming, outlining, or proofreading after you have produced your own substantive analysis. You may not use AI to generate reflective journals, process recordings, or any work presented as evidence of clinical judgment or empathy. If used in permitted ways, include a two-sentence note: tool used, purpose, and what you changed. If not used, explicitly state so.

Artifact C: Rubric Criterion for Relational Work

Authenticity and Professional Voice (AI Boundary Criterion)

- **Exemplary:** Work demonstrates the student's own reflective and relational reasoning.
- **Unacceptable:** AI-generated language or "therapeutic voice" is used in reflective content, compromising the assessment of professional formation.
- **Action:** Evidence of AI-authored reflection results in a learning conference rather than immediate punishment.

Decision-Making Framework: Questions and Boundaries

Ethical governance requires structured decision-making that resists ad hoc adoption. Without a shared framework, AI use can become fragmented, inequitable, and misaligned with program goals. Program leaders should use a set of guiding questions before expanding AI use:

- What educational or assessment problem is this AI use intended to address?
- How does it align with professional values?
- Who benefits from this use, and who might be disadvantaged?
- What human expertise and oversight are required?
- At which stages of the educational or assessment process is AI intentionally excluded, and why?
- How will this use be reviewed and revised over time?

These questions shift the focus from what AI *can* do to what programs *should* do. As shown in Table 1, high-stakes judgments of professional fitness remain strictly excluded from AI functions to protect the integrity of the “gatekeeping” role. They also make explicit that not all technically feasible uses of AI are ethically defensible. In the helping professions, where professional judgment and relational competence are central, governance frameworks must prioritize alignment with values over efficiency.

Data Governance and Intentional Non-Use

Data governance is one of the most consequential dimensions of AI integration. In this program, AI is intentionally excluded from the analysis of student assessment data. Student work is managed through established, secure institutional systems to ensure privacy and accountability. This choice reflects a judgment that assessment interpretation must remain human-led. By limiting AI to “upstream” design functions, programs leverage its generative capabilities without risking student data privacy

Equity, Access, and Institutional Responsibility

Institutional adoption of vetted AI tools promotes equity by ensuring all students have access to quality tools regardless of personal resources. It also allows for the vetting of tools for FERPA compliance. Governance is simplified when a common tool is available, allowing programs to develop shared guidelines rather than managing a fragmented ecosystem of unvetted platforms.

This does not require mandating use; rather, it establishes a baseline of access and safety. Faculty and programs may still choose not to use AI or to use it selectively, but they do so within a clearer ethical and infrastructural context. Such institutional responsibility aligns with the helping professions’ commitment to fairness and access. Just as programs would not expect students to purchase specialized clinical software without institutional support, they should be cautious about expecting students or faculty to navigate AI tools independently. Ethical governance recognizes that access to safe, effective tools is a collective responsibility, not an individual burden (O’Sullivan et al., 2025).

Governance as a Recurring Review Cycle

Ethical governance is not a one-time policy but an ongoing practice of reflection. Programs must build mechanisms for revisiting AI use and revising guidelines as technologies evolve. By treating AI integration as a living practice, program leaders model the adaptability they seek to cultivate in their students.

Ultimately, ethical governance at the program level is about more than managing risk. It is about affirming the values that define the helping professions and ensuring that technological innovation serves those values rather than eroding them. When governance is transparent, participatory, and grounded in professional ethics, AI becomes less a source of anxiety and more a site of responsible leadership (Oncioiu & Bularca, 2025).

Key Takeaways: Ethical Governance

- **Operationalize Transparency:** Use specific artifacts like AI-disclosure notes and critique assignments to make boundaries visible to students.
- **Protect Data Integrity:** Limit AI to planning and drafting roles. Keep the actual analysis of student performance within secure, human-led systems.
- **Build a Decision Trail:** Use a consistent set of evaluative questions to document why specific AI uses were permitted or restricted.

IMPLICATIONS FOR PROGRAM DIRECTORS, LEARNING DESIGNERS, AND INSTITUTIONS

Responsible AI integration in the helping professions is not primarily a technical challenge. It is a leadership and design challenge. Programs that treat AI as an isolated tool risk ethical drift. However, those that approach AI as infrastructure governed by roles and developmental readiness are better positioned to support professional formation.

Implications for Program Directors: Ethical Stewardship

For directors, AI integration requires a reframing of leadership. You do not need to become a technical specialist, but you must become an ethical steward of how AI intersects with curricula and accreditation.

- **Locate AI within Program Goals:** Move beyond individual course experimentation. Articulate shared principles for AI use and clarify where consistency is required, such as in assessment transparency.
- **Adopt Role-Differentiated Governance:** Use the framework established in Table 1 to justify different expectations for faculty, designers, and students.

This supports AI literacy as a developmental outcome rather than a compliance burden.

- **Commit to Reflective Practice:** Treat AI integration as a recurring cycle. Regular reviews ensure that your program's tools remain aligned with evolving professional standards and ethical commitments.

Implications for Learning Designers: Codifying Expertise

For designers, AI presents an opportunity to strengthen the pedagogical foundations of online education. When used intentionally, it supports alignment and scalability in resource-constrained environments.

- **Codify Design Knowledge:** Training AI systems on institutional mission statements and course design documents transforms tacit knowledge into shared infrastructure. This improves consistency across the curriculum.
- **Mediate Subject Matter Expertise:** As shown in the "Before and After" artifacts (see Table 3), designers should act as the primary AI interlocutors. This reduces the cognitive load on SMEs and preserves the "human" disciplinary voice.
- **Advocate for Ethical Design:** Resist treating AI-generated content as a finished product. Monitor for bias and advocate for course pacing that allows students time for genuine reflection.

Implications for Institutions: Equity and Responsibility

At the institutional level, AI raises questions of access that extend beyond individual programs.

- **Adopt Vetted Tools:** Institutional adoption of a supported AI tool promotes equity. It ensures that access to quality tools is not dependent on a student's personal resources and allows for centralized FERPA compliance vetting.
- **Support Cross-Functional Governance:** Create structures that facilitate dialogue between program leaders, faculty, and IT professionals. Policies produced through collaboration are more likely to be practical and values-aligned.

A Note on International Contexts

While this chapter focuses largely on North American accreditation (e.g., CSWE, CACREP, APA), the principles of role-differentiated governance and AI as infrastructure are globally applicable. International bodies, such as the International Federation of Social Workers (IFSW) or global psychological associations, emphasize social justice and human dignity (IFSW, 2020; International Union of Psychological Science, 2008). Program directors outside North America can use the Table 1 boundaries to ensure that AI adoption does not inadvertently import Western-centric biases or erode the culturally specific relational models essential to their local contexts.

CONCLUSION: TOWARD A RESPONSIBLE FUTURE FOR PROFESSIONAL EDUCATION

The integration of artificial intelligence into social work, counseling, and psychology is not merely a change in the tools we use; it is a change in the environment where professional identity is formed. Throughout this chapter, the central argument has remained that academic programs serve as the ethical unit of this integration. By shifting the focus from individual classroom novelties to program-level infrastructure, leadership can ensure that innovation serves the core values of the helping professions: human dignity, equity, and relational accountability.

The role-differentiated framework established in this chapter serves as more than a set of rules; it is a map for maintaining trust. When program directors and learning designers use AI to strengthen the "pipes" of education (e.g., refining rubrics, aligning curriculum maps, and drafting accreditation narratives), they are not automating the profession. They are instead reinvesting their time into the high-stakes human judgments that define our fields. By intentionally excluding AI from the assessment of professional fitness and reflective "use of self," programs honor the social contract they hold with the public.

Looking forward, the success of AI integration will not be measured by the sophistication of the tools we adopt, but by the clarity of the boundaries we maintain. Stewardship requires us to resist the urge to use AI as a shortcut for the relational work of teaching and gatekeeping. Instead, we must use it to make our educational systems more coherent, our assessments more equitable, and our design processes more inclusive.

Ultimately, AI integration is an invitation to be more intentional about what is truly human in our work. In a landscape where machine-generated content is becoming ubiquitous, the ability of a professional to exercise empathy, navigate ethical complexity, and maintain a therapeutic presence becomes more valuable than ever. By building robust governance structures today, program leaders ensure that the helping professions remain firmly anchored in these human commitments, even as the technological infrastructure continues to shift.

ACKNOWLEDGMENT

AI Use Disclosure. Generative artificial intelligence (AI) tools (OpenAI's ChatGPT 5.2 and Google's Gemini 3) were used during the preparation of this chapter to assist with drafting and editorial refinement. AI tools were not used to generate original empirical content, analyze data, or make substantive scholarly judgments. All conceptual decisions, ethical judgments, and final content were determined, reviewed, and approved by the author, who assumes full responsibility for the work.

REFERENCES

Adamakis, M., & Rachiotis, T. (2025). Artificial intelligence in higher education: A state-of-the-art overview of pedagogical integrity, artificial intelligence literacy, and policy integration. *Encyclopedia*, *5*(4), 180. DOI: 10.3390/encyclopedia5040180

Ahn, E., Choi, M., Fowler, P., & Song, I. (2025). Artificial Intelligence (AI) Literacy for Social Work: Implications for Core Competencies. *Journal of the Society for Social Work and Research*, *16*(4). Advance online publication. DOI: 10.1086/735187

Alsharefeen, R. (2025). Faculty as street-level bureaucrats: Discretionary decision-making in the era of generative AI. *Frontiers in Education*. Advance online publication. DOI: 10.3389/feduc.2025.1662657

American Association of University Professors. (2025). *Artificial intelligence and academic professions*. AAUP. https://www.aaup.org/reports-publications/aaup-policies-reports/topical-reports/artificial-intelligence-and-academic

American Counseling Association. (2014). *ACA code of ethics*. https://www.counseling.org/knowledge-center/ethics/ethics-code-2014

American Counseling Association. (2026). *Integrating AI and LLMs into counseling education: Ethical and inclusive approaches*. https://www.counseling.org/resources/research-reports/artificial-intelligence-counseling/for-faculty#

American Psychological Association. (2017). *Ethical principles of psychologists and code of conduct* (2002, amended effective June 1, 2010, and January 1, 2017). https://www.apa.org/ethics/code

Banta, T. W., & Blaich, C. (2010). Closing the assessment loop. *Change: The Magazine of Higher Learning*, *43*(1), 22–27. DOI: 10.1080/00091383.2011.538642

Barocas, S., & Selbst, A. D. (2016). Big data's disparate impact. *104. California Law Review*, *671*. Advance online publication. DOI: 10.2139/ssrn.2477899

Berridge, C., Bricout, J., Goldkind, L., Gregoire, T., Hiltz, B., McInroy, L. B., O'Neil, M., Patton, D. U., Putnam-Hornstein, E., Rodriguez, M. Y., Trahan, M., Victor, B., Gabel, S. G., & Fujita, M. (2025). *CSWE Commission on Educational Policy task force on technology and social work education report*. Council on Social Work Education. https://www.cswe.org/CSWE/media/EdResources/ARL_TechReport_web.pdf

Campbell, K., Schwier, R. A., & Kenny, R. F. (2007). The critical, relational practice of instructional design in higher education: An emerging model of change agency. *Educational Technology Research and Development*, *57*(5), 645–663. DOI: 10.1007/s11423-007-9061-6

Chan, C. K. Y. (2023). A comprehensive AI policy education framework for university teaching and learning. *International Journal of Educational Technology in Higher Education*, *20*(38). Advance online publication. DOI: 10.1186/s41239-023-00408-3

Chick, J. C., Morello, L., & Vance, J. (2025). Universal Design for Learning as an equity framework: Addressing educational barriers and enablers for diverse non-traditional learners. *Education Sciences*, *15*(9), 1265. DOI: 10.3390/educsci15091265

Croaker, S., Dickinson, T., Watson, S., & Zuchowski, I. (2017). Students' suitability for social work: Developing a framework for field education. *Advances in Social Work and Welfare Education, 19*(2), 109–124. https://journal.anzswwer.org/index.php/advances/article/view/174

Dickens, E., Han, A., Shafiq, N. & Taggart, J., (2025) Curriculum developers: An emerging subset of educational developers. *To Improve the Academy: A Journal of Educational Development, 44*(1). DOI: 10.3998/tia.5274

Ewell, P. T. (2009). *Assessment, accountability, and improvement: Revisiting the tension.* National Institute for Learning Outcomes Assessment. https://inside.southernct.edu/sites/default/files/a/inside-southern/assessment-and-planning/Assessment-Accountability-and-Improvement.pdf

Foster, V. A., & McAdams, C. R.III. (2009). A framework for creating a climate of transparency for professional performance assessment: Fostering student investment in gatekeeping. *Counselor Education and Supervision, 48*(4), 271–284. DOI: 10.1002/j.1556-6978.2009.tb00080.x

Giray, L., Sevnarayan, K., & Ranjbaran Madiseh, F. (2025). Beyond policing: AI writing detection tools, trust, academic integrity, and their implications for college writing. *Internet Reference Services Quarterly, 29*(1), 83–116. DOI: 10.1080/10875301.2024.2437174

International Federation of Social Workers. (2020). *Global standards for social work education and training*. https://www.ifsw.org/global-standards-for-social-work-education-and-training/

International Union of Psychological Science. (2008). *Universal declaration of ethical principles for psychologists.* https://www.iupsys.net/about/declarations/universal-declaration-of-ethical-principles-for-psychologists/

Isaacs, J. (2021). The problem with data-driven decision making in education. *Journal of Educational Thought / Revue de La Pensée Educative, 54*(1). DOI: 10.55016/ojs/jet.v54i1.72895

Kasneci, E., Sessler, K., Küchemann, S., Bannert, M., Dementieva, D., Fischer, F., Gasser, U., Groh, G., Günnemann, S., Hüllermeier, E., Krusche, S., Kutyniok, G., Michaeli, T., Nerdel, C., Pfeffer, J., Poquet, O., Sailer, M., Schmidt, A., Seidel, T., & Stadler, M. (2023). ChatGPT for good? On opportunities and challenges of large language models for education. *Learning and Individual Differences*, *103*(102274). Advance online publication. DOI: 10.1016/j.lindif.2023.102274

Kim, J., Klopfer, M., Grohs, J. R., Eldardiry, H., Weichert, J., Cox, L. A.II, & Pike, D. (2025). Examining faculty and student perceptions of generative AI in university courses. *Innovative Higher Education, 50*, 1281–1313. DOI: 10.1007/s10755-024-09774-w

Kuh, G. D., Ikenberry, S. O., Jankowski, N. A., Cain, T. R., Ewell, P. T., Hutchings, P., & Kinzie, J. (2015). *Using evidence of student learning to improve higher education. Jossey-Bass*. Wiley.

Laundon, M., & Grant-Smith, D. (2023). Defining and advancing a systems approach to achieving educator wellbeing: An integrative review of wellbeing in higher education. *Student Success*, *14*(3), 104–119. DOI: 10.5204/ssj.3191

Lee, S. S., & Moore, R. L. (2024). Harnessing generative AI (GenAI) for automated feedback in higher education: A systematic review. *Online Learning : the Official Journal of the Online Learning Consortium*, *28*(3). Advance online publication. DOI: 10.24059/olj.v28i3.4593

Marshall, S., Blaj-Ward, L., Dreamson, N., Nyanjom, J., & Bertuol, M. T. (2024). The reshaping of higher education: Technological impacts, pedagogical change, and future projections. *Higher Education Research & Development*, *43*(3), 521–541. DOI: 10.1080/07294360.2024.2329393

Masters, K. (2023). Ethical use of Artificial Intelligence in health professions education: AMEE Guide No. 158. *Medical Teacher, 45*(6), 574–584. DOI: 10.1080/0142159X.2023.2186203

Moorhouse, B. L., Yeo, M. A., & Wan, Y. (2023). Generative AI tools and assessment: Guidelines of the world's top-ranking universities. *Computers and Education Open, 5*. Advance online publication. DOI: 10.1016/j.caeo.2023.100151

National Association of Social Workers. (2021). *NASW code of ethics*. https://www.socialworkers.org/About/Ethics/Code-of-Ethics/Code-of-Ethics-English

Nicola-Richmond, K., Dawson, P., Helen, P., & Macfarlane, S. (2025). It takes a village... Program-wide approaches to redesigning assessment in a time of generative artificial intelligence (GenAI). *Journal of University Teaching & Learning Practice*. Advance online publication. DOI: 10.53761/zpp2ja61

O'Sullivan, J., Lowry, C., Woods, R., & Conlon, T. (2025). *Generative AI in higher education teaching & learning: Principles for ethical AI adoption*. Higher Education Authority. DOI: 10.82110/qmt6-jw48

Obermeyer, Z., Powers, B., Vogeli, C., & Mullainathan, S. (2019). Dissecting racial bias in an algorithm used to manage the health of populations. *Science, 366*(6464), 447–453. DOI: 10.1126/science.aax2342

Oncioiu, I., & Bularca, A. R. (2025). Artificial intelligence governance in higher education: The role of knowledge-based strategies in fostering legal awareness and ethical artificial intelligence literacy. *Societies (Basel, Switzerland), 15*(6), 144. DOI: 10.3390/soc15060144

Peters, U., & Chin-Yee, B. (2025). Generalization bias in large language model summarization of scientific research. *Royal Society Open Science, 12*(4), 241776. DOI: 10.1098/rsos.241776

Potgieter, I. (2020). Privacy concerns in educational data mining and learning analytics. *International Journal of Information Ethics, 28*. Advance online publication. DOI: 10.29173/irie384

Prieto, L. P., Dlab, M. H., Gutiérrez, I., Abdulwahed, M., & Balid, W. (2011). Orchestrating technology enhanced learning: A literature review and a conceptual framework. *International Journal of Technology Enhanced Learning, 3*(6), 583. DOI: 10.1504/ijtel.2011.045449

Reamer, F. (2023). Artificial intelligence in social work: Emerging ethical issues. *International Journal of Social Work Values and Ethics, 20*(2), 52–71. DOI: 10.55521/10-020-205

Reamer, F. G. (2019). Social work education in a digital world: Technology standards for education and practice. *Journal of Social Work Education*, *55*(3), 420–432. https://www.jstor.org/stable/48543052

Reiss, M. J. (2021). The use of AI in education: Practicalities and ethical considerations. *London Review of Education*, *19*(1). Advance online publication. DOI: 10.14324/lre.19.1.05

Rodriguez, M. Y., Goldkind, L., Victor, B. G., Hiltz, B., & Perron, B. E. (2024). Introducing generative artificial intelligence into the MSW curriculum: A proposal for the 2029 Educational Policy and Accreditation Standards. *Journal of Social Work Education*, *60*(2), 174–182. DOI: 10.1080/10437797.2024.2340931

Salido, A., Syarif, I., Sitepu, M. S., Wana, P. R., Taufika, R., & Melisa, R. (2025). Integrating critical thinking and artificial intelligence in higher education: A bibliometric and systematic review of skills and strategies. *Social Sciences & Humanities Open*, *12*, 101924. DOI: 10.1016/j.ssaho.2025.101924

Schophuizen, M., & Kalz, M. (2020). Educational innovation projects in Dutch higher education: Bottom-up contextual coping to deal with organizational challenges. *International Journal of Educational Technology in Higher Education*, *17*(36). Advance online publication. DOI: 10.1186/s41239-020-00197-z

Schuwirth, L. W. T., & van der Vleuten, C. P. M. (2020). A history of assessment in medical education. *Advances in Health Sciences Education : Theory and Practice*, *25*(5), 1045–1056. DOI: 10.1007/s10459-020-10003-0

Selwyn, N. (2014). *Distrusting educational technology: Critical questions for changing times*. Bloomsbury Academic.

Selwyn, N. (2022). *Should robots replace teachers? AI and the future of education*. Polity Press.

Shoemaker, S., Freeburg, N., & Duquette, K. (2025). Artificial intelligence in counselor education: Innovative strategies for teaching, supervision, and clinical training. *The Journal of Counselor Preparation and Supervisor*, *19*(3), 1–34.

Singer-Freeman, K., & Robinson, C. (2020). Grand challenges for assessment in higher education. *Research & Practice in Assessment, 15*(2). https://www.rpajournal.com/dev/wp-content/uploads/2020/11/Grand-Challenges-for-Assessment-in-Higher-Education.pdf

Slade, S., & Prinsloo, P. (2013). Learning analytics: Ethical issues and dilemmas. *The American Behavioral Scientist*, *57*(10), 1510–1529. DOI: 10.1177/0002764213479366

Timotheou, S., Miliou, O., Dimitriadis, Y., Sobrino, S. V., Giannoutsou, N., Cachia, R., Monés, A. M., & Ioannou, A. (2023). Impacts of digital technologies on education and factors influencing schools' digital capacity and transformation: A literature review. *Education and Information Technologies*, *28*(6), 6695–6726. DOI: 10.1007/s10639-022-11431-8

Watts, K. J. (2025). Paying the cognitive debt: An experiential learning framework for integrating AI in social work education. *Education Sciences*, *15*(10), 1304. DOI: 10.3390/educsci15101304

Williams, R. T. (2024). The ethical implications of using generative chatbots in higher education. *Frontiers in Education*, *8*(1331607). Advance online publication. DOI: 10.3389/feduc.2023.1331607

Williamson, B. (2017). Big data in education: The digital future of learning, policy and practice. *Sage (Atlanta, Ga.)*.

Zhao, C. (2024). AI-assisted assessment in higher education: A systematic review. *Journal of Educational Technology and Innovation*, *6*(4). Advance online publication. DOI: 10.61414/jeti.v6i4.209

KEY TERMS AND DEFINITIONS

AI Literacy: The capacity to understand, critically evaluate, and ethically use artificial intelligence in professional and educational contexts, including awareness of AI's capabilities, limitations, biases, and implications for human judgment.

Educational Infrastructure: The underlying systems, tools, and processes—often invisible to learners—that shape how education is designed, delivered, assessed, and governed, including AI-supported workflows.

Ethical Stewardship: A leadership approach to AI integration that emphasizes responsibility, transparency, accountability, and alignment with professional values rather than compliance, surveillance, or technical efficiency alone.

Professional Formation: The developmental process through which students acquire not only disciplinary knowledge and skills, but also ethical judgment, relational competence, and professional identity.

Program-Level Governance: The structures, policies, and decision-making processes through which academic programs guide, evaluate, and oversee AI use across curriculum design, assessment, accreditation, and professional preparation.

Programmatic Assessment: The systematic collection, interpretation, and use of evidence across courses and learning experiences to evaluate student learning outcomes, inform curricular improvement, and meet accreditation and accountability requirements.

Role-Differentiated AI Use: An approach to AI integration that recognizes different expectations and boundaries for AI use based on users' expertise and developmental readiness (e.g., instructional designers and subject matter experts versus students).

Compilation of References

AASW Practice Standards. (2023). https://my.aasw.asn.au/file-asset/0699g000001T7hsAAC

Abbass, H. A. (2019). Social integration of artificial intelligence: Functions, automation allocation logic and human-autonomy trust. *Cognitive Computation*, *11*(2), 159–171. DOI: 10.1007/s12559-018-9619-0

Abigail, L. K. M. (2016). Do communities of practice enhance faculty development? *Health Profession Education*, *2*(2), 61–74. DOI: 10.1016/j.hpe.2016.08.004

Abubakar, A. M., Gupta, D., & Parida, S. (2024). A reinforcement learning approach for intelligent conversational chatbot for enhancing mental health therapy. *Procedia Computer Science*, *235*, 916–925. DOI: 10.1016/j.procs.2024.04.087

Adamakis, M., & Rachiotis, T. (2025). Artificial intelligence in higher education: A state-of-the-art overview of pedagogical integrity, artificial intelligence literacy, and policy integration. *Encyclopedia*, *5*(4), 180. DOI: 10.3390/encyclopedia5040180

Adhikary, P. K., Srivastava, A., Kumar, S., Singh, S. M., Manuja, P., Gopinath, J. K., Krishnan, V., Gupta, S. K., Deb, K. S., & Chakraborty, T. (2024). Exploring the efficacy of large language models in summarizing mental health counseling sessions: Benchmark study. *JMIR Mental Health*, *11*, e57306. Advance online publication. DOI: 10.2196/57306

Ahluwalia, M., Sehgal, S., Lee, G., Agu, E., & Kpodonu, J. (2025). Disparities in artificial intelligence-based tools among diverse minority populations: Biases, barriers, and solutions. *JACC Advances*, *4*(5), 101742. DOI: 10.1016/j.jacadv.2025.101742

Ahn, E., Choi, M., Fowler, P., & Song, I. (2025). Artificial intelligence (AI) literacy for social work: Implications for core competencies. *Journal of the Society for Social Work and Research*, *16*(1), 9–26. DOI: 10.1086/735187

Akkurt, M., Maurya, R., & Brown, T. (2025). Learning through simulation: Counselor trainees' interactions with ChatGPT as a client. *Behavioral Sciences (Basel, Switzerland)*, *15*(12), 1660. DOI: 10.3390/bs15121660

Al Kez, D., Foley, A. M., Laverty, D., Del Rio, D. F., & Sovacool, B. (2022). Exploring the sustainability challenges facing digitalization and internet data centers. *Journal of Cleaner Production*, *371*, 133633.

Alikhademi, K., Drobina, E., Prioleau, D., Richardson, B., Purves, D., & Gilbert, J. E. (2022). A review of predictive policing from the perspective of fairness. *Artificial Intelligence and Law*, *30*(1), 1–17. DOI: 10.1007/s10506-021-09286-4

Allan, J., Briskman, L., & Pease, B. (2020). *Critical social work: Theories and practices for a socially just world* (Routledge, T.Francis Group, Ed.; 2nd ed.).

Allen, L. K., & Kendeou, P. (2023). ED-AI Lit: An Interdisciplinary Framework for AI Literacy in Education. *Policy Insights from the Behavioral and Brain Sciences*, *11*(1), 3–10. DOI: 10.1177/23727322231220339

Almusaed, A., Almssad, A., Yitmen, I., & Homod, R. Z. (2023). Enhancing student engagement: Harnessing "AIED"'s power in hybrid education—A review analysis. *Education Sciences*, *13*(7), 632. DOI: 10.3390/educsci13070632

Al-Rantisi, A. M., ElShanti, N. H., & Harb, S. A. (2025). Challenges of using artificial intelligence in social work education. *Social Work Education*, •••, 1–18. DOI: 10.1080/02615479.2025.2483354

Alsharefeen, R. (2025). Faculty as street-level bureaucrats: Discretionary decision-making in the era of generative AI. *Frontiers in Education*. Advance online publication. DOI: 10.3389/feduc.2025.1662657

American Association of University Professors. (2025). *Artificial intelligence and academic professions*. AAUP. https://www.aaup.org/reports-publications/aaup-policies-reports/topical-reports/artificial-intelligence-and-academic

American Counseling Association. (2014). *ACA code of ethics*. https://www.counseling.org/knowledge-center/ethics/ethics-code-2014

American Counseling Association. (2014). Code of ethics. https://www.counseling.org/knowledge-center/ethics

American Counseling Association. (2026). *Integrating AI and LLMs into counseling education: Ethical and inclusive approaches*. https://www.counseling.org/resources/research-reports/artificial-intelligence-counseling/for-faculty#

American Psychological Association. (2017). *Ethical principles of psychologists and code of conduct* (2002, amended effective June 1, 2010, and January 1, 2017). https://www.apa.org/ethics/code

American Psychological Association. (2017). Ethical principles of psychologists and code of conduct. https://www.apa.org/ethics/code

American Psychological Association. (2025). *Ethical guidance for AI in the professional practice of health service psychology*. https://www.apa.org/topics/artificial-intelligence-machine-learning/ethical-guidance-professional-practice.pdf

Anders, A. D., & Dux Speltz, E. (2025). Developing generative AI literacies through self-regulated learning: A human-centered approach. *Computers and Education: Artificial Intelligence*, *9*, 100482. DOI: 10.1016/j.caeai.2025.100482

Annapureddy, R., Fornaroli, A., & Gatica-Perez, D. (2025). Generative AI literacy: Twelve defining competencies. *Digit. Gov.: Res. Pract.*, *6*(1), 13. Advance online publication. DOI: 10.1145/3685680

Asakura, K. (2024). Toward a critical approach to simulation-based social work education: Guidelines for designing simulated client case scenarios. *Journal of Social Work Education*, *60*(1), 102–114.

Asakura, K., & Bogo, M. (2021). Editorial: The use of simulation in advancing clinical social work education and practice. *Clinical Social Work*, *49*, 111–116.

Asakura, K., Occhiuto, K., Todd, S., Leithead, C., & Clapperton, R. (2020). A call to action on artificial intelligence and social work education: Lessons learned from a simulation project using natural language processing. *Journal of Teaching in Social Work*, *40*(5), 501–518. DOI: 10.1080/08841233.2020.1813234

Asal, M. G. R., Alsenany, S. A., Elzohairy, N. W., & El-Sayed, A. A. I. (2025). The impact of digital competence on pedagogical innovation among nurse educators: The moderating role of artificial intelligence readiness. *Nurse Education in Practice*, *85*, 104367. DOI: 10.1016/j.nepr.2025.104367

Australian Association of Social Workers. (2024). *Australian social work education and accreditation standards*. Retrieved 29th December 2025 from https://aasw-media.s3.ap-southeast-4.amazonaws.com/wp-content/uploads/2025/10/00.-AASW-ASWEAS-2024.pdf

Babaeva, A., Samerkhanova, E., Guseva, L., Shmeleva, N., & Gromov, B. (2023). Social work in the digital age. *E3S Web of Conferences, 381*, 1023. DOI: 10.1051/e3sconf/202338101023

Báez, J. C., Bjugstad, A., Park, T. K., Jones, J. L., Bidwell, L. N., Sage, M., & Hitchcock, L. I. (2025). Social work educators innovating with generative AI: An exploratory study. *Journal of Social Work Education, 61*(1), 14–29. DOI: 10.1080/10437797.2024.2411170

Baker, E., & Jenney, A. (2023). Virtual simulations to train social works for competency-based learning: A scoping review. *Journal of Social Work Education, 59*(1), 8–31.

Banta, T. W., & Blaich, C. (2010). Closing the assessment loop. *Change: The Magazine of Higher Learning, 43*(1), 22–27. DOI: 10.1080/00091383.2011.538642

Barbosa da Silva, J., Espinal, M., Garcia-Saiso, S., Fitzgerald, J., Marti, M., Bascolo, E., Haddad, A. E., & D'Agostino, M. (2024). A digital transformation for primary health care. *Bulletin of the World Health Organization, 102*(1), 2–2A. DOI: 10.2471/BLT.23.290726

Barocas, S., & Selbst, A. D. (2016). Big data's disparate impact. *104. California Law Review, 671.* Advance online publication. DOI: 10.2139/ssrn.2477899

Baron, P. (2024). Are AI detection and plagiarism similarity scores worthwhile in the age of ChatGPT and other Generative AI? *Scholarship of Teaching and Learning in the South, 8*(2), 151–179. DOI: 10.36615/sotls.v8i2.411

Bashir, N., Donti, P., Cuff, J., Sroka, S., Ilich, M., Sze, V., Delimitru, C., & Alveti, E. (2024). The climate and sustainability implications of generative AI. MIT. https://mit-genai.pubpub.org/pub/8ulgrckc

Beale, R. (2022). *Adapting university policies for generative AI: Opportunities, challenges, and policy solutions in higher education.* Arxiv.org. https://arxiv.org/html/2506.22231v1

Bender, E. M., Gebru, T., McMillan-Major, A., & Shmitchell, S. (2021). On the dangers of stochastic parrots: Can language models be too big? *Proceedings of the 2021 ACM Conference on Fairness, Accountability, and Transparency*, 610–623. https://doi.org/DOI: 10.1145/3442188.3445922

Benjamin, R. (2019). *Race after technology: Abolitionist tools for the new Jim code.* Polity Press.

Benjamin, R. (2019). *Race after technology: Abolitionist tools for the new Jim Code.* Polity Press.

Bernacki, M. L., Greene, M. J., & Lobczowski, N. G. (2021). A systematic review of research on personalized learning: Personalized by whom, to what, how, and for what purpose (s)? *Educational Psychology Review*, *33*(4), 1675–1715.

Berrett-Abebe, J., Novella, J. K., & Perera, D. M. (2023). Shared and unique competencies in interprofessional behavioral health: Implications for counselor education. *The Journal of Counselor Preparation and Supervisor*, *17*(5). https://research.library.kutztown.edu/jcps/vol17/iss5/5

Berridge, C., Bricout, J., Goldkind, L., Gregoire, T., Hiltz, B., McInroy, L. B., O'Neil, M., Patton, D. U., Putnam-Hornstein, E., Rodriguez, M. Y., Trahan, M., Victor, B., Gabel, S. G., & Fujita, M. (2025). *CSWE Commission on Educational Policy task force on technology and social work education report*. Council on Social Work Education. https://www.cswe.org/CSWE/media/EdResources/ARL_TechReport_web.pdf

Berry, D. M. (2023). The limits of computation: Joseph Weizenbaum and the ELIZA chatbot. *Weizenbaum Journal of the Digital Society, 3*(3). https://doi.org/DOI: 10.34669/WI.WJDS/3.3.2

Berthelot, A., Caron, E., Jay, M., & Lefèvre, L. (2025, July). Understanding the environmental impact of generative AI services. *Communications of the ACM, 68*(7), 46–53.

Berzin, S. C., Singer, E., & Chan, C. (2020). Preparing social work students for an AI-driven world. *Journal of Social Work Education, 56*(sup1), S103–S113.

Bewersdorff, A., Nerdel, C., & Zhai, X. (2025). How AI literacy correlates with affective, behavioral, cognitive and contextual variables: A systematic review. *Computers and Education: Artificial Intelligence*, *9*. Advance online publication. DOI: 10.1016/j.caeai.2025.100493

Blodgett, S. L., Barocas, S., Daumé, H.III, & Wallach, H. (2020). Language (technology) is power: A critical survey of "bias" in NLP. *ArXiv:2005.14050 [Cs]*. https://arxiv.org/abs/2005.14050

Boetto, H. (2025). Artificial intelligence in social work: An EPIC model for practice. *Australian Social Work*, 1–14. DOI: 10.1080/0312407X.2025.2488345

Bogo, M., Regehr, C., Katz, E., Logie, C., & Mylopoulos, M. (2011). Developing a tool for assessing students' reflections on their practice. *Social Work Education*, *30*(02), 186–194.

Brodie, P. (2023). Data infrastructure studies on an unequal planet. *Big Data & Society*, *10*(1). Advance online publication. DOI: 10.1177/20539517231182402

Buele, J., & Llerena-Aguirre, L. (2025). Transformations in academic work and faculty perceptions of artificial intelligence in higher education. *Frontiers in Education, 10*. Advance online publication. DOI: 10.3389/feduc.2025.1603763

Buelvas Parra, J. A., Santamaría Escobar, Á. E., & Pertuz Martínez, A. P. (2024). Artificial intelligence in education: Benefits, challenges, and ethical considerations according to scientific evidence. *Journal of International Crisis and Risk Communication Research, 7*(S5). Advance online publication. DOI: 10.63278/jicrcr.vi.606

Buolamwini, J., & Gebru, T. (2018). Gender shades: Intersectional accuracy disparities in commercial gender classification. *Proceedings of the 1st Conference on Fairness, Accountability, and Transparency*, 77–91.

Campbell, K., Schwier, R. A., & Kenny, R. F. (2007). The critical, relational practice of instructional design in higher education: An emerging model of change agency. *Educational Technology Research and Development, 57*(5), 645–663. DOI: 10.1007/s11423-007-9061-6

Cashwell, S. (2024). Bringing environmental justice to the practice setting: Putting the environment in Person-in-Environment. *Journal of Human Rights and Social Work*, •••, 1–8.

Chan, C. K. Y. (2023). A comprehensive AI policy education framework for university teaching and learning. *International Journal of Educational Technology in Higher Education, 20*(38). Advance online publication. DOI: 10.1186/s41239-023-00408-3

Chick, J. C., Morello, L., & Vance, J. (2025). Universal Design for Learning as an equity framework: Addressing educational barriers and enablers for diverse non-traditional learners. *Education Sciences, 15*(9), 1265. DOI: 10.3390/educsci15091265

Chinoracky, R., & Stalmasekova, N. (2025). Ethical problems in the use of artificial intelligence by university educators. *Education Sciences, 15*(10), 1322. DOI: 10.3390/educsci15101322

Chouldechova, A., Putnam-Hornstein, E., Benavides-Prado, D., Fialko, O., & Vaithianathan, R. (2018). A case study of algorithm-assisted decision-making in child maltreatment hotline screening. *Proceedings of Machine Learning Research, 81*, 134–148.

Chu, T. S., & Ashraf, M. (2025). Artificial intelligence in curriculum design: A data-driven approach to higher education innovation. *Knowledge (Beverly Hills, Calif.), 5*(3), 14. DOI: 10.3390/knowledge5030014

Corbin, T., Walton, J., Bannister, P., & Deranty, J.-P. (2025). On the essay in a time of GenAI. *Educational Philosophy and Theory*, 1–13. DOI: 10.1080/00131857.2025.2572802

Cordero, D., Zhao, Y., Diaz, P., & Weiss, G. M. (2025). Unveiling bias: Analyzing race and gender disparities in AI-generated imagery. *2025 IEEE 49th Annual Computers, Software, and Applications Conference (COMPSAC), Computers, Software, and Applications Conference (COMPSAC), 2025 IEEE 49th Annual, COMPSAC*, 318–323. https://doi.org/DOI: 10.1109/COMPSAC65507.2025.00051

Costanza-Chock, S. (2020). *Design justice: Community-led practices to build the worlds we need*. MIT Press.

Council on Social Work Education. (2022). Educational policy and accreditation standards (EPAS:6, 7, 8 AND 9:).

Council on Social Work Education. (2022). *Educational policy and accreditation standards for baccalaureate and master's social work programs*. Retrieved 29th December 2025 from https://www.cswe.org/getmedia/bb5d8afe-7680-42dc-a332-a6e6103f4998/2022-Educational-Policy-and-Accreditation-Standards-(EPAS).pdf

Crawford, K. (2021). *Atlas of AI: Power, politics, and the planetary costs of artificial intelligence*. Yale University Press.

Crawford, K. (2021). *The atlas of AI: Power, politics, and the planetary costs of artificial intelligence*. Yale University Press.

Croaker, S., Dickinson, T., Watson, S., & Zuchowski, I. (2017). Students' suitability for social work: Developing a framework for field education. *Advances in Social Work and Welfare Education, 19*(2), 109–124. https://journal.anzswwer.org/index.php/advances/article/view/174

Cui, Y., He, W., Du, X., Zeng, M., & Liu, D. (2025). The impact of AI writing assistants on academic writing performance. *International Journal of Distance Education Technologies, 23*(1), 1–28. DOI: 10.4018/ijdet.391326

Currie, G. M. (2023). Academic integrity and artificial intelligence: Is ChatGPT hype, hero or heresy? *Seminars in Nuclear Medicine, 53*(5), 719–730. DOI: 10.1053/j.semnuclmed.2023.04.008

Curtis, G. J. (2025). The two-lane road to hell is paved with good intentions: Why an all-or-none approach to generative AI, integrity, and assessment is insupportable. *Higher Education Research & Development*, 1–8. DOI: 10.1080/07294360.2025.2476516

Dai, C., & Ke, F. (2022). Educational applications of artificial intelligence in simulation-based learning: A systematic mapping review. *Computers and Education: Artificial Intelligence, 3*. Advance online publication. DOI: 10.1016/j.caeai.2022.100087

Dali, K., & Caidi, N. (2023). Social work education for the digital age: Insight from information science. *Social Work Education, 42*(5), 663–693. DOI: 10.1080/02615479.2022.2057942

Damiano, A. D., Lauría, E. J. M., Sarmiento, C., & Zhao, N. (2024). Early perceptions of teaching and learning using generative AI in higher education. *Journal of Educational Technology, 52*(3), 346–375.

Darwin, Rusdin, D., Mukminatien, N., Suryati, N., Laksmi, E. D., & Marzuki. (2024). Critical thinking in the AI era: An exploration of EFL students' perceptions, benefits, and limitations. *Cogent Education, 11*(1). Advance online publication. DOI: 10.1080/2331186X.2023.2290342

Davis, F. D. (1989). Perceived usefulness, perceived ease of use, and user acceptance of information technology. *Management Information Systems Quarterly, 13*(3), 319–340.

Delello, J. A., Sung, W., Mokhtari, K., Hebert, J., Bronson, A., & De Giuseppe, T. (2025). AI in the classroom: Insights from educators on usage, challenges, and mental health. *Education Sciences, 15*(2), 113. DOI: 10.3390/educsci15020113

Derricks, V., Hirsh, A. T., Perkins, A. J., Daggy, J. K., & Matthias, M. S. (2024). Health care discrimination affects patient activation, communication self-efficacy, and pain for Black Americans. *The Journal of Pain, 25*(12), 1–11. DOI: 10.1016/j.jpain.2024.104663

Dickens, E., Han, A., Shafiq, N. & Taggart, J., (2025) Curriculum developers: An emerging subset of educational developers. *To Improve the Academy: A Journal of Educational Development, 44*(1). DOI: 10.3998/tia.5274

Drisko, J., & Grady, M. D. (2018). Teaching evidence-based practice using cases in social work education. Families in Society, 99(3), 269-282. https://doi.org/ (Original work published 2018)DOI: 10.1177/1044389418785331

Dueck, A. C., & Sundararajan, L. (Eds.). (2024). *Values and Indigenous psychology in the age of the machine and market: When the Gods have fled*. Springer International Publishing., DOI: 10.1007/978-3-031-53196-5

Duggan, G. B. (2016). Applying psychology to understand relationships with technology: From ELIZA to interactive healthcare. *Behaviour & Information Technology, 35*(7), 536–547. DOI: 10.1080/0144929X.2016.1141320

Dwivedi, Y. K., Hughes, L., Baabdullah, A. M., Ribeiro-Navarrete, S., Giannakis, M., & Metri, B. (2021). Artificial intelligence (AI): Multidisciplinary perspectives on emerging challenges, opportunities, and agenda for research, practice, and policy. *International Journal of Information Management, 57*. Advance online publication. DOI: 10.1016/j.ijinfomgt.2019.08.002

Egonsdotter, G., & Israelsson, M. (2022). Computer-based simulations in social work education: A scoping review. *Research on Social Work Practice, 34*(1), 41–53. DOI: 10.1177/10497315221147016

Elyoseph, Z., & Levkovich, I. (2023). Beyond human expertise: The promise and limitations of ChatGPT in suicide risk assessment. *Frontiers in Psychiatry, 14*. Advance online publication. DOI: 10.3389/fpsyt.2023.1213141

Eubanks, V. (2018). *Automating inequality: How high-tech tools profile, police, and punish the poor*. Beacon Press.

European Commission. (2019). *Ethics guidelines for trustworthy AI*. https://digital-strategy.ec.europa.eu/en/library/ethics-guidelines-trustworthy-ai

European Union. (2024). *Artificial Intelligence Act* (Regulation (EU) 2024/1689). Official Journal of the European Union. https://eur-lex.europa.eu/eli/reg/2024/1689/oj/eng

Evans, T. R., Branney, P., Clements, A., & Hatton, E. (2023). Improving evidence-based practice through preregistration of applied research: Barriers and recommendations. *Accountability in Research, 30*(2), 88–108. DOI: 10.1080/08989621.2021.1969233

Ewell, P. T. (2009). *Assessment, accountability, and improvement: Revisiting the tension*. National Institute for Learning Outcomes Assessment. https://inside.southernct.edu/sites/default/files/a/inside-southern/assessment-and-planning/Assessment-Accountability-and-Improvement.pdf

Fahad, S. (2024). Transforming medical social work with artificial intelligence. *Social Work Chronicle, 13*(1), 24–49.

Feuerriegel, S., Hartmann, J., Janiesch, C., & Zschech, P. (2024). Generative AI. *Business & Information Systems Engineering, 66*(1), 111–126. DOI: 10.1007/s12599-023-00834-7

Fitas, R. (2025). Inclusive Education with AI: Supporting Special Needs and Tackling Language Barriers. *arXiv preprint arXiv:2504.14120.*

Fitzpatrick, K. K., Darcy, A., & Vierhile, M. (2017). Delivering cognitive behavior therapy to young adults with symptoms of depression and anxiety using a fully automated conversational agent (Woebot): A randomized controlled trial. *JMIR Mental Health*, *4*(2), e19. DOI: 10.2196/mental.7785 PMID: 28588005

Fitzpatrick, K. K., Shuman, M., & Wang, Y. (2024). Human-computer empathy in trauma contexts. *Computers in Human Behavior*, *149*, 107928.

Flenady, G., & Sparrow, R. (2025). Cut the bullshit: Why GenAI systems are neither collaborators nor tutors. *Teaching in Higher Education*, 1–10. DOI: 10.1080/13562517.2025.2497263

Floridi, L., & Cowls, J. (2022). A unified framework of five principles for AI in society. *Machine learning and the city: Applications in architecture and urban design*, 535-545.

Floridi, L., Cowls, J., Beltrametti, M., Chatila, R., Chazerand, P., Dignum, V., & Vayena, E. (2021). Ethics of artificial intelligence: Mapping the debate. *Big Data & Society*, *8*(2).

Folomieieva, N., Koriakin, O., Matsenko, L., Siaska, I., & Fed, I. (2024). Problem-based learning in higher education: A path towards training innovative and competent specialists. *Amazonia Investiga*, *13*(77), 201–217. DOI: 10.34069/AI/2024.77.05.15

Foster, V. A., & McAdams, C. R.III. (2009). A framework for creating a climate of transparency for professional performance assessment: Fostering student investment in gatekeeping. *Counselor Education and Supervision*, *48*(4), 271–284. DOI: 10.1002/j.1556-6978.2009.tb00080.x

Francis, N. J., Jones, S., & Smith, D. P. (2025). Generative AI in higher education: Balancing innovation and integrity. *British Journal of Biomedical Science*, *81*, 14048. DOI: 10.3389/bjbs.2024.14048

Funa, A. A., & Gabay, R. A. E. (2025). AI literacy in health-professions education: Deepening the case for curricular reform in the Philippines. *Health Science Reports*, *8*(11), e71551. DOI: 10.1002/hsr2.71551

Future of Life Institute. (2025). *EU Artificial Intelligence Act*. Retrieved 29th December 2025 from https://artificialintelligenceact.eu

Galindo-Domínguez, H., Delgado, N., Losada, D., & Etxabe, J. M. (2024). An analysis of the use of artificial intelligence in education in Spain: The in-service teacher's perspective. *Journal of Digital Learning in Teacher Education, 40*(1), 41–56. DOI: 10.1080/21532974.2023.2284726

Garay, S. M. (2025). Advancing instructional design with AI: A study on AI literacy in higher education [Doctoral dissertation, University of South Alabama]. ProQuest.

García-Torres, D., Fernández, C., Mira, J. J., Morales, A., & Vicente, M. A. (2025). Using AI-based virtual simulated patients for training in psychopathological interviewing: Cross-sectional observational study. *JMIR Medical Education, 11*, e78857. DOI: 10.2196/78857

Gealone, D. (2024). Exploring faculty perceptions of AI integration in pedagogical practices at higher education institutions: A qualitative study. *International Journal of Arts. Sciences and Education, 5*(1), 140–147. https://ijase.org/index.php/ijase/article/view/396

George, A. S., Baskar, T., & Srikaanth, P. B. (2024). The erosion of cognitive skills in the technological age: How reliance on technology impacts critical thinking, problem-solving, and creativity. *Partners Universal Innovative Research Publication, 2*(3), 147–163. DOI: 10.5281/zenodo.11671150

Gillani, N., Eynon, R., Chiabaut, C., & Finkel, K. (2023). Unpacking the "Black Box" of AI in education. *Journal of Educational Technology & Society, 26*(1), 99–111.

Gillingham, P. (2021). Algorithmic decision-making in social work: The challenge of trust. *British Journal of Social Work, 51*(5), 1741–1758.

Giray, L., Sevnarayan, K., & Ranjbaran Madiseh, F. (2025). Beyond policing: AI writing detection tools, trust, academic integrity, and their implications for college writing. *Internet Reference Services Quarterly, 29*(1), 83–116. DOI: 10.1080/10875301.2024.2437174

Gladhart, M. A. (2010). Determining faculty needs for delivering accessible electronically delivered instruction in higher education. *Journal of Postsecondary Education and Disability, 22*(3), 185–196. https://eric.ed.gov/?id=EJ906692

Goldingay, S., Hodgson, D., Boddy, J., Nipperess, S., & Watts, L. (2020). Online and blended social work education in Aotearia New Zealand and Australia negotiating the tensions. *Advances in Social Work & Welfare Education, 21*(2), 62–74.

Goldkind, L. (2021). Social work and artificial intelligence: Into the matrix. *Social Work, 66*(4), 372–374. DOI: 10.1093/sw/swab028 PMID: 34279661

Gregorcic, B., Polverini, G., & Sarlah, A. (2024). ChatGPT as a tool for honing teachers' Socratic dialogue skills. *Physics Education, 59*(4), 045005.

Grobbel, C., Piscotty, R. J., & Hanna, D. (2024). Artificial intelligence bootcamp: A strategy for educating faculty. *Nurse Educator, 50*(4), E248–E249. DOI: 10.1097/NNE.0000000000001815

Guest, O., Suarez, M., Müller, B., van Meerkerk, E., Oude Groote Beverborg, A., de Haan, R., Reyes Elizondo, A., Blokpoel, M., Scharfenberg, N., Kleinherenbrink, A., Camerino, I., Woensdregt, M., Monett, D., Brown, J., Avraamidou, L., Alenda-Demoutiez, J., Hermans, F., & van Rooij, I. (2025). Against the uncritical adoption of 'AI' technologies in academia. *Zenodo.* https://doi.org/https://doi.org/10.5281/zenodo.17065099

Hacker, P. (2024). Sustainable AI regulation. *Common Market Law Review, 61*(2), 345–386. DOI: 10.54648/cola2024025

Han, E., & Shin, J. (2025). Understanding artificial intelligence and machine learning: Foundational concepts for counselor education. *The Journal of Counselor Preparation and Supervisor, 19*(3), 1–15. DOI: 10.70013/7b5l47yn

Hanley, T. (2025). Artificial intelligence and the changing landscape of therapy. *Counselling & Psychotherapy Research, 25*(4). Advance online publication. DOI: 10.1002/capr.70056

Haque, M., & Rubya, S. (2023). An overview of chatbot-based mobile mental health apps: Insights from app description and user reviews. *JMIR mHealth and uHealth, 11*, e44838. DOI: 10.2196/44838 PMID: 37213181

Harizan, S. H. M., & Ally, M. (2025). Artificial intelligence in micro-credentials for open and distance learning: A technologically enhanced systematic review. *Turkish Online Journal of Distance Education, 26*(3). https://files.eric.ed.gov/fulltext/EJ1479078.pdf

Harvard Business School. (2021). Case Method: 100 Years. Harvard Business School. https://www.hbs.edu/case-method-100

Healy, K. (2022). *Social work theories in context* (3rd ed.). Bloomsbury.

Hill Collins, P. (2019). *Intersectionality as critical social theory*. Duke University Press.

Hodgson, D., Goldingay, S., Boddy, J., Nipperess, S., & Watts, L. (2021). Problematising artificial intelligence in social work education: Challenges, issues and possibilities. *British Journal of Social Work, 52*(4). Advance online publication. DOI: 10.1093/bjsw/bcab168

Hodgson, D., Watts, L., & Gair, S. (2023). Artificial intelligence and implications for the Australian Social Work Journal. *Australian Social Work, 76*(4), 425–427. DOI: 10.1080/0312407X.2023.2247833

Holmes, W., Bialik, M., & Fadel, C. (2019). *Artificial intelligence in education: Promises and implications for teaching and learning*. Center for Curriculum Redesign.

Hou, C., Zhu, G., & Sudarshan, V. (2025). The role of critical thinking on undergraduates' reliance behaviours on generative AI in problem-solving. *British Journal of Educational Technology, 56*(5), 1919–1941. DOI: 10.1111/bjet.13613

Howell, R. A. (2021). Engaging students in education for sustainable development: The benefits of active learning, reflective practices and flipped classroom pedagogies. *Journal of Cleaner Production, 325*, 129318.

Hung, I. C., & Chen, N. S. (2018). Embodied interactive video lectures for improving learning comprehension and retention. *Computers & Education, 117*, 116–131. DOI: 10.1016/j.compedu.2017.10.005

International Federation of Social Workers. (2020). *Global standards for social work education and training*. https://www.ifsw.org/global-standards-for-social-work-education-and-training/

International Union of Psychological Science. (2008). *Universal declaration of ethical principles for psychologists*. https://www.iupsys.net/about/declarations/universal-declaration-of-ethical-principles-for-psychologists/

Isaacs, J. (2021). The problem with data-driven decision making in education. *Journal of Educational Thought / Revue de La Pensée Educative, 54*(1). DOI: 10.55016/ojs/jet.v54i1.72895

Ivanov, S. (2023). The dark side of artificial intelligence in higher education. *Service Industries Journal, 43*(15-16), 1055–1082. DOI: 10.1080/02642069.2023.2258799

Jadon, A. (2025). Ethical AI development: Mitigating bias in generative models. In Reddy, C. K. K., Joseph, S., Joshi, H., Ouaissa, M., & Hanafiah, M. M. (Eds.), *Interplay of artificial general intelligence with quantum computing. Sustainable artificial intelligence-powered applications*. Springer., DOI: 10.1007/978-3-031-87931-9_10

James, P., Lal, J., Liao, A., Magee, L., & Soldatic, K. (2024). Algorithmic decision-making in social work practice and pedagogy: Confronting the competency/critique dilemma. *Social Work Education, 43*(6), 1552–1569. DOI: 10.1080/02615479.2023.2195425

Jefferies, G., Fox, M., Dodds, L., & Davis, C. (2025). A theoretical framework for understanding the importance of implementing simulation in social work education. *Social Work Education, 44*(2), 354–367.

Johnstone, M., Catrina, B., & Ross, N. (2022). The McDonaldization of social work: A critical analysis of mental health care services using the Choice and Partnership Approach (CAPA) in Canada. *Journal of Progressive Human Services, 33*(3), 223–243. DOI: 10.1080/10428232.2022.2050117

Jonassen, D. H., & Hernandez-Serrano, J. (2002). Case-based reasoning and instructional design: Using stories to support problem solving. *Educational Technology Research and Development, 50*(2), 65–77. DOI: 10.1007/BF02504994

Jordan, J. R. (2020). Relational ethics in clinical practice: Restoring trust in helping relationships. *Clinical Social Work Journal, 48*(3), 201–214.

Joshi, M. A. (2024). Adaptive learning through artificial intelligence. *International Journal on Integrated Education, 7*(2), 41–43.

Kamalov, F., Calonge, D. S., & Gurrib, I. (2023). New era of artificial intelligence in education: Towards a sustainable multifaceted revolution. *Sustainability, 15*(16), 12451. DOI: 10.3390/su151612451

Kamoun, F., Ayeb, W. E., Jabri, I., Sifi, S., & Iqbal, F. (2024). Exploring students' and faculty's knowledge, attitudes, and perceptions towards ChatGPT: A cross-sectional empirical study. *Journal of Information Technology Education*, 23.

Kasneci, E., Sessler, K., Küchemann, S., Bannert, M., Dementieva, D., Fischer, F., Gasser, U., Groh, G., Günnemann, S., Hüllermeier, E., Krusche, S., Kutyniok, G., Michaeli, T., Nerdel, C., Pfeffer, J., Poquet, O., Sailer, M., Schmidt, A., Seidel, T., & Stadler, M. (2023). ChatGPT for good? On Opportunities and Challenges of Large Language Models for Education. *Learning and Individual Differences, 103*. Advance online publication. DOI: 10.1016/j.lindif.2023.102274

Keegan, D. J., & Farwa, A. (2025). Human Services 2.0: Navigating ethics, innovation, and applications of AI in human services. In Ahmed, E., Babar, A. R., Samad, A., Ahmed, R. I., & Beydoun, G. (Eds.), *Strengthening Human Relations in Organizations With AI* (pp. 247–272). IGI Global., DOI: 10.4018/979-8-3693-6507-6.ch010

Khatri, B. B., & Karki, P. D. (2023). Artificial intelligence (AI) in higher education: Growing academic integrity and ethical concerns. *Nepalese Journal of Development and Rural Studies, 20*(01), 1–7.

Kim, J., Klopfer, M., Grohs, J. R., Eldardiry, H., Weichert, J., Cox, L. A.II, & Pike, D. (2025). Examining faculty and student perceptions of generative AI in university courses. *Innovative Higher Education, 50*, 1281–1313. DOI: 10.1007/s10755-024-09774-w

Knight, C. (2015). Trauma-informed social work practice: Lessons from the field. *Clinical Social Work Journal, 43*(1), 25–37. DOI: 10.1007/s10615-014-0481-6

Koivisto, M., & Grassini, S. (2023). Best humans still outperform artificial intelligence in a creative divergent thinking task. *Scientific Reports, 13*(1), 13601. Advance online publication. DOI: 10.1038/s41598-023-40858-3

Kolb, D. A. (1984). *Experiential learning: experience as the source of learning and development.* Prentice-Hall.

Kominkiewicz, F., & O'Neil, M. (2025). The application of artificial intelligence to social work education and practice. In *Encyclopedia of Social Work.* NASW Press and Oxford University Press.

Kong, S. C., & Zhu, J. (2025). Developing and validating an artificial intelligence ethical awareness scale for secondary and university students: Cultivating ethical awareness through problem-solving with artificial intelligence tools. *Computers and Education: Artificial Intelligence, 9*, 100447. DOI: 10.1016/j.caeai.2025.100447

Kong, S.-C., Korte, S.-M., Burton, S., Keskitalo, P., Turunen, T., Smith, D., Wang, L., Lee, J. C.-K., & Beaton, M. C. (2025). Artificial Intelligence (AI) literacy – An argument for AI literacy in education. *Innovations in Education and Teaching International, 62*(2), 477–483. DOI: 10.1080/14703297.2024.2332744

Kourgiantakis, T., Sewell, K. M., Hu, R., Logan, J., & Bogo, M. (2020). Simulation in social work education: A scoping review. *Research on Social Work Practice, 30*(4), 433–450.

Kuh, G. D., Ikenberry, S. O., Jankowski, N. A., Cain, T. R., Ewell, P. T., Hutchings, P., & Kinzie, J. (2015). *Using evidence of student learning to improve higher education. Jossey-Bass.* Wiley.

Lainjo, B. (2020). The global social dynamics and inequalities of artificial intelligence. *International Journal of Innovation Scientific Research and Review, 5*(8), 4966–4974.

Lampou, R. (2023). The integration of artificial intelligence in education: Opportunities and challenges. *Review of Artificial Intelligence in Education*, *4*. Advance online publication. DOI: 10.37497/rev.artif.intell.educ.v4i00.15

Laranjo, L., Dunn, A. G., Tong, H. L., Kocaballi, A. B., Chen, J., Bashir, R., Surian, D., Gallego, B., Magrabi, F., Lau, A. Y. S., & Coiera, E. (2018). Conversational agents in healthcare: A systematic review. *Journal of the American Medical Informatics Association : JAMIA*, *25*(9), 1248–1258. DOI: 10.1093/jamia/ocy072 PMID: 30010941

Lateef, F. (2010). Simulation-based learning: Just like the real thing. *Journal of Emergencies, Trauma and Shock*, *3*(4), 348–352.

Laundon, M., & Grant-Smith, D. (2023). Defining and advancing a systems approach to achieving educator wellbeing: An integrative review of wellbeing in higher education. *Student Success*, *14*(3), 104–119. DOI: 10.5204/ssj.3191

Lazcoz, G., & de Miguel, I. (2025). Is more data always better? On alternative policies to mitigate bias in Artifical Intelligence health systems. *Bioethics*, *39*, 414–424.

Lee, M. K., Forlizzi, J., Kiesler, S., Rybski, P., Antanitis, J., & Savetsila, S. (2012, March). Personalization in HRI: A longitudinal field experiment. In *Proceedings of the seventh annual ACM/IEEE international conference on Human-Robot Interaction*, 319-326.

Lee, S. S., & Moore, R. L. (2024). Harnessing generative AI (GenAI) for automated feedback in higher education: A systematic review. *Online Learning : the Official Journal of the Online Learning Consortium*, *28*(3). Advance online publication. DOI: 10.24059/olj.v28i3.4593

Lelescu, A., Sava, S., Grosseck, G., & Malita, L. (2025). Exploring trust in generative AI for higher education institutions: A systematic literature review focused on educators. *Humanities & Social Sciences Communications*. Advance online publication. DOI: 10.1057/s41599-025-06253-1

Lionarons, T. A. (2025). Artificial intelligence in crisis decision-making: Practical applications and ethical objections. In Lin, L. (Ed.), *Ethics in the age of AI: Navigating politics and security* (pp. 269–290). Ethics Press.

Li, P., Yang, J., Islam, M. A., & Ren, S. (2025). Making AI less “thirsty”: Uncovering and addressing the secret water footprint of AI models. *Communications of the ACM*, *68*(7), 54–61.

Liu, D., & Bridgeman, A. (2023). *What to do about assessments if we can't out-design or out-run AI?* University of Sydney. Retrieved 11th November 2025 from https://educational-innovation.sydney.edu.au/teaching@sydney/what-to-do-about-assessments-if-we-cant-out-design-or-out-run-ai/

Liu, B. (2021). In AI we trust? Effects of agency locus and transparency on uncertainty reduction in human–AI interaction. *Journal of Computer-Mediated Communication, 26*(6), 384–402. https://doi.org/https://doi.org/10.1093/jcmc/zmab013

Liu, N. (2025). Exploring the factors influencing the adoption of artificial intelligence technology by university teachers: The mediating role of confidence and AI readiness. *BMC Psychology, 13*(1), 311. DOI: 10.1186/s40359-025-02620-4

Liu, X., Zhang, L., & Wei, X. (2025). Generative artificial intelligence literacy: Scale development and its effect on job performance. *Behavioral Sciences (Basel, Switzerland), 15*(6), 811. DOI: 10.3390/bs15060811

Logie, C., Bogo, M., Regehr, C., & Regehr, G. (2013). A critical appraisal of the use of standardized client simulations in social work education. *Journal of Social Work Education, 49*(1), 66–80.

Long, D., & Magerko, B. (2020). *What is AI literacy? Competencies and design considerations* Proceedings of the 2020 CHI Conference on Human Factors in Computing Systems, Honolulu, HI, USA. DOI: 10.1145/3313831.3376727

Luckin, R. (2017). Towards artificial intelligence-based assessment systems. *Nature Human Behaviour, 1*(3), 003.

Lund, B. D., Lee, T. H., Mannuru, N. R., & Arutla, N. (2025). AI and academic integrity: Exploring student perceptions and implications for higher education. *Journal of Academic Ethics, 23*(3), 1545–1565. DOI: 10.1007/s10805-025-09613-3

Mackey, W. (2014). *Culturally relevant education and critical pedagogy: Devolution of hierarchies of power.* Revista Internacional de Educación para la Justicia Social.

Mahmud, S. (2024). Fostering academic integrity in the age of artificial intelligence. In *Academic integrity in the age of artificial intelligence* (pp. 1–20). IGI Global Scientific Publishing., DOI: 10.4018/979-8-3693-0240-8.ch001

Mamaleka, M. M., & Skobi, F. (2024). New intervention strategies in rendering social work services to families amidst the pandemic crisis: A social work perspective. In Lutz, R., & Weimann-Sandig, N. (Eds.), *Family dynamics, gender and social inequality during COVID-19* (pp. 211–226). Springer Nature., DOI: 10.1007/978-3-031-51237-7_14

Marshall, S., Blaj-Ward, L., Dreamson, N., Nyanjom, J., & Bertuol, M. T. (2024). The reshaping of higher education: Technological impacts, pedagogical change, and future projections. *Higher Education Research & Development, 43*(3), 521–541. DOI: 10.1080/07294360.2024.2329393

Martella, A. M., & Schneider, D. W. (2024). A reflection on the current state of active learning research. *The Journal of Scholarship of Teaching and Learning, 24*(3), 119–136.

Masters, K. (2023). Ethical use of Artificial Intelligence in health professions education: AMEE Guide No. 158. *Medical Teacher, 45*(6), 574–584. DOI: 10.1080/0142159X.2023.2186203

Mehdaoui, A. (2024). Unveiling Barriers and Challenges of AI Technology Integration in Education: Assessing Teachers' Perceptions, Readiness and Anticipated Resistance. *Futurity Education, 4*(4), 95–108.

Mehdaoui, A. (2024). Unveiling barriers and challenges of AI technology integration in education: Assessing teachers' perceptions, readiness and anticipated resistance. *Futurity Education, 4*(4), 95–108. DOI: 10.57125/FED.2024.12.25.06

Mooney, L., Cummings, C., Koller, J. M., Dunkle, J., & Bobadilla, T. (2024). Perspectives of social work faculty/staff and students about online learning and practicum education. *Journal of Teaching in Social Work, 44*(5), 462–475. DOI: 10.1080/08841233.2024.2408170

Moorhouse, B. L., Yeo, M. A., & Wan, Y. (2023). Generative AI tools and assessment: Guidelines of the world's top-ranking universities. *Computers and Education Open, 5*. Advance online publication. DOI: 10.1016/j.caeo.2023.100151

Morandini, S., Fraboni, F., De Angelis, M., Puzzo, G., Giusino, D., & Pietrantoni, L. (2023). The impact of artificial intelligence on workers' skills: Upskilling and reskilling in organisations. Informing Science: The International Journal of an Emerging Transdiscipline, 26, 039–068. https://doi.org/DOI: 10.28945/5078

Morris, R., Perry, T., & Wardle, L. (2021). Formative assessment and feedback for learning in higher education: A systematic review. *Review of Education, 9*(3), 1–26. DOI: 10.1002/rev3.3292

Mzwri, K., & Turcsányi-Szabo, M. (2025). Bridging LMS and generative AI: Dynamic course content integration (DCCI) for enhancing student satisfaction and engagement via the ask ME assistant. *Journal of Computers in Education*. Advance online publication. DOI: 10.1007/s40692-025-00367-w

National Association of Social Workers. (2017). *Standards for technology in social work practice*. https://www.socialworkers.org/Practice/NASW-Practice-Standards-Guidelines/Standards-for-Technology-in-Social-Work-Practice

National Association of Social Workers. (2021). Code of ethics of the National Association of Social Workers. https://www.socialworkers.org/About/Ethics/Code-of-Ethics/Code-of-Ethics-English

National Association of Social Workers. (2021). Code of ethics. https://www.socialworkers.org/About/Ethics/Code-of-Ethics/Code-of-Ethics-English

National Association of Social Workers. (2021). *NASW code of ethics*. https://www.socialworkers.org/About/Ethics/Code-of-Ethics

National Association of Social Workers. (2021). *NASW code of ethics*. https://www.socialworkers.org/About/Ethics/Code-of-Ethics/Code-of-Ethics-English

Navasca, R. (2025). Bridging digital and vocational learning: The role of AI in enhancing culturally responsive TLE instruction and pedagogical approaches. *International Journal on Culture. History of Religions*, *7*(SI3), 479–494. DOI: 10.63931/ijchr.v7isi3.398

Nazaretsky, T., Ariely, M., Cukurova, M., & Alexandron, G. (2022). Teachers' trust in AI-powered educational technology and a professional development program to improve it. *British Journal of Educational Technology*, *53*(4), 914–931.

Nicola-Richmond, K., Dawson, P., Helen, P., & Macfarlane, S. (2025). It takes a village... Program-wide approaches to redesigning assessment in a time of generative artificial intelligence (GenAI). *Journal of University Teaching & Learning Practice*. Advance online publication. DOI: 10.53761/zpp2ja61

Noble, S. U. (2018). *Algorithms of oppression: How search engines reinforce racism*. NYU Press.

Noel, L., Chen, Q., Petruzzi, L. J., Phillips, F., Garay, R., Valdez, C., & Jones, B. (2022). Interprofessional collaboration between social workers and community health workers to address health and mental health in the United States: A systematised review. *Health & Social Care in the Community*, *30*(6), e6240–e6254.

Nuwasiima, M., Ahonon, M. P., & Kadiri, C. (2024). The role of artificial intelligence (AI) and machine learning in social work practice. *World Journal of Advanced Research and Reviews*, *24*(1), 80–97.

O'Sullivan, J., Lowry, C., Woods, R., & Conlon, T. (2025). *Generative AI in higher education teaching & learning: Principles for ethical AI adoption*. Higher Education Authority. DOI: 10.82110/qmt6-jw48

Obermeyer, Z., Powers, B., Vogeli, C., & Mullainathan, S. (2019). Dissecting racial bias in an algorithm used to manage the health of populations. *Science, 366*(6464), 447–453.

Okada, A., Sherborne, T., Panselinas, G., & Kolionis, G. (2025). Fostering transversal skills through open schooling supported by the CARE-KNOW-DO pedagogical model and the UNESCO AI competencies framework. *International Journal of Artificial Intelligence in Education, 35*(4), 1953–1998. DOI: 10.1007/s40593-025-00458-w

Oliveira Silva, G., Fonseca, L. M. M., Siqueira, K. M., de Góes, F. D. S. N., Ribeiro, L. M., & Aredes, N. D. A. (2023). The simulation design in health and nursing: A scoping review. *Nursing Open, 10*(4), 1966–1984. DOI: 10.1002/nop2.1466

Oncioiu, I., & Bularca, A. R. (2025). Artificial intelligence governance in higher education: The role of knowledge-based strategies in fostering legal awareness and ethical artificial intelligence literacy. *Societies (Basel, Switzerland), 15*(6), 144. DOI: 10.3390/soc15060144

Ooi, P. B., & Wilkinson, G. (2025). Enhancing ethical codes with artificial intelligence governance: A growing necessity for the adoption of generative AI in counselling. *British Journal of Guidance & Counselling, 53*(1), 66–80. DOI: 10.1080/03069885.2024.2373180

Osborn, P. R., & Karandikar, S. (2023). Practice-based knowledge perspectives of cultural competence in social work. *Journal of Ethnic & Cultural Diversity in Social Work, 32*(6), 285–297.

Penn, M. L., Currie, C. S. M., Hoad, K. A., & O'Brien, F. A. (2016). The use of case studies in OR teaching. *Higher Education Pedagogies, 1*(1), 16–25. DOI: 10.1080/23752696.2015.1134201

Pentina, I., Hancock, T., & Xie, T. (2023). Exploring relationship development with social chatbots: A mixed-method study of Replika. *Computers in Human Behavior, 140*, 107600. Advance online publication. DOI: 10.1016/j.chb.2022.107600

Pérez-García, P., & Hernández-Fernández, A. (2023). AI chatbots in digital mental health: A narrative literature review. *Computers & Education: Artificial Intelligence, 4*, 100104.

Peters, U., & Chin-Yee, B. (2025). Generalization bias in large language model summarization of scientific research. *Royal Society Open Science*, *12*(4), 241776. DOI: 10.1098/rsos.241776

Ping, Y. (2024). Experience in psychological counseling supported by artificial intelligence technology. *Technology and Health Care*, *32*(6), 3871–3888.

Pirozzoli, A. (2024). The human-centric perspective in the regulation of artificial intelligence. *European Papers (Online. Periodico), 9*(1), 105–116. https://doi.org/ DOI: 10.15166/2499-8249/745

Popil, I. (2011). Promotion of critical thinking by using case studies as teaching method. *Nurse Education Today*, *31*(2), 204–207. DOI: 10.1016/j.nedt.2010.06.002

Potgieter, I. (2020). Privacy concerns in educational data mining and learning analytics. *International Journal of Information Ethics*, *28*. Advance online publication. DOI: 10.29173/irie384

Powell, S., & Forsyth, R. (2024). Generative AI and the implications for authentic assessment. In *Using generative ai effectively in higher education* (1st ed.). Routledge., DOI: 10.4324/9781003482918-15

Prieto, L. P., Dlab, M. H., Gutiérrez, I., Abdulwahed, M., & Balid, W. (2011). Orchestrating technology enhanced learning: A literature review and a conceptual framework. *International Journal of Technology Enhanced Learning*, *3*(6), 583. DOI: 10.1504/ijtel.2011.045449

Rafi, S., & Rafi, S. (2022). Mental health and stress in the digital workplace: Implications for social work practice. In *Managing the digital workplace in the post-pandemic era* (pp. 26–40).

Rafi, S., & Saif, S. (2021). Physical and mental health issues of elderly women in India: A review. In *Handbook of research on policies, protocols, and practices for social work*.

Rafi, S. (2019). Critical analysis of the legal approach to protect the elderly population in India. *BSSS Journal of Social Work*, *11*(1), 1–20.

Rafi, S., & Saif, S. (2020a). Age-friendly communities: Creating a conducive environment for the elderly in India. *Journal of Geriatric Medicine*, *2*(2), 7.

Rafi, S., & Saif, S. (2020b). Critical review of literature on the prevalence of elder abuse in India: Sorrow of greying. *Journal of Psychosocial Well-being*, *1*(2), 35–44.

Rahman, A., Ishak, W. I., Aziz, A., Arif, Z., Salleh, S. M., & Safii, M. (2025). Responsible AI literacy's role in ethical, transparent, and sustainable AI adoption in SMEs: Mediating effects of technology, organization and environment. *Proceedings of the 3rd International Conference on Business, Finance, Management and Economic (BizFAME 2024)*, 196–220. https://doi.org/DOI: 10.2991/978-94-6463-827-1_14

Rajaraman, V. (2014). JohnMcCarthy: Father of artificial intelligence. *Resonance, 19*(3), 198–207. DOI: 10.1007/s12045-014-0027-9

Rane, J., Kaya, Ö., Mallick, S. K., & Rane, N. (2024). *Artificial intelligence in education: A SWOT analysis of ChatGPT and its implications for practice and research*. Deep Science Publishing., DOI: 10.70593/978-81-981271-7-4_4

Reamer, F. G. (2019). Social work education in a digital world: Technology standards for education and practice. *Journal of Social Work Education, 55*(3), 420–432. https://www.jstor.org/stable/48543052

Reamer, F. G. (2023). Artificial intelligence in social work: Emerging ethical issues. *International Journal of Social Work Values & Ethics, 20*(2), 52–71. DOI: 10.55521/10-020-205

Reamer, F. G. (2023). Artificial intelligence in social work: Emerging ethical issues. *International Journal of Social Work Values and Ethics, 20*(2), 52–71.

Regilme, S. S. F. (2024). Artificial intelligence colonialism: Environmental damage, labor exploitation, and human rights crises in the Global South. *SAIS Review (Paul H. Nitze School of Advanced International Studies), 44*(2), 75–92. DOI: 10.1353/sais.2024.a950958

Reimer, E. C. (2024). Examining the role of generative AI in enhancing social work education: An analysis of curriculum and assessment design. *Social Sciences, 13*(12), 648. DOI: 10.3390/socsci13120648

Reiss, M. J. (2021). The use of AI in education: Practicalities and ethical considerations. *London Review of Education, 19*(1). Advance online publication. DOI: 10.14324/lre.19.1.05

Ren, X., & Wu, M. L. (2025). Examining teaching competencies and challenges while integrating artificial intelligence in higher education. *TechTrends, 69*, 519–538. DOI: 10.1007/s11528-025-01055-3

Rodriguez, M. Y., Goldkind, L., Victor, B. G., Hiltz, B., & Perron, B. E. (2024). Introducing generative artificial intelligence into the MSW curriculum: A proposal for the 2029 Educational Policy and Accreditation Standards. *Journal of Social Work Education, 60*(2), 174–182. DOI: 10.1080/10437797.2024.2340931

Rogers, L., & MacCormac, A. (2025). Finding a balance: Using a pre-post test to evaluate the effectiveness of scenario-based learning using a blended approach among undergraduate nursing students. *Nurse Education Today, 147*. Advance online publication. DOI: 10.1016/j.nedt.2025.106573

Rubin, M., Arnon, H., Huppert, J. D., & Perry, A. (2024). Considering the role of human empathy in AI-driven therapy. *JMIR Mental Health, 11*(1), e56529. DOI: 10.2196/56529

Ruschemeier, H., & Hondrich, L. (2024). Automation bias in public administration - An interdisciplinary perspective from law and psychology. SSRN *Electronic Journal*. https://doi.org/DOI: 10.2139/ssrn.4736646

Russell, S., & Norvig, P. (2016). *Artificial intelligence: A modern approach* (3rd ed.). Pearson.

Russ-Smith, J., & Lazarus, M. (2025). *The AI (R)evolution*. Monash University. DOI: 10.26180/27274938.v5

Sadiku, M. N. O., & Musa, S. M. (2021). Digital Intelligence. In Sadiku, M. N. O., & Musa, S. M. (Eds.), *A primer on multiple intelligences* (pp. 163–174). Springer International Publishing., DOI: 10.1007/978-3-030-77584-1_13

Saidin, S. S., Ahmad, N., & Aziz, S. (2025). Ethical governance of artificial intelligence in organizations: Challenges and strategies. In Ahmed, E., Babar, A. R., Samad, A., Ahmed, R. I., & Beydoun, G. (Eds.), *Strengthening human relations in organizations with AI* (pp. 59–82). IGI Global., DOI: 10.4018/979-8-3693-6507-6.ch003

Salido, A., Syarif, I., Sitepu, M. S., Wana, P. R., Taufika, R., & Melisa, R. (2025). Integrating critical thinking and artificial intelligence in higher education: A bibliometric and systematic review of skills and strategies. *Social Sciences & Humanities Open, 12*, 101924. DOI: 10.1016/j.ssaho.2025.101924

Saxena, D., & Guha, S. (2024). Algorithmic harms in child welfare: Uncertainties in practice, organization, and street-level decision-making. *ACM Journal on Responsible Computing, 1*(1), 1–32. DOI: 10.1145/3616473

Schindler, L. A., Burkholder, G. J., Morad, O. A., & Marsh, C. (2017). Computer-based technology and student engagement: A critical review of the literature. *International Journal of Educational Technology in Higher Education, 14*(1). Advance online publication. DOI: 10.1186/s41239-017-0063-0

Schophuizen, M., & Kalz, M. (2020). Educational innovation projects in Dutch higher education: Bottom-up contextual coping to deal with organizational challenges. *International Journal of Educational Technology in Higher Education, 17*(36). Advance online publication. DOI: 10.1186/s41239-020-00197-z

Schuwirth, L. W. T., & van der Vleuten, C. P. M. (2020). A history of assessment in medical education. *Advances in Health Sciences Education : Theory and Practice, 25*(5), 1045–1056. DOI: 10.1007/s10459-020-10003-0

Sebesta, J., & Davis, V. L. (2023). *Supporting instruction and learning through artificial intelligence: A survey of institutional practices & policies. WICHE Cooperative for Educational Technologies*. WCET.

Selbst, A., & Barocas, S. (2018). The intuitive appeal of explainable machines. *Fordham Law Review, 87*(3), 1085–1139.

Selwyn, N. (2014). *Distrusting educational technology: Critical questions for changing times*. Bloomsbury Academic.

Selwyn, N. (2019). *Should robots replace teachers? AI and the future of education*. Polity Press.

Serrano, E., & Bajo, J. (2019). Deep neural network architectures for social services diagnosis in smart cities. *Future Generation Computer Systems, 100*, 122–131.

Shata, A., & Hartley, K. (2025). Artificial intelligence and communication technologies in academia: Faculty perceptions and the adoption of generative AI. *International Journal of Educational Technology in Higher Education, 22*(14). Advance online publication. DOI: 10.1186/s41239-025-00511-7

Sherwood, G. (2024). Reflective practice and knowledge development: Transforming research for a practice-based discipline. *International Journal of Nursing Sciences, 11*(4), 399–404.

Shi, J., Liu, W., & Hu, K. (2025). Exploring how AI literacy and self-regulated learning relate to student writing performance and well-being in generative AI-supported higher education. *Behavioral Sciences (Basel, Switzerland), 15*(5), 705. DOI: 10.3390/bs15050705 PMID: 40426482

Shoemaker, S., Freeburg, N., & Duquette, K. (2025). Artificial intelligence in counselor education: Innovative strategies for teaching, supervision, and clinical training. *The Journal of Counselor Preparation and Supervisor, 19*(3), 1–34.

Shoval, D. H. (2025). Artificial intelligence in higher education: Bridging or widening the gap for diverse student populations? *Education Sciences*, *15*(5), 637. DOI: 10.3390/educsci15050637

Siddals, S., Torous, J., & Coxon, A. (2024). *"It happened to be the perfect thing": Experiences of generative AI chatbots for mental health. npj Mental Health Research*, *3*(1), 48. DOI: 10.1038/s44184-024-00097-4

Siddik, M. A. B., Shehabi, A., & Marston, L. (2021). The environmental footprint of data centers in the United States. *Environmental Research Letters*, *16*(6), 064017.

Sidiropoulos, D., & Anagnostopoulos, C.-N. (2024). Applications, challenges and ethical issues of AI and ChatGPT in education. *arXiv preprint*. https://doi.org//arXiv.2402.07907DOI: 10.48550

Singer-Freeman, K., & Robinson, C. (2020). Grand challenges for assessment in higher education. *Research & Practice in Assessment*, *15*(2). https://www.rpajournal.com/dev/wp-content/uploads/2020/11/Grand-Challenges-for-Assessment-in-Higher-Education.pdf

Singh, T. M., Reddy, C. K. K., Murthy, B. R., Nag, A., & Doss, S. (2025). AI and education: Bridging the gap to personalized, efficient, and accessible learning. In *Internet of behavior-based computational intelligence for smart education systems* (pp. 131–160). IGI Global.

Slade, S., & Prinsloo, P. (2013). Learning analytics: Ethical issues and dilemmas. *The American Behavioral Scientist*, *57*(10), 1510–1529. DOI: 10.1177/0002764213479366

Smith, J., & Nguyen, T. (2023). Leveraging AI in social work: A pathway to empowering vulnerable populations. *Journal of Technology in Human Services*, *41*(1), 50–68.

Smith, S. M., Tate, M., Freeman, K., Walsh, A., Ballsun-Stanton, B., & Lane, M. (2025). A university framework for the responsible use of generative AI in research. *Journal of Higher Education Policy and Management*, •••, 1–20. DOI: 10.1080/1360080X.2025.2509187

Social Work England. (2021). *Qualifying education and training standards 2021*. Retrieved 29th December 2025 from https://www.socialworkengland.org.uk/media/3423/1227_socialworkengland_standards_drft_qual_ed_training_standards_2021.pdf

Soman, G., Judy, M. V., & Abou, A. M. (2025). Human guided empathetic AI agent for mental health support leveraging reinforcement learning-enhanced retrieval-augmented generation. *Cognitive Systems Research, 90*, 101337. DOI: 10.1016/j.cogsys.2025.101337

Song, Y., Weisberg, L. R., Zhang, S., & Tian, X., Kristy Elizabeth Boyer, & Israel, M. (2024). A framework for inclusive AI learning design for diverse learners. *Computers & Education: Artificial Intelligence*, *6*(6), 100212–100212. DOI: 10.1016/j.caeai.2024.100212

Soomro, A. A., Khan, M. H., Umar, M., Sjid Khan, S., & Ali, O. (2025). AI-driven academic advising in higher education: Leveraging intelligent systems to personalize student support, improve retention, and optimize career pathways. *The Critical Review of Social Sciences Studies*, *3*(2), 229–248. DOI: 10.59075/vy3v7k17

Southworth, J., Migliaccio, K., Glover, J., Glover, J., Reed, D., McCarty, C., Brendemuhl, J., & Thomas, A. (2023). Developing a model for AI Across the curriculum: Transforming the higher education landscape via innovation in AI literacy. *Computers and Education: Artificial Intelligence*, *4*(1), 100127. DOI: 10.1016/j.caeai.2023.100127

Spathopoulou, F., Pitychoutis, K. M., & Papakonstantinidis, S. (2025). AI and higher education: Understanding faculty roles in teaching, research, and administration. *Contemporary Educational Technology*, *17*(4), ep600. DOI: 10.30935/cedtech/17406

Stamer, T., Steinhäuser, J., & Flägel, K. (2023). Artificial intelligence supporting the training of communication skills in the education of health care professions: Scoping review. *Journal of Medical Internet Research*, *25*(8), 1–16. DOI: 10.2196/43311

Stone, B. W. (2025). Generative AI in higher education: Uncertain students, ambiguous use cases, and mercenary perspectives. *Teaching of Psychology*, *52*(3), 347–356. DOI: 10.1177/00986283241305398

Sullivan, M., Kelly, A., & McLaughlan, P. (2023). ChatGPT in higher education: Considerations for academic integrity and student learning. *Journal of Applied Learning & Teaching*, *6*(1), 31–40.

Sweller, J., Van Merriënboer, J. J., & Paas, F. (2019). Cognitive architecture and instructional design: 20 years later. *Educational Psychology Review*, *31*(2), 261–292.

Tadimalla, S. Y., Cary, J., Hull, G., Register, J., Maxwell, D., Pugalee, D., & Heafner, T. (2025). Comprehensive AI literacy: The case for centering human agency. *ArXiv.org*. https://arxiv.org/abs/2512.16656

Tahirsylaj, A., Matson, J., & Gashi, L. (2019). Educating minds for the age of innovation. *International Journal of Innovation. Creativity and Change, 5*(1), 15–32.

Tanana, M. J., Soma, C. S., Srikumar, V., Atkins, D. C., & Imel, Z. E. (2019). Development and evaluation of ClientBot: Patient-like conversational agent to train basic counseling skills. *Journal of Medical Internet Research, 21*(7), e12529. DOI: 10.2196/12529

Tanana, M., Hallgren, K. A., Imel, Z. E., Atkins, D. C., & Srikumar, V. (2016). A comparison of natural language processing methods for automated coding of motivational interviewing. *Journal of Substance Abuse Treatment, 65*, 43–50. DOI: 10.1016/j.jsat.2016.01.006

Therasa, M. M. (2023). Adapting Assistive Technology to Diverse Learning Needs in Inclusive Education. *Shanlax International Journal of Arts. Science and Humanities, 11*, 63–66.

Thistlethwaite, J. E., Davies, D., Ekeocha, S., Kidd, J. M., & MacDougall, C., Matthews, Purkis, J., & Clay, D. (2012). The effectiveness of case-based learning in health professional education. A BEME systematic review: BEME Guide No. 23. *Medical Teacher, 34*(6), e421–e444. DOI: 10.3109/0142159X.2012.680939

Timotheou, S., Miliou, O., Dimitriadis, Y., Sobrino, S. V., Giannoutsou, N., Cachia, R., Monés, A. M., & Ioannou, A. (2023). Impacts of digital technologies on education and factors influencing schools' digital capacity and transformation: A literature review. *Education and Information Technologies, 28*(6), 6695–6726. DOI: 10.1007/s10639-022-11431-8

Topping, K. J., Gehringer, E., & Khosravi, H., Srilekha Gudipati, Jadhav, K., & Surya Susarla. (2025). Enhancing peer assessment with artificial intelligence. *International Journal of Educational Technology in Higher Education, 22*(1). Advance online publication. DOI: 10.1186/s41239-024-00501-1

Torun, F., & Şanal, S. O. (2025). The perspectives of academicians and students regarding the use of generative artificial intelligence in higher education. [IJTE]. *International Journal of Technology in Education, 8*(1), 65–87.

Trianggono, M. M., Prahani, B. K., Zahro, I., Ashadi, F., & Siswono, H. (2025). AI-integrated project-based learning as a pathway to quality education: Enhancing critical and creative thinking in pre-service teachers. *Multidisciplinary Reviews, 9*(7), 2026308. DOI: 10.31893/multirev.2026308

Tsakeni, M., Nwafor, S. C., Mosia, M., & Egara, F. O. (2025). Mapping the scaffolding of metacognition and learning by AI tools in STEM classrooms: A bibliometric-systematic review approach (2005-2025). *Journal of Intelligence, 13*(11), 148. DOI: 10.3390/jintelligence13110148 PMID: 41295429

Tsamados, A., Aggarwal, N., Cowls, J., Morley, J., Roberts, H., Taddeo, M., & Floridi, L. (2021). The ethics of algorithms: Key problems and solutions. *AI & Society, 37*(1), 215–230. DOI: 10.1007/s00146-021-01154-8

Tsao, J. (2025). Trajectories of AI policy in higher education: Interpretations, discourses, and enactments of students and teachers. *Computers and Education: Artificial Intelligence, 9*, 100496. DOI: 10.1016/j.caeai.2025.100496

Urdang, E. (2010). Awareness of self—A critical tool. *Social Work Education, 29*(5), 523–538. DOI: 10.1080/02615470903164950

Venkatesh, V., Thong, J. Y., & Xu, X. (2016). Unified theory of acceptance and use of technology: A synthesis and the road ahead. *Journal of the Association for Information Systems, 17*(5), 328–376. DOI: 10.17705/1jais.00428

Venter, J., Coetzee, S. A., & Schmulian, A. (2024). Exploring the use of artificial intelligence (AI) in the delivery of effective feedback. *Assessment & Evaluation in Higher Education, 50*(4), 1–21. DOI: 10.1080/02602938.2024.2415649

Verboom, A. D. P. R., Pais, L., Zijlstra, F. R. H., Oswald, F. L., & dos Santos, N. R. (2025). Perceptions of artificial intelligence in academic teaching and research: A qualitative study from AI experts and professors' perspectives. *International Journal of Educational Technology in Higher Education, 22*(1). Advance online publication. DOI: 10.1186/s41239-025-00546-w

Walter, Y. (2024). Embracing the future of artificial intelligence in the classroom: The relevance of AI literacy, prompt engineering, and critical thinking in modern education. *International Journal of Educational Technology in Higher Education, 21*(1). Advance online publication. DOI: 10.1186/s41239-024-00448-3

Wang, H., Dang, A., Wu, Z., & Mac, S. (2024). Generative AI in higher education: Seeing ChatGPT through universities' policies, resources, and guidelines. *Computers and Education: Artificial Intelligence, 7*, 100326. DOI: 10.1016/j.caeai.2024.100326

Wang, T., Lund, B. D., Marengo, A., Pagano, A., Mannuru, N. R., Teel, Z. A., & Pange, J. (2023). Exploring the potential impact of artificial intelligence (AI) on international students in higher education: Generative AI, chatbots, analytics, and international student success. *Applied Sciences (Basel, Switzerland), 13*(11), 6716. DOI: 10.3390/app13116716

Wang, X., Liu, J., Jia, S., Hou, C., Jiao, R., Yan, Y., & Liu, X. Y. (2024). Hybrid teaching after COVID-19: Advantages, challenges and optimization strategies. *BMC Medical Education*, *24*(1), 753.

Watts, K. J. (2025). Paying the cognitive debt: An experiential learning framework for integrating AI in social work education. *Education Sciences*, *15*(10), 1304. DOI: 10.3390/educsci15101304

Watts, L., & Hodgson, D. (2019). *Social justice theory and practice for social work: Critical and philosophical perspectives* (1st ed.). Springer Nature., DOI: 10.1007/978-981-13-3621-8

Watty, K., McKay, J., & Ngo, L. (2016). Innovators or inhibitors? Accounting faculty resistance to new educational technologies in higher education. *Journal of Accounting Education*, *36*, 1–15.

Whitbread, M., Hayes, C., Prabhakar, S., & Upsher, R. (2025). Exploring university staff's perceptions of using generative artificial intelligence at university. *Education Sciences*, *15*(3), 367. DOI: 10.3390/educsci15030367

Whittaker, M., Crawford, K., Dobbe, R., Fried, G., Kaziunas, E., Mathur, V., & Schwartz, O. (2018). *AI Now Report 2018*. AI Now Institute.

Williamson, B. (2017). Big data in education: The digital future of learning, policy and practice. *Sage (Atlanta, Ga.)*.

Williams, R. T. (2024). The ethical implications of using generative chatbots in higher education. *Frontiers in Education*, *8*(1331607). Advance online publication. DOI: 10.3389/feduc.2023.1331607

Wu, Y. (2024). Critical thinking pedagogics design in an era of ChatGPT and other AI tools: Shifting from teaching "what" to teaching "why" and "how.". *Journal of Education and Development*, *8*(1), 1–10. DOI: 10.20849/jed.v8i1.1404

Xiao, B., Can, D., Gibson, J., Imel, Z. E., Atkins, D. C., Georgiou, P. G., & Narayanan, S. S. (2016). Behavioral coding of therapist language in addiction counseling using recurrent neural networks. In *Interspeech 2016* (pp. 908–912). International Speech Communication Association (ISCA). https://doi.org/. 2016-1560.DOI: 10.21437/interspeech

Xu, Z., Procko, K., Munje, M., Patterson, K., Sabatini, L., Biswas, J., & Stone, P. (2025). The essentials of AI for life and society: A full-scale AI literacy course accessible to all. *ArXiv.org*. https://www.arxiv.org/abs/2512.04110

Yan, L., Sha, L., Zhao, L., Li, X., Martinez-Maldonado, R., Chen, G., & Gašević, D. (2023). Practical and ethical challenges of large language models in education: A systematic scoping review. *Journal of Educational Technology & Society*, *26*(1), 123–145.

Yaseen, H., Mohammad, A. S., Ashal, N., Abusaimeh, H., Ali, A., & Sharabati, A.-A. A. (2025). the impact of adaptive learning technologies, personalized feedback, and interactive AI tools on student engagement: The moderating role of digital literacy. *Sustainability*, *17*(3), 1133. DOI: 10.3390/su17031133

Yuan, Y., Huang, J., Ma, X., & Yan, K. (2020, November). Children's drawing psychological analysis using shallow convolutional neural network. In 2020 International Conferences on Internet of Things (iThings) and IEEE Green Computing and Communications (GreenCom) and IEEE Cyber, Physical and Social Computing (CPSCom) and IEEE Smart Data (SmartData) and IEEE Congress on Cybermatics (Cybermatics) (pp. 692-698). IEEE.

Yusuf, H., Money, A., & Daylamani-Zad, D. (2025). Towards reducing teacher burden in Performance-Based assessments using aivaluate: An emotionally intelligent LLM-Augmented pedagogical AI conversational agent. *Education and Information Technologies*, •••, 1–45.

Zamfiroiu, A., Sharma, R. C., Constantinescu, D., Pană, M., & Toma, C. (2022). Using learning analytics for analyzing students' behavior in online learning. *Studies in Informatics and Control*, *31*(3), 63–74.

Zawacki-Richter, O., Marín, V. I., Bond, M., & Gouverneur, F. (2019). Systematic review of research on artificial intelligence applications in higher education: Where are the educators? *International Journal of Educational Technology in Higher Education*, *16*(1), 39. DOI: 10.1186/s41239-019-0171-0

Zhai, X. (2024). Transforming teachers' roles and agencies in the era of generative AI: Perceptions, acceptance, knowledge, and practices. *Journal of Science Education and Technology*, •••, 1–11.

Zhao, C. (2024). AI-assisted assessment in higher education: A systematic review. *Journal of Educational Technology and Innovation*, *6*(4). Advance online publication. DOI: 10.61414/jeti.v6i4.209

Zheng, K., Shen, Z., Chen, Z., Che, C., & Zhu, H. (2024). Application of AI-empowered scenario-based simulation teaching mode in cardiovascular disease education. *BMC Medical Education*, *24*, 1003–1013.

Zhou, X., Teng, D., & Al-Samarraie, H. (2024). The mediating role of generative AI self-regulation on students' critical thinking and problem-solving. *Education Sciences*, *14*(12), 1302. DOI: 10.3390/educsci14121302

About the Contributors

Jenifer Norton earned their Ph.D. in Social Work from Bryn Mawr College and holds a Master of Social Work from Widener University. They are currently Executive Director of AI Integration & Innovation in the Office of Online Education Innovation, Psychology Program Director in the School of Professional Studies & Innovation, and Professor of Practice at Moravian University. In these roles, Dr. Norton leads institution-wide efforts to integrate generative AI into online education, curriculum design, assessment, and faculty development in ways that are ethical, accessible, and human-centered, while also overseeing interdisciplinary psychology programming focused on human behavior, mental health, and well-being. Dr. Norton brings over a decade of experience in online and hybrid higher education, with particular expertise in instructional design, curriculum development, and program administration. Their career spans leadership roles including Online MSW Program Director, Academic Director for Noodle, and Assistant Professor across multiple institutions. They have supported curriculum innovation at the intersection of technology, artificial intelligence, and human-centered disciplines, notably contributing to AI integration initiatives across general education and professional studies at Moravian University. Their scholarly work and teaching emphasize ethical technology use, culturally aware pedagogy, social justice, and data-informed practice in social work, counseling, and psychology. Dr. Norton has served as evaluator on several federally funded behavioral health grants and contributed to academic publications and conferences in areas such as online learning, AI in education, and culturally sustainable curricula.

***

Stevara Haley Clark, Ed.D., M.S.W., is the Director of Online Programs and Distance Education and Associate Professor at the School of Social Work. Holding both a Master of Social Work and a Doctor of Education in Educational Leadership from Virginia Commonwealth University, Dr. Clark brings a unique blend of clinical insight, academic expertise, and administrative leadership to her roles. She leads strategic initiatives to expand access to high-quality, equity-centered online education and to strengthen academic programs through inclusive, student-centered practices. With over a decade of experience in higher education, Dr. Clark brings a strong foundation in academic administration, online program development, and organizational culture change. Her leadership is grounded in principles of trust, transparency, and compassionate communication, fostering collaborative and empowering learning environments for students and faculty alike. Prior to joining Pitt, Dr. Clark held several leadership roles at Virginia Commonwealth University's School of Social Work, where she directed online education and served as Interim Associate Dean for Academic and Student Affairs. There, she oversaw curricular development, supported accreditation compliance, advanced strategic enrollment management, and implemented innovations in digital learning and inclusive teaching practices.

Bonny Cotter is an experienced social worker, educator, and practitioner with a career spanning over three decades across government, community, and academic sectors. She currently serves as a Lecturer and Unit Coordinator in the Master of Social Work (Qualifying) program at Excelsia University College. She holds a Bachelor of Social Work from UNSW, a Graduate Diploma in Creative Music Therapy, and a Graduate Certificate in Developmental Trauma. Bonny is a member of the AASW and has contributed to sector development through supervision training, conference presentations, and board leadership.

Deepak D, an academician of two years old, with teaching experience in the areas of taxation, accounting, and IFRS. He has expertise in academic publishing, research content writing, coaching, teaching, editing, and analytical abilities. He possesses a PhD from JAIN (Deemed To Be University) in the School of Commerce. He has participated in a number of FDPs, workshops, seminars, and conferences. He as published more than 10 research paper in different UGC Care journal, web of science, Scopus.

Caroline Fitzgerald Campbell, PhD, LSW, is an Assistant Professor and MSW On-Campus Program Director at Widener University's Center for Social Work Education. With over 20 years in social work education and practice, she specializes in trauma-informed care, community resilience, and relational care models. Dr. Fitzgerald Campbell earned her PhD from Widener University, and an MSW from Temple University. Her research focuses on community models for trauma interventions, healing-centered pedagogy, and social worker well-being.

With a background in clinical leadership, Dr. Campbell previously managed domestic violence and health programs and works to integrate wellness and equity as she nurtures future social work leaders.

RamakrishnaG. N. is an Associate Professor in the Department of Economics at the School of Humanities and Social Sciences (SHSS), JAIN (Deemed-to-be University), Bengaluru. He has a Ph.D. in Economics from Bangalore University and an M.Phil. from Dravidian University. With over 15 years of academic and administrative experience, he has served as HOD, Principal, BOE/BOS Member, and Research Guide for Ph.D. scholars. His research interests include Financial Economics, Development Economics, and Public Policy. Dr. Ramakrishna has presented numerous papers at both national and international conferences and has been widely published in reputable journals. He has also contributed book chapters and holds a patent on "The Mediating Effect of Service Innovation on the Indian Insurance Industry." An active academic leader, he has organized faculty development programs, national seminars, and international conferences. He is also a registered Independent Assessor with the Karnataka Monitoring and Evaluation Authority (KMEA).

Kimberly E. Giamportone, PhD, LMSW is an Assistant Professor of Social Work at the University of Southern Maine in Portland. Her clinical experience in medical social work was honed in the areas of hospice and palliative care departments prior to moving into academia full time. She also functions as chair of the ethics committee as a member of the board for a local hospice agency. Kimberly's research and scholarship interests are focused on the facilitators and barriers to team cohesion within interprofessional teams, application of the code of ethics in guiding social work practice, and preparing social work students for future employment in healthcare settings.

Sheeba Joseph has been associated with BSSS College since 2006. At present, in addition to teaching, she serves the institute in the additional role of Academic In-Charge. She has presented papers at national and international conferences and has published articles in peer-reviewed Scopus- and WoS-indexed journals. She has also contributed chapters to edited volumes and has one authored book and two edited books to her credit. Dr. Joseph has organized several national seminars, conferences, and workshops, and has been invited to deliver lectures for various training programmes and workshops. Her areas of interest include geriatric social work and research in the field of social work education.

David Keegan is a Senior Lecturer in Social Work at Excelsia University College and an experienced social work leader with over 25 years in community services, international NGOs and higher education. His practice and research focus on refugee wellbeing, displacement, and the emerging role of artificial intelligence in social work. He is completing a PhD examining how AI is shaping social work practice and professional identity.

Rachel Salmon is an Instructional Designer with the Teaching and Learning with Technology team at Widener University, with a special focus working with the Center for Social Work Education. She holds a B.S. in Psychology from University of the Sciences in Philadelphia, an M.S. in Education from Drexel, and an M.Ed. in Instructional Technology from Widener University. She specializes in innovative, engaging, and inclusive learning experiences such as integrating simulation-based learning and the appropriate use of AI.

Index

A

C

D

E

F

G

H

I

L

M

N

www.ingramcontent.com/pod-product-compliance
Lightning Source LLC
LaVergne TN
LVHW080853300926
849162LV00003B/418